The Internationalisation of Retailing in Asia

Retailing in Asia is currently undergoing a major process of internationalisation. Retailers from Europe and North America are entering the Asian market and stimulating changes to the traditional retail structures; public policy agencies are considering what types of intervention are appropriate; and all of this is affecting fundamentally the managerial culture of retailing in the region. The book brings together a range of experts in retail research, mostly drawn from across Asia, who provide original, in-depth, analyses of this key development. It explores the conflicts and benefits that arise as retailing in Asia becomes internationalised.

John Dawson is Professor of Marketing at the University of Edinburgh, Visiting Professor at ESADE, Barcelona and Distinguished Professor at the University of Marketing and Distribution Sciences, Japan.

Masao Mukoyama is Dean and Professor of Retailing in the Faculty of Commerce at the University of Marketing and Distribution Sciences, Japan.

Sang Chul Choi is Professor of Marketing and Distribution Systems at the University of Marketing and Distribution Sciences, Japan.

Roy Larke is Professor of Retailing at the University of Marketing and Distribution Sciences, Japan and Visiting Professor at the University of Edinburgh.

RoutledgeCurzon advances in Asia-Pacific business

The Internationalisation of Retailing in Asia

**Edited by
John Dawson,
Masao Mukoyama,
Sang Chul Choi and
Roy Larke**

RoutledgeCurzon
Taylor & Francis Group

LONDON AND NEW YORK

First published 2003
by RoutledgeCurzon
11 New Fetter Lane, London EC4P 4EE

Simultaneously published in the USA and Canada
by RoutledgeCurzon
29 West 35th Street, New York, NY 10001

RoutledgeCurzon is an imprint of the Taylor & Francis Group

© 2003 University of Marketing and Distribution Sciences, Kobe, Japan

Typeset in Times New Roman by
Newgen Imaging Systems (P) Ltd, Chennai, India
Printed and bound in Great Britain by
Antony Rowe Ltd, Chippenham, Wiltshire

British Library Cataloguing in Publication Data
A catalogue record for this book is available from the British Library

Library of Congress Cataloging in Publication Data
A catalog record for this book has been requested

ISBN 0–415–30904–2

Contents

Figures

Tables

Contributors

Amelia Yuen Shan Au-Yeung is Lecturer in Strategic Management in the School of Business Strategy and Operations in the Faculty of Business, Kingston Hill at Kingston University, Kingston-upon-Thames, Surrey, KT2 7LB, England. E-mail: ameliaay@usa.net

Roger C. K. Chan is Associate Professor in the Center of Urban Planning and Environmental Management at the the University of Hong Kong, Pokfulam Road, Hong Kong. E-Mail: hrxucck@hkucc.hku.hk

Sang Chul Choi is Professor of Marketing and Distribution Systems in the Faculty of Commerce at the University of Marketing and Distribution Sciences, 3-1 Gakuen Nishimachi, Nishi ku, Kobe, 651-2188, Japan. E-mail: Sang_Chul_Choi@reds.umds.ac.jp

John Dawson is Professor of Marketing in the School of Management at the University of Edinburgh, Edinburgh, Scotland, EH8 9JY, Visiting Professor at ESADE, Barcelona and Distinguished Professor at the University of Marketing and Distribution Sciences, Japan. E-mail: John.Dawson@ed.ac.uk. Website: http://www.retaildawson.com

Tsuchiya Hitoshi is Instructor in the Department of Marketing and Distribution Management at the National Kaohsiung First University of Science and Technology, 1 University Road, Yuanchau, Kaohsiung 824, Taiwan. E-Mail: hitoshi@ccms.nkfust.edu.tw

Wen Hong is Doctoral Candidate in the Center of Urban Planning and Environmental Management at the University of Hong Kong, Pokfulam Road, Hong Kong. E-mail: whong@hkusua.hku.hk

Han Jinglun is Professor of International Business, Marketing and Trade at Nankai University, 94 Weijin Road, Nankai, Tianjin, P. R. China, 300071. E-mail: hjl39@263.net

Roy Larke is Professor of Retailing in the Faculty of Commerce at the University of Marketing and Distribution Sciences, 3-1 Gakuen Nishimachi, Nishi ku, Kobe, 651-2188 Japan and editor of *Japan Consuming*. E-mail: Roy_Larke@red.umds.ac.jp. Website: http://gandalf.umds.ac.jp/

Masao Mukoyama is Professor of Retailing in the Faculty of Commerce at the University of Marketing and Distribution Sciences, 3-1 Gakuen Nishimachi, Nishi ku, Kobe, 651-2188 Japan and Convenor of the First SARD workshop on International Retailing. E-mail: Masao_Mukoyama@red.umds.ac.jp

Victor R. Savage is the Head in the Department of Geography at the National University of Singapore, AS3, #06-04, 3 Arts Link, Singapore 117570. E-mail: seasava@nus.edu.sg

Seong Mu Suh is Professor at Choong-Ang University, Ansung-sie, Kyungki-do, 456-756, Korea. E-mail: smsuh@cau.ac.kr

Jirapar Tosonboon is Associate Professor in the Faculty of Commerce and Accountancy at Thammasat University, Thailand. E-mail: jirapar@alpha.tu.ac.th

Shuguang Wang is Associate Professor in the School of Applied Geography at Ryerson University Toronto, Ontario, Canada M5B 2K3. E-mail: swang@geography.ryerson.ca

Acknowledgements

The editors gratefully acknowledge the help of Isao Nakauchi, Chairman of the Nakauchi Gakuen Educational Foundation, and Yoshiaki Shiraishi, Vice-President and Dean of the Graduate School of Marketing and Distribution Sciences, UMDS and Chairman of the Society of Asian Retailing and Distribution, in supporting the original workshop. Participants in the workshop were also instrumental in the discussions with the authors that have enabled them to develop more fully their original papers. The input of these participants is gratefully acknowledged.

Introduction

John Dawson

> For itself no country can provide;
> For that merchants travel far and wide;
> Their work and toil feeds the nation
> so refrain from baseless fulmination.
> Merchants cross the seas and back
> To bring each nation what it lacks.
> (Gilles le Muisit – Dit de Marchands.
> Quoted in Le Goff (1980))

This fourteenth-century support for international sourcing by retailers is part of the long tradition of retailers operating internationally, and of foreign entrepreneurs operating in domestic retail markets. International retailers are not a new phenomenon. Furthermore, such activities have generated economic and social conflicts for as long as they have existed. In late mediaeval England, the merchants sought protection from the foreign competitors. The foreign merchants competed in new ways, perceived to be unfair by the existing merchants. Westerfield (1915), in his classic historical study of English retailing, reports that in the early eighteenth century, 'The English merchant was not satisfied with the rate of profit which the Dutch Merchant made. The Dutch did a big business for a small profit, and the English preferred to do a smaller business at a large profit' (p. 373). Three hundred years later, there are similar calls for protectionism and similar concerns about foreign retailers taking market share by seeking volume business.

The foreign retailer often brings innovations into domestic markets. Throughout the more than 2000-year history of innovation diffusion in retailing there are references to foreign traders as agents in urban change and business evolution. The associations and international links of several trading diasporas since the Middle Ages are described in the essays in Fallers (1967). These studies illustrate the importance of foreign entrepreneurs in introducing, not only new products, but also new managerial methods, into a variety of domestic markets. The European ventures into Africa in the nineteenth century introduced permanent market structures into traditional trading systems, bringing ideas of market administration and standardisation of weights and measures (Hodder 1961;

Hodder and Ukwu 1971). Such changes had considerable effect on the indigenous trading groups and their traditional practices. Alongside the attempts to modernise the administration of distribution there are also many examples of innovation in trading technologies. In more modern times, there are many examples of supermarkets being introduced into countries by foreign entrepreneurs. For example, Lawson (1967, 1971) pointed to Syrian and Lebanese traders introducing supermarkets into Ghana in the early 1950s. Wish and Harrison (1969) showed how American supermarket companies introduced the idea to Puerto Rico with a huge effect on local firms and the subsequent emergence of Puerto Rican owned supermarket groups. The transfer of Western formats into China in the present day (Goldman 2001) is only the latest in a long history of innovation diffusion by foreign retailers.

Whether the foreign influence has been politically motivated or whether it is the result of a market response it was not unusual for there to be antagonism between the foreign entrepreneurs and the traditional methods of the local trading groups. The conflict that occurs as retail innovations are introduced by foreign agencies has a long and complex history and has been the subject of considerable study. Many of the studies of retail internationalisation in the last twenty-five years have considered activities in Europe or North America. Relatively few have looked at the recent increasing amounts of retail internationalisation in East Asia.

The chapters in this volume begin to address some issues associated with the rapid increase in international retailer activity in East Asia. In this context, retail internationalisation raises some new themes. An important one is the contrast between business cultures, with Western-based retailers, for the most part, entering countries having strong Eastern cultures. Whilst European and American managerial cultures are very different, both are different from Asian managerial culture. The entry and growth of foreign retailers into China, Japan, Thailand or Korea brings with it not only a potential clash in retail operations with local retailers but also a clash of managerial philosophy which pits European approaches against American approaches, as both attempt to accommodate very different cultural environments. Thus, in addition to the inter-relationship of the foreign retailers with local retailers it is also necessary to consider relationships amongst the foreign retailers involved in internationalisation.

These chapters result from a workshop on *The Impacts of International Retailers in Asia* sponsored by the Society for Asian Research on Distribution. The workshop was held at University of Marketing and Distribution Science in Kobe, Japan in November 2001. The aim of the workshop was to provide a springboard for discussion and research. The issues raised by retail internationalisation in Asia are important ones for political and economic development and the processes of social change in the region. They affect the ways that the WTO agreements will operate in practice and the nature of the 'globalisation' process. At one level the activities of the international retailers have significance for these macro-economic processes but at another level they affect the daily life and lifestyle of each ordinary consumer. The need for research to understand the processes involved in international retailing has never been greater. Through this

Table 0.1 Propositional phases of internationalisation of a retailer

	Stabilisation phase	Consolidation phase	Control phase	Domination phase
Dynamics	• Uncertainty in formats, formula and markets • High rate of formula innovation and high degree of operational flexibility • Fluctuations in demand • Low volume of sales • Formula functionality more important than brand name • Erratic competitive actions • Test relationships with suppliers	• Appearance of dominant format • Clearer understanding of customer needs • Increased process innovation • Introduction of retailer branding • Competition based on quality and availability • Network expansion	• Strong pressure on margins • Formula differences emphasised • Retail brand product development specific to market • Convergence of product, formula and process innovations	• Multi-format and multi-formula development • Obsolescence of earlier assets • New competition from many directions • Increase of channel power • Options to break subservient position in respect of group
Priorities	• Development of formula • Understanding customer • Acquiring knowledge (tacit and explicit) from competition • Establishing the formula as benchmark format	• Fine tuning of formula • Market exploration and learning about market • Pursuit of growth strategy to increase sales space • Improve logistics	• Cost control focus • Branding of formula • Customer service levels defined and delivered • Extend power over suppliers	• Brand development of formulae and items • Increase social role • Explore new formula for growth sub-markets • Outsource non-core activity
Strategic alliances	• Formation of alliances with business services providers • Evaluation of franchising	• Joint ventures and alliances to increase network density • Alliances with marketing service agencies	• Retailer controlled alliances with suppliers	• Alliances with innovative channels
Mergers and acquisitions	• Acquisitions to gain tacit knowledge • Acquisitions to gain operational scale	• Opportunistic acquisition of competitors	• Acquisitions to become dominant retailer in the market • Acquisitions to enter new markets	• Acquisitions of niche players • Divestment of non-performing formulae

research the processes can be understood and managed in appropriate ways to avoid in Asia the difficulties and conflicts that arose, when American retailers moved into Central and South America, in the 1950s and 1960s.

The processes involved in retail internationalisation are complex. Some of the complexity is suggested in Table 0.1 which shows some propositions concerning post-entry processes associated with foreign retailer activity. Initially there is considerable fluidity as the firm gains understanding about the new market. The characteristics listed in the table are illustrative of the variety of activity. The firm, in a second phase, then adjusts to the new conditions, consolidating its position, and in a third phase begins to try to exert control over vertical and horizontal channel relationships. When the retailer becomes established in the market, mature strategies seeking market domination, and similar to those used in the home country, are applied. Whilst this sequence of stabalisation–consolidation–control–domination can be hypothesised to model the overall process, few firms pass through the complete model, deciding to withdraw from the market at some stage or failing to achieve their objectives. The activities listed in Table 0.1 can be seen as illustrative being neither inclusive nor mandatory. The time taken in the various stages also vary greatly from firm to firm and country to country. As seen in the chapters of this book, in the East Asian countries the processes are still in early phases. Considerably, more research is needed to identify the nature of the processes in retail internationalisation as it gathers speed throughout the region.

A theme in the chapters in this book is that internationalisation brings with it conflicts as well as benefits. Internationalisation brings with it a conflict of the traditional with the modern. There is also the conflict between the nationalistic view and the international one. Almost inevitably the foreign retailer is viewed with some suspicion by competitors and often by government. The benefits are often longer term and become present in terms of improving productivity and efficiency, and often encouraging indigenous retailers to change traditional practices to the benefit of consumers. International retailing has a long history but it continues to present perplexing challenges to governments around the world. The essays in this volume raise a variety of issues relevant to government, retailers and academics but they represent only a first step along the route to a fuller understanding of the processes of retailer internationalisation.

References

Fallers, L. A. (ed.) (1967) *Immigrants and Associations*. Mouton: The Hague.

Goldman, A. (2001) 'The transfer of retail formats into developing economies: the example of China', *Journal of Retailing*, 77(2): 221–42.

Hodder, B. W. (1961) 'Rural periodic day markets in part of Yorubaland', *Transactions of Institute of British Geographers*, 29: 149–59.

Hodder, B. W. and Ukwu, U. I. (1969) *Markets in West Africa*. Ibadan: Ibadan University Press.

Lawson, R. (1967) 'The distributive system in Ghana', *Journal of Development Studies*, 3: 195–205.

Lawson, R. (1971) 'The supply response of retail trading to urban population growth in Ghana'. In: C. Meillassoux (ed.) *The Development of Indigenous Trade and Markets in West Africa*. London: Oxford University Press, pp. 377–98.

Le Goff, J. (1980) *Time Work and Culture in the Middle Ages*. Chicago: University of Chicago Press.

Westerfield, R. B. (1915) *Middlemen in English Business*. New Haven: Yale University Press. Reprinted edition 1968, New York: Augustus M Kelley.

Wish, J. R. and Harrison, K. M. (1969) *Marketing: One Answer to Poverty*. University of Oregon Business Publication 3.

1 International retailing in Japan

Roy Larke

Introduction

Internationalization is the single largest issue in Japanese retailing today. Both practitioners and academic observers alike are struggling with this one problem. From an outsider's point of view, the question is how to enter the Japanese market and which overseas retailers are likely to find success. For many Japanese, however, the question is very different. Both experts and consumers alike have an ingrained distrust of overseas entrants into the market, which alone presents a formidable barrier.

History and recent changes

Although it would often seem otherwise, non-Japanese retailers have not suddenly began operating in Japan in the last ten years. There is also the case of US supermarket chain Safeway making a brief and unhappy attempt to operate in the market in the 1950s (Larke 1991: 146). Safeway opened stores in Setagaya and Funabashi, but contemporary reports blame the underdeveloped consumer market and disinterest in overseas supermarkets as the key elements for failure (see MITI 1989: 275–6).

Other similar examples of uninspired attempts to enter Japan have undoubtedly been attempted over the past forty years. The only significance of these is that non-Japanese retailers did realize the existence of the Japanese market. Drawing on Tanner's work (1992), Alexander (1997: 83–4) points out that Japanese retailers were very open and enthusiastic about drawing on Western retail know-how and ideas from the 1950s onwards. This is clear in the large number of Western formats and store fascias that were imported into Japan during this period. Some of the most famous examples are Seven-Eleven, Lawson, Circle K, all from the convenience store sector and all imported purely as fascias with only minor input of know-how from their original namesakes in the USA. Others include Robinson's, a small Californian department store, and Printemps, both of which were also introduced to Japan in name only. Over the years, since their introduction in the 1970s, both formats have become Japanese, although in these cases neither have been made successful by their Japanese licensees.

The second wave of retail internationalization came in the form of global brand retailing. Japanese consumers have a love of brands. It is surprising how little research has been done into this area, but it is safe to say that famous, exclusive global brands have become a symbol of Japanese economic success. For example, in 2001, 1 in 6 Japanese owned a piece of Louis Vuitton luggage (Japan Consuming 2001). Furthermore, the majority of these 20 million people will have paid well above the French price for any particular item. In July 2001, LVMH Japan increased prices on the majority of its lines from 41 per cent above those in Europe to take them to 50 per cent higher.

From the late 1970s, exclusive brands quickly entered the Japanese market. At the height of the bubble economy in the late 1980s, Japanese department stores could offer the best brands in the world, and, in most cases, not worry at all about prices. Such was the demand for exclusivity that consumers were quoted as simply asking for the most expensive items in any particular line (Nikkei Ryutsu Shinbun 1989).

The Japanese love of brands, and particularly exclusive, overseas brands, continues to demand far greater research although observational studies are many (Fields 1983, 1988: 32–40, 2000: 145–65; Cendron 1984; Larke 2002). The most commonly held belief is that consumers view these items as high status symbols. Their high prices and their foreign origin both contribute to the exclusive nature of the brand. Exclusivity and conspicuous consumption symbolize individual success and status, and replace products such as spacious homes and cars that would usually take a similar role in the consumer mind in many other industrial nations.

Over the past ten years, however, there has been a significant change in the sales channels for these brands. Whereas LVMH provides a very successful example of such market entry, it is the exception rather than the rule. To understand this, it is necessary to consider the more theoretical aspects of retail internationalization.

Retail internationalization literature

Alexander (1997) provides one of the most comprehensive reviews of the literature as a whole. To summarize his work, the literature on retail internationalization looks into two main questions: the who and how, and how and why?

The 'who and how' of internationalization

The first considers which companies undertake internationalization and seeks to develop differing taxonomies for their behaviour. Hollander (1970) provides an early example of such work in which he categorizes retail internationalization strategy largely by merchandise sector. This simple typology was expanded to include more details on the motives for overseas expansion by several studies (see Treadgold 1988; Salmon and Tordjman 1989; Bailey *et al.* 1995). All four of these studies have direct relevance to the Japanese case, although none was developed to look at the specific case of the internationalization of a particular country or region.

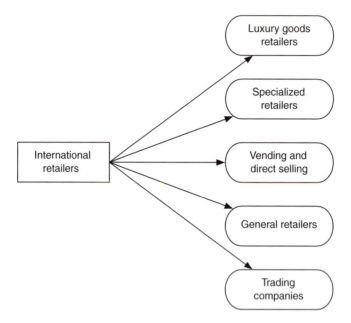

Figure 1.1 Hollander's classification of international retailers.

Hollander (1970) classifies international retailers into 1 of 5 types as shown in Figure 1.1. As already noted, Japan's case began with the entry of luxury goods retailers, although their exact method of entry differed greatly as discussed in the next section. Specialized or niche retailers also entered early and direct selling has also been a common form of entry. General retailers have been less common, and the power of Japan's own large wholesalers and trading companies means that only the largest international companies made their presence felt in the market.

Treadgold (1988, 1990) distinguished companies by entry strategy and geographical spread. He suggested that companies would vary in terms of their risk affinity and in their geographical ambitions. Again this is a simple typology, but, combined with Hollander's work, it becomes a useful framework for considering cross-border retailing as a whole. Treadgold suggested that most companies would prefer high levels of control when entering external markets and would therefore be willing to incur higher costs in order to maintain that control. He then identifies global companies that are willing to forego control in preference for operations in a larger number of countries and over greater distances. He identifies four category clusters among four levels of geographical spread and three market entry strategies (see Figure 1.2).

Alexander (1997: 50–2) expands on this idea to suggest that Hollander's and Treadgold's typologies can be combined. He suggests that general and luxury goods retailers prefer high risk, high control strategies, and so will limit their geographical dispersion. He infers as such that these retailers will not fall into

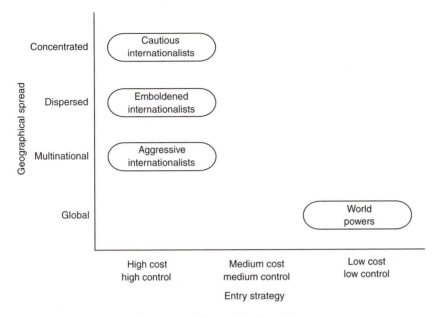

Figure 1.2 Treadgold's typology of international retailers.

Treadgold's Global World Power category. Specialized retailers, however, are so varied as to employ all types of entry strategy from high to low control and will be the only type, under Hollander's typology, to achieve global authority.

Salmon and Tordjman (1989) offer a simple typology of retailers based on their internationalization strategy. The authors categorize companies as global, multi-national or investment. This typology is useful in its simplicity and relates directly to the companies and entry methods employed (see Table 1.1).

The problem with this typology is its simplicity. Since the research was undertaken, international retailing has become increasingly sophisticated and it would be difficult to find companies that have the characteristics of only a single type. In the case of Japan, however, the typology is useful for two reasons.

On the one hand, the Global Strategy is the usual method of internationalization for Japanese companies, and there are few cases in any industry where a Japanese firm has broken this basic model. This is also true for the new expansion of Japanese retailers overseas. On the other hand, Japanese expectations for entry of overseas firms into their own market, and particularly in the retail industry, could be categorized as overwhelmingly favouring the multinational approach. I will consider this point, in the next section, in greater detail.

While all four studies introduced are groundbreaking in their own right, they suffer from one critical problem. As Alexander (1997) points out, each is developed based on samples of retailers operating in international markets at the time. This in itself is most un-retail like as it dwells on a particular point in time and

Table 1.1 Salmon and Tordjman's classification of international retail strategies

---

Global strategy
Replicate operations around the world to achieve high economies of scale using a standardized retail marketing mix and vertical integration of distribution, production and design. Management is centralized, relying on fast information exchange, but technology transfer is limited.

Multinational strategy
Adapt their operations depending on local conditions using a broader and more flexible retail marketing mix, but maintaining similarities where possible. Economies of scale are reduced, but sought wherever possible. Management is decentralized with regular communication between markets. Technology transfer is high.

Investment strategy
Use an acquisition strategy to establish presence in the overseas market. Development is isolated and little communication or replication is achieved between markets. Market entry is swift, but transfer of skills is limited and unimportant.

Source: Salmon and Tordjman (1989).

that previous to it. Retailing is probably one of the most dynamic and fast changing industrial sectors there is, and it is clear from more recent developments in internationalization that companies can be equally categorized by international strategy objectives. Those companies that are more forward looking and open to change are generally those actively seeking to internationalize.

This is as true for Japanese companies as it is for others. Over the past ten years, the Japanese domestic retail industry has seen an unprecedented level of stagnation and a distinct lack of change. In retailing, lack of change may be interpreted as regression in many respects. But even within such a declining period, there have been a number of companies who have been forward looking and willing to change rapidly. These are now looking to expand abroad.

The 'how and why' of retail internationalization

The how and why of the retail internationalization process is the second phase in the research history. Over time (see again Alexander 1997: 76–94), retailing has passed through a number of phases of internationalization. Each was triggered by a large range of factors and variables, but, in general, it could be argued that retail firms have seen a significant differential competitive advantage to be exploited. Arguably, the development of retailing as an industrial sector in leading advanced economies has now reached a stage where a single domestic economy has become too restrictive for companies that have developed significant competitive advantage in their home markets. An overly simplistic view would suggest that the continuing demand from investors for leading retailers to maintain on-going high levels of growth have forced companies to reach out overseas. Even in the case of Fast Retailing in Japan, this is seen as the overriding factor (see Japan Consuming 2001).

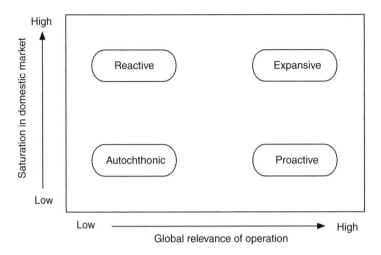

Figure 1.3 Internationalization: motivation structure.
Source: Alexander 1997: 133.

There is a wide and diverse literature on the internationalization process and the reasons behind it. Some would argue that the reasons for internationalization deserve more focus and expansion (see Mukoyama 1996: 11–22). Despite the complexity and interest of market entry into certain nations, this particular topic has been mainly considered outside the academic sphere. It can also be said that the theoretical analysis of past retail expansion has led some analysts away from the practicalities, towards ideas that are less than useful in the real world.

As for reasons behind international expansion, Alexander (1997: 129) again provides a useful and comprehensive summary of other key sources up to the mid-1990s (Kacker 1985; Treadgold 1988, 1990; Alexander 1990a,b; CIG 1991, 1994; McGoldrick and Fryer 1993). This table has been reproduced extensively in the Japanese literature because its push-pull framework is intuitive and generalizable to many explicit cases (Kawabata 2000: 37–40). Alexander identifies political, economic, social, cultural and retail structure-related incentives coming from within the retailer's home markets and in target expansion markets that induce the international expansion decision. It is important to remember his point that each is relative, and none will operate individually. Based on this and other works, Alexander concludes by placing a retailer's individual need for international expansion into 1 of 4 categories (see Figure 1.3).

The four positions are as follows:

1   *Autochthonic*: where home market saturation and global potential of the business are both low and limited. This is, presumably, a position of retail businesses at the very earliest stages of development.

2   *Reactive*: where home market saturation is high, although global potential of the business is still low, some companies may be forced to attempt internationalization as a means to expand. More likely, however, such companies may choose domestic diversification as a primary strategy as happened with the majority of Japanese retailers in the 1980s.

3   *Proactive*: a retail business operating in a low level of saturation at home, but having high global potential may decide to make an early and unforced international expansion. This is the case of many niche retailers seeking to take advantage of their competitive advantage in one or more aspects of their business.

4   *Expansive*: a retail business operating in a highly saturated home market, but also possessing business potential for the global market may adopt an active and far reaching internationalization strategy.

Although there is a long history of retail internationalization that has occurred in a number of waves during the past 100 years or more, arguably, Alexander's fourth strategic position of expansive retailers has now become more prominent during the past 10–15 years. While saturation levels have been reached in more than a few retail categories in many industrialized nations, there is a small but increasing number of retailers who also possess management capability that sets them apart on the global stage. The obvious examples are: Wal-Mart, Carrefour, Tesco and, possibly, Fast Retailing. The number of these companies remains small. The other more numerous groups of proactive retailers has also grown in recent years and would include Body Shop, Lush, Gap, Ikea, Starbucks and the leading exclusive brands who are taking an increasing interest in their own retail operations. Alexander's work is therefore a useful way to understand the motives behind retail internationalization and, as we will see, is highly relevant to the most recent entry of so-called global retailers into the Japanese market.

It is not, however, the only analysis of such motives. Dawson (1994) also offered a detailed list of concrete motives for retail internationalization. The Dawson list is as follows:

1   Saturation of the domestic market.
2   Restrictions, legal and otherwise, on store expansion in the domestic market.
3   Underdevelopment or backward nature of target expansion markets.
4   Competitive or structural differences in the target market allow for high income potential to better prepared overseas entrants.
5   Spreading risk across several markets.
6   Use overseas of excess or cheap capital from the home market.
7   Expansionist or adventurous psychology of senior management.
8   Acquisition of new management know-how, philosophy or technology that can be applied to advantage in other markets.
9   To strengthen either individual or group buying power.
10   Retails may expand abroad as a channel for large manufacturers to further expand and utilize production capacity.

11 The breaking or removal of entry barriers can encourage retailers to move overseas.
12 To meet the needs of customer overseas, even following domestic nationals abroad as tourists.
13 The opportunity to establish a near monopoly position in a new or under-developed market in the hope of high returns over the short term.

Again it is possible to find examples of companies and cases of international market entry for many different countries and companies on each of these points. Some, such as following domestic nationals to markets overseas, the exploitation of underdeveloped markets and development overseas as a channel for manufacturers, are particularly relevant to the expansion of Japanese retailers in Asia and, previously, in Europe.

In one of the most comprehensive studies of retail internationalization yet to be undertaken anywhere, Kawabata (2000: 42) considers the motives for the Japanese expansion in Asia and summarizes his basic framework into four key areas:

1 *Deregulation*: removal of barriers to retail trade within a country and to market entry.
2 *Expansion of overseas markets*: again, following Japanese nationals to other countries is a key factor as Japanese consumers tend to be suspicious of non-Japanese retailers and prefer Japanese food wherever possible. Retailers also took some advantage of the high exchange rate differentials in the early 1990s when the Yen was high, and overseas tourism from Japan was at its height.
3 *Restrictions on the domestic market*: the difficulty of opening stores at home, particularly with the restrictions on large store development in Japan, along with high land and labour costs.
4 *Other factors*: include the low cost of Asian expansion due to the high Yen and the empire building attempts of retailers during the bubble economy.

In these four points, Kawabata succinctly summarizes the main reasons why Japanese companies have moved into Asia. He is clear that other reasons, such as those offered by Dawson above, are less relevant in the majority of cases. It is also clear that there are few examples of Japanese retailers who see international expansion as a proactive strategy. Yaohan was probably the only true example (Davies 1996) and as this strategy led to the bankruptcy of the company as a whole, it is not a case to which many Japanese are happy to refer. While some companies have opened a number of stores around Asia, none have attempted a multinational strategy, preferring to maintain management in the domestic market and operate single, limited resource stores outside the country.

So what about the overseas companies entering the Japanese market? Again there are examples of companies coming to Japan for all the reasons suggested above. In general, however, Japan has long been seen as a relatively closed, very costly market to enter, although Japanese sources have, at times, tried a little too hard to exaggerate the difficulty. In the following section, we see that there are now a number of changes taking place. First and foremost, the difficulty and cost of entering Japan is quickly being reduced or alleviated altogether. In addition, while Japan has attracted and even encouraged smaller, proactive international retailers, partly through its long-held image as 'the final frontier' of international retailing, the country is now attracting the attention of, in Alexander's typology, expansionist retailers. This is a major change for the market and one for which domestic retailers are unprepared.

Before discussing these points in detail, however, it is necessary to look at the development of international retailing in Japan in much greater depth.

International retailing in Japan

Japan has passed through three distinct stages over the past thirty years in terms of retail internationalization. First was the infancy stage during the 1950s and 1960s when a small number of more adventurous non-Japanese retailers sought to take advantage of the underdeveloped nature of the market. Today, none of these survive in any prominent way. Unlike the UK, for example, Japan does not have a Woolworth's or the reincarnation of a Safeway that were leftover from the penetration of outside bodies. The cultural obstacles faced by any overseas company entering the Japanese market are significant and, often, overwhelming, and in the early stages, the high cost and intimate marketing detail needed to run a local retailer were simply too much even for the most advanced outsider. Culturally speaking, Japan is often as difficult to understand for other Asian nations as it is for Westerners.

The second stage began in the 1970s, built up to a peak in the 1980s, and is still on-going. This is the entry of proactive and highly aggressive niche retailers and brand vendors. The majority of these offer exclusive consumer brands, although it would be possible to stretch the definition to include consumer goods giants like Proctor and Gamble and Nippon Lever in this category. Most, however, are the famous names such as Louis Vuitton, Chanel, Gucci and so on. They also include, later in the period, retail operations such as Benetton, Body Shop and Laura Ashley.

Broadly speaking, these retailers and brand companies which link directly to the retail stage of the channel entered the Japan in one of two ways. The minority, of which Louis Vuitton is the obvious case, approached the Japanese market directly and independently. The majority, however, were invited to Japan by Japanese businesses. As in many aspects of Japanese distribution, it was the General Trading Companies or 'Sogo Shosha' who either overtly or covertly provided the invitations. While these massive conglomerate companies are famous for bulk imports of grains, fossil fuels and foodstuffs, and for logistics and supply chain management, they also control some of the largest stables of exclusive imported brands in the country. More recently, large apparel manufacturer/wholesalers such as Onward Kashiyama, Renown, World and Five Foxes have also built their own brand stables. Onward, for example, controls Jean Paul Gautier and now operates the brand worldwide. Renown acquired Aquascutum in the late 1980s, although it has managed to conceal this fact from the majority of Japanese customers even today.

It could be said that the acquisition of the overseas brand, or at least the exclusive rights to selling the brand in Japan, is by far the most preferred method of market entry into Japan for, of course, the Japanese. In the past, the high cost of land, and the intangible costs of research and marketing implementation in Japan, all meant that many overseas entrants were more than happy to leave the details to Japanese companies acting as licensees, franchisors, exclusive dealers or, at most, in a joint venture where the Japanese partner took the lead. Such conditions no longer apply.

The change in the Japanese economy over the 1990s, along with greater understanding by non-Japanese corporations of the intricacies of international business, has led to the third and current phase of modern internationalization of Japanese retailing.

For the first time in modern Japanese history, overseas retailers are entering the Japanese market and competing alongside Japanese competitors. Not only that, since the mid-1990s, an increasing number of companies that have operated in Japan with Japanese suppliers or Japanese partners have decided to make a break towards independent operations. These are clear trends and ones that are set to change Japanese retailing more than at any time other over the past forty years.

The Japanese view

One of the clearest indications of the importance of recent developments is the reaction of press and academic experts. This reaction has been almost universally opposed to the entry of large overseas retailers into the Japanese market. In the most extreme examples, journalists talk of 'Black Ships' in reference to the fleet of Admiral Perry, an American naval officer who is credited with opening Japan at the point of a cannon barrel in the 1850s (e.g. see Nemoto and Tamehiro 2001: 37). This sense of fear and indignation is largely journalistic, but it is surprising how many more serious journals are keen to support it.

In June 2001, Takayama (2001) presented a very typical view in perhaps the most respected semi-academic journal writing in the leading distribution journal *Ryutsu to Shisutemu*. Takayama offers a brief view of retail internationalization in Japan. He, as most others, refers to the movement as a problem to be solved, and describes the expansion of Western retailers such as Carrefour and Metro in the rest of Asia. Most tellingly, however, Takayama points out that Japanese distribution continues to rely to some extent on multi-layered wholesale intermediaries within channels. While this is, in truth, no longer a significant factor, beginning with the entry of ToysRUs in 1990, he suggests that overseas retailers are directly responsible for the breakdown of such traditional distribution systems. Indeed, insisting that the rest of Asia is a long way behind Japan in terms of distribution advancement, he goes as far as saying very clearly:

> The general point of view is that Western retailers are seeking to "create distribution systems" in Asia, but in Japan, their aim is to "break the distribution system."

> (Takayama 2001: 5 with original quotes)

Such views are, indeed, generally accepted. Since Carrefour opened its first store in December 2000, perhaps partly because of its record breaking start, with 50,000 customers during the first two days, journalistic coverage has been scathing and almost universally condemning, including a significant amount of outright propaganda (among many examples see: Nihon Marketing Journal 2001; Nikkei Ryutsu Shinbun 2001; Asahi Shinbun 2001a,b). The overwhelming view is that such companies should not be allowed to compete on equal terms with Japanese, and should, possibly through regulation, sell only imported goods.

Only recently have more reasonable accounts began to appear. One of these, Nemoto (2001), offers a highly detailed account of the most recent entry of non-Japanese retailers. Even so, Nemoto still assumes such moves are almost unconditionally bad for Japan. He also ignores two important factors. First, the majority of non-Japanese retail operations have been supported by Japanese partners. Second, the possibility that new entrants make changes to the sector that benefit Japanese firms.

Takayama (2001) lists a number of overseas retail 'failures' including JC Penny, Sears Roebuck and Office Max, but infers the Japanese partner company was the victim of the failure in each case. The recent high profile withdrawal of Boots from Japan has also been welcomed in the Japanese press, along with sympathy for the efforts of partner Mitsubishi. Nemoto's analysis also makes the same assumptions. This theme that non-Japanese firms cannot comprehend the Japanese market is one that commentators have held for as far back as the distribution system has been a topic of academic study (e.g. see Maruyama, 1990).

Analysis of retail internationalization within Japan

A number of past studies have made limited attempts at analysing the Japanese market in terms of overseas retail penetration (e.g. Fahy and Taguchi 2000) and the topic has been touched upon in both the academic and journalist press (e.g. JETRO 2000; Dawson and Larke 2001). It is somewhat surprising that there are no obvious examples of detailed, in-depth studies. One of the reasons for this has been the problem of language. The majority of Japanese researchers have concentrated their efforts on studying the expansion of Japanese retailers overseas rather than the more thorny and politically incorrect issue of overseas entrants, and there are also a significant number of articles from non-Japanese researchers covering the same topic (see Mukoyama 1996, 2000; Clarke and Rimmer 1997; Davies 2000; Kawabata 2000; Sternquist 2000).

Not only is the subject somewhat taboo in Japan itself, but there is also the overwhelming problem of collecting accurate up-to-date data on retail activities in Japan. There are several directories of overseas companies, but none provide comprehensive details on any particular company. From the researcher's point of view, there are three key problems in collecting this data:

1 Overseas subsidiaries are often not required to make full public disclosure of results.
2 There are a significant number of companies which are not classified primarily as retailers but which, especially in recent years, are taking an active role in retail channels. It is often difficult to even find public data on store numbers for these companies. This problem is compounded by the fact that overseas retailers often operate a mixture of free-standing, licensed and concession outlets within their total distribution structure.
3 The fast paced and dynamic nature of the retail sector means that up-to-date information is almost impossible to compile without constant contact with companies in question.

The data set

The data in this chapter are the first known attempt, in either English or Japanese, to compile a more complete list of overseas companies, that are active in the retail sector in Japan. In total 180 retail concerns were identified for this chapter. For each company the variables presented in Table 1.2 were collected. The starred variables indicate areas where it is difficult to collect accurate information, usually because the companies are unwilling to make this public. For point of reference, some cases of companies no longer active in Japan, have also been included. In addition, the indication of entry formats, from independently operated to license controlled by a Japanese company should also be treated with some suspicion as the exact ownership and its current location is also treated with some secrecy by some firms.

Table 1.2 Data variables collected in survey

Year of establishment
Company name (Japan)
Home nationality
Broad product category
Representative (Japanese/non-Japanese)
Parent company
Entry format (direct/joint venture/license)
Japanese partner(s)
Japanese partner shares
Store numbers (free standing/concessions)
Sales (where publicly available)*
Notes (change in ownership, entry format etc.)*

In the initial stage of the research, the data were built up from two main sources, Toyo Keizai Directory of Overseas Companies 2001 and the Nikkei Directory of Overseas Companies 2000. These directories list around 4,000 non-Japanese companies operating in Japan, but neither one is complete. In addition to the companies that are listed, seventeen obvious companies which are clearly visible in the retail marketplace have been added. Some attempt has also been made to omit brands that are non-Japanese in origin, but which are sold as imports only in the Japanese market. Adding these data to the total would probably be of some value, but the volume of data would increase to such an extent as to greatly increase the time necessary to compile it. They have, therefore, been omitted for the current study. Furthermore, for simplicity's sake, gasoline, automobile and Internet retailers have all been omitted from the analysis, although kept in the database where possible. Restaurants, including prominent examples such as Starbucks Coffee have been included, however, because they are very relevant to the research issue at hand.

Basic analysis

A basic analysis of even this initial and incomplete data set is still revealing, not least in that such an exercise has not been undertaken previously. Figure 1.4 presents a frequency diagram for all sample companies from the earliest established (in 1967) to 2000.

Figures 1.4, 1.5 and 1.6 ignore cases where a particular retailer has recently pulled out of the market.

As already described the three phases of overseas retail entry in Japan can be seen in Figure 1.4. From a slow start in the 1960s, more and more brands entered the market. There are still more of these that are sold in Japan through direct import agreements with Japanese firms, but which have no direct presence in Japan in the form of a subsidiary or other form of overseas ownership. As is discussed, 1973, with the entry of Bally, to 1992, when Hugo Boss was established, marks the extended period when exclusive apparel, cosmetics and similar brand owners came into the market. Some entered as imports through Japanese agents, others through joint ventures. Most are now directly operated subsidiaries.

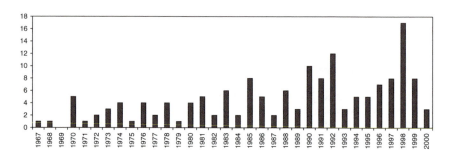

Figure 1.4 Overseas retail entry into Japan by year.

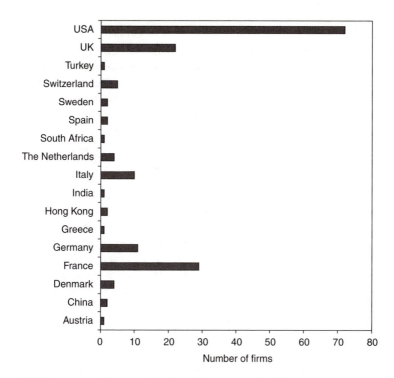

Figure 1.5 Overseas retailers entering Japan by country of origin.

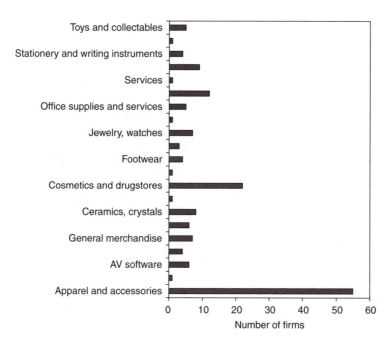

Figure 1.6 Overseas retailers by product category.

The third wave began with the entry of companies such as Eddie Bauer and Gap in the early 1990s. These lower priced, more mass market brands were the leaders of the third phase which still continues today. It represents the mass influx of popular retailers from around the world. Occurring at the end of the bubble economy of the 1980s, it represents a new demand for cheaper and/or more interesting overseas products to replace the overpriced and poorly marketed Japanese alternatives. It also shows that less exclusive companies are at last seeing Japan as an open market, and realizing the potential of selling to the richest consumers in the world.

The years 1992 and 1998 represent sub-phases within this third period. The year 1992 is the breakwater beyond the bubble economy when land prices had begun to fall and more overseas retailers saw the weakness of the Japanese domestic retail market as compared to North America and much of Europe. It was also the height of international expansion for companies like Gap, Disney Store and ToysRUs. The year 1998 represents a second trough in the Japanese economy, particularly in terms of land prices, and follows on from a peak in the value of the Yen that made the market look increasingly cost attractive. While not included in the figure, this was also the year that Japan saw the first big influx of US Internet-based retailers.

Figure 1.5 shows country of origin and includes 163 companies. It illustrates the dominance of American brands and retailers at this point in time. France, Britain, Germany and Italy follow on with 10 or more companies, and companies with parent firms in 12 other nations can also be identified.

If we consider the same data in relation to the year the overseas company was established, 41 of the 72 (57 per cent) US firms were established after 1990. This compares with the proportion of the total data set of 92 firms out of 184 (50 per cent).

Also in comparison, only 10 of the 22 British firms entered after 1990, and only 8 of the 29 French firms did the same. This illustrates the high number of exclusive haute couture brands that entered from Europe early in the process. It also, perhaps, represents a difference in initial entry strategy. In recent years, the majority of newly established overseas companies have maintained 100 per cent ownership and have been directly operated. Early sources, for example the various literature available at JETRO and older MITI reports, suggest that this is a new trend and previously joint-venture and licensing were more common. With the current data set it is not possible to confirm this, as ownership is collected for the year 2001. In some cases, for example, adidas and L. L. Bean, companies which are listed as having been established quite recently in the 1990s were previously operated under license by Japanese firms for a number of years. This is one topic for further research.

Another difficultly of the data is judging precise product category or sector. Because of this, it was decided to ignore common industrial categorization and use a broader description as shown in Figure 1.6.

Apparel merchandise along with related accessories, but excluding bags and leather goods retailers, is by far the dominant retail category operated by overseas concerns. This again reflects the early entry of exclusive brand retailers, but the continuing entry of more mass market retailers has continued to push the number up. Related to this also is the second highest category, that of Cosmetics, into which Boots and Walgreen's were also added as the two overseas drugstore operators. The top minor categories were restaurant chains, sportswear, jewellery, ceramics and audio visual software. At present, accurate data on store numbers are not available but analysis of product category by the number of actual outlets in each will greatly add to this.

Most other broad categories are included, but food and supermarkets are both remarkably poorly represented. This reflects the advance of domestic retailers in these categories as well as the greater difficulty in finding competitive advantage that can be translated into overseas operations. It is, hypothetically, the next frontier, however. For the time being, Carrefour has been categorized as a general merchandise retailer as the company is currently concentrating on its hypermarket format.

In the long run, however, Carrefour, along with possible new entrants such as Tesco, Wal-Mart and Metro are likely to cause more change in the food distribution channel than in any other. While Japan has some impressively large food retailers, the distribution of food remains one of the most traditional and least efficient of any product category. From the consumer's point of view it is also the most highly priced as a result. This is at least partly due to the inability and unwillingness of major Japanese food distributors to effect change in the system. In the 1990s, the largest of these have all suffered major structural problems brought on largely due to low levels of competition which lead to inertia in the sector. It is one area where rapid change can be expected in the near future, and overseas retailers are more than likely to be the key agents of that change.

Keys to success in Japan and entry strategy

There is little debate that Japan is not an easy market to enter. This is the main reason why so many Western companies have chosen to enter less developed markets in the rest of Asia before Japan. Nevertheless, the overall economic power of the Japanese market makes it a very attractive one. This situation suggests that market entry in terms of overall cost and potential success is seen by many companies as being particularly difficult. When the actual success of a small number of high profile companies such as Louis Vuitton, ToysRUs and Starbucks is considered, the reluctance of other large, wealthy and very competitive international retailers to enter Japan is even more surprising. Of course, the fact that this is now changing very quickly, with all of the world's top retailers now turning their attention to Japan, is the single main reason why it is such an issue.

There is a significant literature on Japanese distribution in English. Larke (1994: 246–66) provides a comprehensive list up to the mid-1990s. A more recent study is Czinkota and Kotabe (2000). A lot of this literature has taken a critical view of Japanese distribution as seen from a Western point of view, but surprisingly few have looked at entry methods and successful cases. Unsurprisingly,

Table 1.3 Differences between Japanese and Western values

	Japanese values	*Western values*
Social roles	Group seniority	Individualism
Competition	Success through cooperation	Success through competition
Perception	Appearance is truth	Reality is truth

Source: Adapted from Sonnenborn (2000).

Japanese sources which consider successful cases of overseas entry are even more rare. JETRO continues to provide an excellent and wide ranging source of information concerning market entry both in print and at its web site (see http://www.jetro.go.jp/), but the broad remit of JETRO's mission and its existence as a Japanese government organization both limit the extent of practical help that it can give.

There are exceptions, however, of which two recent studies stand out. Sonnenborn's (2000) study looks at the automobile market in particular, but offers a number of observations that are applicable to any sector. On the social and cultural side, he correctly recommends overseas companies to learn about and attempt to understand three dichotomies (see Table 1.3).

He points out that Japanese people often place emphasis at the opposite end of the scale to many Westerners and do not react as most non-Japanese would naturally expect. In some cases, the non-Western values are similar in other parts of Asia, but some, for example the Japanese dislike of competition relative to social harmony and, most importantly, the Japanese tendency to place so much emphasis on appearance at all costs, cannot be said to be Asian.

Sonnenborn (2000) goes on to list the 4Ps and management factors for success in the Japanese market, and these can be expanded from a retail viewpoint:

1 *Product concept*: a product that is clearly differentiated and superior in either a tangible or, as in the case of some exclusive brands, intangible way to local competitors will have a much higher chance of success in Japan.

2 *Pricing*: as Sonnenborn points out (2000: 320), in the automobile category, high market entry costs mean that most imported models tend to be exclusive brands and to carry high retail prices. This is a commonly held belief for most products imported into Japan, but it would be incorrect to apply it to all. Japan is the most expensive country in the world, and Japanese consumers have proven very welcoming of discount retailers and other low price imports. It is, however, very important for an overseas company to understand the Japanese image regarding the price–quality trade-off in its own product category and for its own brands. In some cases, such as the case of Louis Vuitton, it will be possible and even desirable to increase prices in Japan above the levels elsewhere. In other cases, this will not be true.

3 *Communication policy*: Sonnenborn's most important point is that good marketing communications and associated brand building can mean make

or break for an overseas company in Japan. He is also correct in pointing out that it would be difficult to attempt to build a brand from scratch within Japan. Japanese are well aware of the consumer market outside their countries and, as in the case of Boots or Carrefour, will take a strong interest in press coverage of these new entrants. Any overseas company needs to be prepared for extensive and controlled PR efforts first and foremost, and the richer firms will begin outright marketing at an early stage.

4   *Distribution policy*: beginning with BMW, overseas car distributors were some of the first to break away from Japanese partnerships and set up their own distribution networks. For such high value-added items, this was an obvious strategy to follow, but now more and more other companies, especially exclusive brands are following suit. Each product and each brand position warrants a different distribution approach, however. The options, as discussed in the next section, are generally direct control, joint venture or licensing, the last two of which come with a number of separate sub-strategies and alternatives.

5   *Management*: despite its importance, this one non-marketing factor is not covered in detail on its own, but the issues are reflected in Sonnenborn's three dichotomies mentioned above. Employee loyalty has overriding importance to operations in Japan and is the single most important factor in terms of employee motivation much more so than salary or other tangible reward. Few non-Japanese companies properly appreciate this fact and many have found it hard to attract and keep good staff. It is true that foreign companies are a popular place of employment partly because they often pay by experience and ability, allowing some Japanese to receive much higher salaries than they would at domestic firms, but also because work practices often provide more freedom and are much more objectively structured than in traditional Japanese firms. Along with the requirement for English language abilities, too many overseas entrants seek employees who have worked at other foreign firms. This has led to a pool of bilingual Japanese employees who are willing to make regular job changes in search of ever higher salaries. This undermines the basic Japanese notion of loyalty to the company and creates significant personnel problems at many firms.

A second and far more useful source of suggestions for market entry is offered by Fields *et al.* (2000: 104–24). The authors list seven factors:

1   Tailoring to the market by adapting to cultural and structural differences.
2   Finding opportunities in declining markets.
3   Not underestimating local competition.
4   Offering a unique product and positioning.
5   Using foreignness as an advantage.
6   Using alliances strategically.
7   Using Japan as a stepping stone to Asia.

This is probably the most relevant and astute list of recommendations currently available in the literature today. The seven points are fairly self-explanatory, but Fields goes on to point out a number of sub-issues which are equally important. He notes that while many companies have found quite remarkable success as a result of tailoring their product, service or retail format to Japan, many others have ignored this problem and attempted, often with little success, to enter the market with a standard 'globalized' offering.

Under his sixth point, Fields makes the assertion which more and more well informed analysts are also coming to believe. He says:

> Some argue that for foreigners to understand the market, they must have Japanese executives and Japanese partners.... [But to] the extent that entrants are using market innovations and focusing on new consumers, the Japanese perspectives become less important and even a disadvantage.
>
> (Fields *et al.* 2000: 115. Brackets added.)

He goes on to illustrate the growing trend for firms to split from initial joint-ventures with Japanese companies. In the consumer products and retail sectors this is a new and increasingly popular strategy, with more and more examples.

Unlike Sonnenborn, Fields also reiterates time and again the need to find highly motivated employees and treat them as Japanese. He recommends:

- training and empowering local management;
- hiring 'passionate' expatriates who really know Japan as well as the internationalization process;
- motivating in ways other than just through monetary reward;
- choose employees from beyond the boundaries of a particular industry or product sector to find people who really know the customer and not just the internal workings of similar or competing firms.

Finally and most importantly, Fields emphasizes the need for tenacity and long-term commitment. This is an aspect of the Japanese market that is at once difficult to quantify and too frequently overlooked. With the constant demand for short-term return on investment for shareholders, companies must place Japanese activities within the context of their overall global strategy. Japan is not a market that can be rushed, but equally many companies have found that with patience and perseverance, it is one of the most lucrative markets in the world. Too many have made only half-hearted attempts at Japan and pulled out long before they have given their business time to mature. It is significant that US outdoor goods retailer REI is one very recent example (see Japan Consuming 2001). REI opened its first overseas store in Tokyo in 2000 only to close down twelve months later. This is particularly sad as, writing before REI's entry into Japan, Fields *et al.* (2000: 105) points out how translating their mail-order catalogue into Japanese brought an 80 per cent increase in sales to the same company several years before.

Retail entry strategies for Japan

There is no single correct entry strategy for a retailer coming to Japan, but the number of possibilities basically fall under one of the following types:

1 Direct operation
2 Joint venture with a Japanese firm or firms
3 Licence or franchise agreement.

Although the majority of overseas companies operating in Japanese retail channels today are 100 per cent foreign-owned subsidiaries of non-Japanese companies, there has been a gradual change back from the license agreements and simple importing to the most favoured method today of direct operation. As already mentioned, the 1990s have also seen a significant and growing number of established companies reorganizing their operations towards direct operation.

The final section of this chapter considers four illustrative cases as brief examples of international retail operation in Japan. Each has its own, very different characteristics. No attempt is made to introduce specific figures into this analysis as, in most cases, companies are unwilling to make them public. The information offered here was gathered from mass media sources, industry analysts and contacts from within the companies involved.

ToysRUs

ToysRUs is seen by many as anathema of Japanese retailers. TRU entered Japan on the back of US–Japan Structural Impediments Initiative trade talks in which the USA demanded deregulation of distribution systems in Japan. Not only that, but as a large format category killer retailer, TRU entered a market with no large, corporate competitors in the retail channel, and one which maintained traditional manufacturer–wholesaler control over distribution channels. The opening of a single TRU store anywhere in Japan would damage the livelihoods of any small toy stores nearby.

The political fallout from TRU's entry was mitigated partly by the force of the US government behind it, but also because TRU chose McDonald's Japan as its joint-venture partner. McDonald's is one of the most successful overseas brands in Japan and has made many significant adaptations and innovations in order to succeed in Japan. In the same style, TRU quickly became a Japanese-style American company. The company president, Manabu Tazaki, is Japanese and although it is true to say TRU changed the whole structure of toy distribution in Japan, this change was not unwelcome to large Japanese suppliers such as Bandai and Tomy because of the greatly expanded market it provides. True, the chain of more than 100 TRU stores that have now been built around Japan have meant thousands of small toy stores have seen their markets disappear, but there have been significant market and business advantages.

TRU is the archetypal example of overseas retail success in Japan. While the political backing, no matter how informal, with which it entered Japan was significant in its initial success, the company has maintained a carefully Japanese stance on many issues. Some academic commentators (e.g. Takayama 2001) still see the company as opening the first hole in the dam, but these same commentators often ignore the benefits.

TRU has opened up and modernized the Japanese toy market. Manufacturers at first were unhappy with their lessening power within retail channels and, as is often the case, fought not to lose control over retail prices, but the scale of TRU operations are now such that even the largest toy makers are very happy to work with the chain although few would probably admit it in public.

TRU Japan is now so successful that it was listed on the Tokyo Stock Exchange in 2001 and has even helped its US parent through a number of financial difficulties over recent years. There have even been rumours of a reverse takeover of the US parent by the Japanese subsidiary as happened with Seven-Eleven in 1989.

For other overseas companies, however, TRU is a case that is difficult to emulate. Basically, the joint-venture agreement meant that TRU Japan worked almost autonomously from its US parent. The backing of McDonalds Japan continues to be a vital part of the company's success and allows it to proceed with a speed and respectability that few foreigners can enjoy. On the other hand, the level of Japanese control may be more than is desirable for many non-Japanese firms.

Boots MC Japan

Boots, the British pharmacy and drugstore chain, presents a sad story indeed. After forays into the Netherlands and a quite successful entry into Thailand, Boots arrived in Japan in fairly typical style. With a small team eager to work in the market, initial moves proceeded very quickly. Unlike ToysRUs, however, Boots' fatal error was in choosing a joint-venture strategy with a Japanese company.

As with any story of failure, there are two very different sides, but whatever the details, the joint-venture strategy was a mistake in this case. In 1999, Boots tied up with one of the largest trading companies in the world, Mitsubishi Shoji, to form Boots MC Japan. Boots held 51 per cent of the firm. Only the managers, on the ground at the time, can say what were the true motivations behind this move, but the chance to tie with one of the largest and most prestigious firms in Japan was undoubtedly a major temptation.

Mitsubishi, along with other large trading companies, is taking a growing interest in retail channels. Mitsubishi is already a major supplier and wholesaler in several consumer goods categories, and in 2000 acquired a controlling stake in the number two convenience store chain, Lawson.

Without repeating rumour and innuendo, the single major problem within the joint venture can be inferred from results of its operations. On the positive side, Boots did an excellent job of establishing its brand in Japan. While expensive, the company spent heavily on advertising and store opening campaigns, and was prepared to introduce its brand to the Japanese consumer. This, on the whole, worked well, and consumers were willing and enthusiastic about trying the brand.

On the other hand, over a two-year period, Boots opened only four stores. Three of them were in very high profile, very expensive locations in Tokyo and Yokohama and as such were impressive, but the very low number of stores over such a long period, and the unconfident nature of store merchandising that mixed unique Boots brands with mundane Japanese competitors, were major disappointments.

The story is a sad one because Boots has many of the ingredients necessary for success in Japan. Foremost, the Boots brand was different, foreign and well presented. Whilst pure speculation, it seems likely that the company concentrated too much on offering a format similar to that in other countries rather than aiming at a more up-market and exclusive target. Such positioning would have led the brand into concessions in department stores and other areas, allowing for a more rapid and much lower cost roll-out, while maintaining brand identity and prestige.

Rumours of major conflict of interests between the British and Japanese management is confirmed by the opposing stories from each side of why the venture failed. But there again, such stories, along with a major hole in the bank account, are always the only things left after any divorce.

Office Depot

Office Depot is one example of a growing number of companies that have decided to take over their Japanese operations before the problems that beset Boots come to a head. Office Depot, along with Office Max its US rival, both entered the Japanese market in 1997. Both chose the most frequently recommended strategy of joint venture. Office Depot signed with electrical distributor Deodeo, while Office Max seemed to get the better deal, linking with number two general merchandise chain Jusco. Jusco is an avid collector of overseas retailers and, unlike some near competitors, has also made a success of several including Laura Ashley, Talbot's and Body Shop in Japan.

In 2001, however, Office Max pulled out of the deal, and, once again, mass media reports of the fallout suggest little love lost between the two. Academic reports (Nemoto and Tamehiro 2001; Takayama 2001) have unconditionally blamed lack of understanding of the Japanese market by Office Max, but this belies the responsibility and the role of the Japanese partner – surely that is why the joint venture was undertaken in the first place?

Office Depot, on the other hand, took another route. In 2000, the company bought out its Japanese partner, and is now going it alone. As Fields has also pointed out, Japan can be a perfect stepping stone for the rest of Asia. In Office Depot's case, unlike ToysRUs, for example, the product sector in which it operates is already mature and highly competitive, but, as with TRU, it is also a sector which relies predominantly on traditional distribution methods.

After buying out Deodeo, Office Depot has yet to make a mark with its own ideas and operational changes, but the company recognizes significant potential. There are possibilities for employing channels and merchandising methods not yet common in the office supplies category and so making changes and adaptations similar to those achieved by TRU. This is less likely, however, because of the higher level of competition that Office Depot faces. It is true that office supplies retailing is an old sector well set for more innovation and new sales methods. With any luck, along with enough financial and intellectual flexibility from the US parent, Office Depot has every chance of success.

Carrefour

If ToysRUs was the first hole in the dam, Carrefour is the first super tanker to run aground. Since the 1960s, Japanese research literature is replete with references to several 'revolutions' that were predicted to change the face of distribution forever (from Hayashi 1992; Kubomura 1996; Nakauchi 2001). None, in hind sight, offer much evidence of any form of change that could be called revolution. In fact, Japanese distribution seems to have spent most of the past forty years actively working against sudden or extreme changes that could be deemed revolutionary. Until, that is, the arrival of Carrefour.

While Boots managed to open four small specialty stores in three years, Carrefour opened three 10,000–20,000 square metre stores in three months from December 2000 to February 2001. The company was heralded with hordes of consumers, with more than 50,000 visiting the first store over its first weekend, followed by derision in the media and incredible condemnation in even more academic circles.

It is true that Carrefour has not done everything right, nor has it been an out and out success, but the three experimental stores it has opened have provided a strong platform for greater adaptation and market innovation. They are also a basis for further expansion. Sales figures are unavailable, but Nemoto and Tamehiro (2001) offer an informed total of Yen 30 billion for the first year. While he points out this would hardly put Carrefour among the top 300 retailers in Japan, he ignores the fact that in terms of sale per store, only the top department stores perform better in such a small chain. If similar results are achieved in the preliminary stores, and there are a number of reasons to expect them to actually improve, Carrefour will quickly jump into the top fifty retailers and be ready to move higher.

Carrefour's 'revolution' was a matter of three factors. First, it is the first large format, globally influential retailer to open in Japan. Second, it did it directly without choosing a Japanese partner or joint venture, even though a number of companies were more than eager to step into the role. Third, and most importantly, it is one of the few retailers who have not only chosen direct operations, but it has also insisted on maintaining some key fundamental operating principles that apply to all its international operations.

Germany's Metro is also planning to open stores in 2002. As Nemoto and Tamehiro (2001) illustrates, Metro is likely to have a far smoother time, partly as it does not have the stigma of being first, but mainly because it is operating within an 80–20 joint venture with Marubeni, another major trading house. Marubeni has significant supermarket and food wholesaling interests of its own and financial analysts have been highly sceptical of the choice of partner, but Metro no doubt hopes the tie-up will ease relations with suppliers, even though it more or less locks the company out of working with members of the other major trading groups.

There is also the possibility of both Tesco entering the market in the very near future following Wal-Mart in 2002. Tesco, which has competitive advantage in marketing, customer service and personnel training, is likely to be able to adapt best of all to Japan. Wal-Mart has a proven preference for entry by acquisition and could cause an even bigger change than Carrefour as it becomes established. Whatever happens, the shock of Carrefour being the first big retailer will soon be over as others follow on in turn.

The second and third criticisms levelled at Carrefour by Japanese in general, the decision to operate directly and to maintain international business practices, are inter-related. The single biggest shock to Japanese suppliers and retailers alike was Carrefour's insistence that it would maintain merchandising and pricing autonomy. Despite the outlawing of Retail Price Maintenance by manufacturers and wholesalers since 1965, price setting and careful control are maintained in respect of social harmony over competition (see Sonnenborn 2000). Retailers generally agree not to sell at a loss under any circumstances, and suppliers will often agree to reabsorb unsold merchandise in order to allow prices to stay high.

Carrefour has refused to play this game. In a way that would have been unacceptable and outright illegal in other industrial nations, several leading wholesalers publicly refused to work with Carrefour. Various reasons were given, but the fact that Carrefour refused to guarantee price demands was the key, unspoken issue. In another case, and in keeping with the need for social harmony, senior executives at Nihon Shurui Hanbai, the largest liquor wholesaler in Japan, freely announced that they would only supply Carrefour if their other (Japanese) retail customers agreed, and then on the understanding that Carrefour would not sell below wholesale price, so undercutting competitors (see Nikkei Ryutsu Shinbun 2001).

Meanwhile, Carrefour introduced the first lowest price guarantee in Japan, offering a core 800 lines at the lowest price within 15 kilometres of each store. Even so, the Japanese press was filled for a time with a series of articles aimed at proving that the French retailer was actually more expensive than Japanese competitors (see Nikkei Trendy 2001; Asahi Shinbun 2001b). On the other hand, Carrefour opened the door to a number of second rank wholesalers who had been shut out of some of the leading Japanese chains due to the near monopoly position of the largest processed food manufacturers. These have reaped the greatest benefits with Carrefour stores achieving record sales on some limited promotional items. One example was the sale of more than 10,000 packs of prepared noodles in a single day.

The fervour has cooled. Consumer numbers at Carrefour stores have waned, and at least one store at Minami Machida in western Tokyo is unlikely to continue in operation under current conditions. Carrefour continues to insist on using

French store managers, and has a significant problem keeping staff due to the driven and intensive nature of management systems. Problems with suppliers, in-store merchandising, and in personnel and training are all being addressed. The company opened two stores in Kanagawa and Saitama at the end of 2001, and vastly increased the proportion of imported Carrefour label brands at its stores. This last change was something the company had not planned for, expecting to win over more Japanese suppliers and compete on level terms with domestic retailers. The move is in response to considerable consumer disappointment that Carrefour stocks just the same merchandise as its rivals and not as much French product as they expected. It is surprising that the company did not realize this problem earlier on.

Carrefour is big enough and bold enough to withstand the press onslaught it has suffered, and is hopefully international enough to adapt to the many aspects of consumer demand and company operations that set Japan apart from other countries. Whatever the outcome, Carrefour currently seems to have made the long-term commitment that too many overseas companies have failed to do. In doing so it has also paved the way for other overseas competitors to make the move.

Conclusions and future research

The conclusion to this report is very simple: Japan is fast approaching the point where its retail market will be properly open to the world stage. As with Japan as a country in the 1850s, the retail market has had to be prised open with a certain amount of force. More than a few overseas retailers have been operating in Japan for a number of years, and many are now taking the advantage to expand and build their business, often breaking out of unproductive joint venture agreements in the process.

The development of international retailing in Japan bears many of the theoretical characteristics introduced in the general research literature, especially Dawson (1994). In many cases, overseas retailers have significant competitive advantages as compared with their Japanese counterparts, and some are also in the happy position of entering retail sectors that have declined or stalled over recent years. Others have established themselves with the help of Japanese-based partners and are now in a position to face the market alone, especially in taking advantage of falls in land value and bored, savings-rich consumers.

On the other hand, Japan is not an easy or blindly accessible market by any means. The need to recognize the differences, adapt and change product and operations, adjust to customer expectations, and be aware of the challenges, particularly in personnel, of operating in Japan, all set it apart from, probably, every other market in the world. It is a mistake to even consider Japan as part of Asia as many of the values, expectations and level of consumer nationalism are all incomparable.

Perhaps the three biggest mistakes that can be drawn from the various unsuccessful and re-developed cases of retail operations in Japan are as follows:

1   *Do not have a strategy and objectives that are too short term*: while Western shareholders demand an unfairly rapid return, success in Japan needs to be

sought over a much longer period than is usual in many markets. Shareholders and senior executives need to be made aware of this fact and, perhaps more importantly, of the potential returns to those who are patient enough to wait. These returns are considerable, and there are numerous cases that prove the point.

2   *Do not expect to operate the business 'out of the box'*: being so tied up in the market development aspects of the business, many overseas managers overlook the importance of internal operations, particularly recruitment, employee motivation and career structure. This can make or break the operation because it is the Japanese staff who will ultimately make the venture a success or failure. Trying to emulate a Japanese business, or allowing senior Japanese staff to try, will not work, but the same is also true for a company that does not adapt some aspects of employment structures towards the Japanese model.

3   *Do not undervalue information or stop listening*: there are a handful of companies who have really investigated the Japanese market. These fall into two categories: those that have decided Japan was not yet ready for their business and those who have seen outright success. Working in Japan should be a constant and ongoing learning process in all aspects of the business from pre-entry surveys to ongoing day-to-day operations. Too many overseas companies have such outright assurance of their existing systems and practices that they are unwilling to listen to suggestions for change. Others listen, but do not make the commitment to implement change where it is obviously necessary. One of the most common problems is companies who are tied to the final decisions of parent office executives living on the other side of the world. Successful companies will be operated in Japan by people who know the market first hand.

This chapter is based on a data set of overseas companies operating in the Japanese retail sector in one way or another. The data set is larger and more complete than any other currently known, outside major consulting houses, but the next aim will be to add to these data and increase their scope and accuracy. While the chapter provides a basic background to international retail expansion in Japan, it does not attempt the level of analysis of past cases that would be really useful.

Research is, however, vitally necessary. Such a topic is increasingly unworthy of many Japanese researchers as it challenges the status quo within which they live. It is necessary to consider not only the problems and detrimental aspects of large, powerful overseas retailers entering the market, but also the advantages and improvements that they are likely to bring. These are considerable, but it is difficult for a career minded Japanese academic to talk about them objectively. The majority of cases so far have restricted themselves to case studies (Aihara 2001; Yokomori 2001) or to speculative work on the ways Japanese retailers should compete. Foremost among the latter, Nemoto and Tamehiro (2001) make the point that the single most important thing Japanese firms can do is simply remain calm. He also then points out that, yes, in terms of marketing ability, information systems and operational management, many overseas retailers are more efficient and more skilled than the majority of Japanese. This illustrates ways in which overseas entry will push Japanese retailers to change for the better.

Acknowledgement

The author would like to thank the UMDS, Distribution Sciences Research Institute, and the Technology Transfer Project (Kagaku Kenkyu Fund) for valuable research funding assistance for this project.

References

Aihara, Osamu (2001) 'Carrefour expanding through M&A and overseas entry' [M&A to kaigai shinshutsu de kyodai-ka suru Karufuru], *Ryutsu to Shisutemu*, 108, June: 12–19.

Alexander, Nicholas (1990a) 'Retailers and international markets: motives for expansion', *International Marketing Review*, 7(4): 75–85.

Alexander, Nicholas (1990b) 'Retailing post-1992', *Services Industries Journal*, 10(2): 172–87.

Alexander, Nicholas (1997) *International Retailing*. Oxford & Malden: Blackwell Publishers.

Asahi Shinbun (2001a) 'Enemies all round: 100 days since the landing of French supermarket "Carrefour"' [Shobai-teki ni mo sojo koka: fu-supa "Karufuru" joriku hyaku nichi], *Asahi Shinbun*, 16 March: 13.

Asahi Shinbun (2001b) 'Overseas supermarket "Carrefour" comes to Saitama' [Gaishikei supa "Karufuru", Saitama he], *Asahi Shinbun*, 2 July: 36.

Bailey, J., Clarke-Hill, C. and Robinson, T. (1995) 'International retail alliance: toward a taxonomy', *Service Industries Journal*, 15(4): 25–41.

Cendron, Bernard (1984) 'Changing the dream: the Japanese and brand names', *Dentsu Japan Marketing/Advertising*, 2(1): 43–7.

CIG (1991) *Cross-Border Retailing in Europe*, London: Corporate Intelligence Group.

CIG (1994) *Cross-Border Retailing in Europe*, London: Corporate Intelligence Group.

Clarke, Ian and Rimmer, Peter (1997) 'The anatomy of retail internationalization: Daimaru's decision to invest in Melbourne, Australia', *Service Industries Journal*, 17(3): 361–82.

Czinkota, M. R. and Kotabe, M. (eds) (2000) *Japanese Distribution Strategy*. London: Business Press.

Davies, Keri (1996) 'Yaohan International Holdings'. In: L. Lusch and P. Dunne (eds) *Cases in Retailing*, South-Western College Publishing, pp. 219–38.

Davies, Keri (2000) 'The international activities of Japanese retailers'. In: Michael R. Czinkota and Masaaki Kotabe (eds) *Japanese Distribution Strategy*, London: Business Press, pp. 227–32.

Dawson, John A. (1994) 'Internationalization of retailing operations', *Journal of Marketing Management*, 10: 267–82.

Dawson, John A. and Larke, Roy (2001) 'Japanese retailing in the 1990s: retailer performance in a decade of slow growth', 11th International Conference on Research in the Distributive Trades, University of Tilberg, 28 June.

Fahy, John and Taguchi, Fuyuki (2000) 'Japan's second distribution revolution: the penetration of global retail formats'. In: Michael R. Czinkota and Masaaki Kotabe (eds) *Japanese Distribution Strategy*, London: Business Press, pp. 298–309.

Fields, George (1983) *From Bonsai's to Levi's*. London: Futura.

Fields, George (1988) *The Japanese Market Culture*. Tokyo: Japan Times.

Fields, George, Kitahira, Hotaka and Wind, Jerry (2000) *Leveraging Japan*. San Francisco: Jossey-Bass.

Hayashi, Shuji (1992) *New Theory of Distribution Revolution* [Ryutsu Kakumei Shinron]. Tokyo: Chikura.

Hollander, Stanley C. (1970) *Multinational Retailing*. East Lansing: MSU Press.

Japan Consuming (2001) 'Santa Claus does exist – if you are an overseas brand', *Japan Consuming*, 2(12): 2–3.

JETRO (2000) Home page: http://www.jetro.go.jp/

Kacker, M. (1985) *Transatlantic Trends in Retailing*. Westport, CT: Quorum.

Kawabata, Moto (2000) *The Overseas Expansion and Strategy of Retailers* [Kourigyo no Kaigai Sinshutsu to Senryaku]. Tokyo: Shinhyoron.

Kubomura, Takayuki (1996) *The Second Distribution Revolution: Themes for the 21st Century* [Dai 2 ji Ryutsu Kakumei: 21 Seiki he no Kadai]. Tokyo: Nihon Keizai Shinbunsha.

Larke, Roy (1991) *Consumer Perceptions of Large Retail Stores*, unpublished PhD thesis, Univesity of Stirling.

Larke, Roy (1994) *Japanese Retailing*. London and New York: Routledge.

Larke, Roy (2002) 'Brands: can't live with 'em, can't live without 'em', *Japan Consuming*, 3(3): 12–15.

McGoldrick, Peter and Fryer, E. (1993) 'Organisational culture and the internationaliza-tion of retailers', 7th International Conference on Research in Distributive Trades, Institute for Retail Studies, University of Stirling, 6–8 September.

MITI (1989) *Vision for Distribution in the 1980s* [90 Nendai no Ryutsu Bijon]. Tokyo: MOF.

Mukoyama, Masao (1996) *Towards the Landing of Pure Global* [Pyua Gurobaru he no Chakuchi]. Tokyo: Chikura Shobo.

Mukoyama, Masao (2000) 'The standardization–adaptation problem of product assortment in the internationalization of retailers'. In: Michael R. Czinkota and Masaaki Kotabe (eds) *Japanese Distribution Strategy*, London: Business Press, pp. 233–41.

Nakauchi, Isao (2001) 'The distribution revolution doesn't end' [Ryutsu Kakumei ha Owaranai]. Tokyo: Nihon Keizai Shinbunsha.

Nemoto, Shigeaki and Tamehiro, Yoshihiro (2001) 'Global retailer: giant overseas retailers enter the Japanese market'. Tokyo: Toyo Keizal Shinposha,

Nihon Marketing Journal (2001) 'Carrefour's dilemma' [Karufuru no jirema], *Nihon Marketing Journal*, 14 June: 1–2.

Nikkei Ryutsu Shinbun (1989) '29th Annual Consumer Survey: high income consumers' [Dai 29 Kai Shohisha Chosa: Kogaku Shotoku Sha], *Nikkei Ryutsu Shinbun*, 10 September: 1–5.

Nikkei Ryutsu Shinbun (2001) 'Asking top wholesaler managers about the true trading conditions with French Carrfour' [Fu Karufuru, torihiki no jittai ha oroshi 2 sha toppu ni kiku], *Nikkei Ryutsu Shinbun*, 23 January: 11.

Nikkei Trendy (2001) 'Price breakthrough: the winners of the low price battle' [Price Breakthrough: tei-kakaku batoru no shosha], *Nikkei Trendy*, 179: 48–73.

Salmon, W. J. and Tordjman, A. (1989) 'The internationalization of retailing', *International Journal of Retailing*, 4(2): 3–16.

Sonnenborn, Hans-Peter (2000) 'Successful market entry and performance in Japan'. In: Michael R. Czinkota and Masaaki Kotabe (eds) *Japanese Distribution Strategy*, London, Business Press, pp. 310–24.

Sternquist, Brenda (2000) 'The internationalization of Japanese department stores and GMS stores: are there characteristics that profile success'. In: Michael R. Czinkota and Masaaki Kotabe (eds) *Japanese Distribution Strategy*, London, Business Press, pp. 242–52.

Takayama, Kunisuke (2001) 'The impact and reaction within the Japanese distribution industry of the overseas expansion of Western retailers' [Obei kourigyo no kaigai shin-shutsu ga, waga kuni ryutsu-gyo ni ataeru inpakuto to taio], *Ryutsu to Shisutemu*, 108, June: 3–11.

Tanner, D. (1992) 'Ito Yokado, Kotobukiya, Marui and Nagasakiya'. In: A. Hast *et al.* (eds) *International Directory of Company Histories* Vol. 5. Detroit, St James Press.

Treadgold, A. (1988) 'Retailing without frontiers', *Retail and Distribution Management*, 16(6): 31–7.

Treadgold, A. (1990) 'The emerging internationalization of retailing: present status and future changes', *Irish Marketing Review*, 5(2): 11–27.

Yokomori, Toyo (2001) 'Metro announces Japan entry' [Nihon shinshutsu wo hyomei shita Metoro], *Ryutsu to Shisutemu*, 108, June: 20–7.

2 The development of foreign retailing in Taiwan

The impacts of Carrefour

Tsuchiya Hitoshi

Introduction

The internationalization of Carrefour increased rapidly, through the 1990s, and by 2002, the firm had stores in more than twenty countries. It had approximately a hundred stores in Asia, most of them being hypermarkets. In the Asian market, Taiwan was the first country where Carrefour set up businesses. Carrefour opened its first store in Kaohsiung, a southern city of Taiwan in 1989. Since then it has gradually increased its presence, with 5 stores by 1992, 10 stores by 1995 and it had 26 stores in 2001. The number of employees exceeded 6,000 and sales totalled NT$43 billion. Compared with Makro, the second largest hypermarket operator in Taiwan with sales amounting to NT$13.8 billion, Carrefour is considerably larger. Carrefour has become the largest hypermarket operator in Taiwan over a period of only ten years.

There are a variety of topics for investigation in the study of the internationalization of retailing. These topics include:

- the entry mode;
- the struggle between adaptation and standardization;
- the influences on local enterprises and local distribution systems;
- the effects of feedback of information and techniques to retailer's head-office and distribution system in the home country (Davies and Yahagi 2001).

Generally, entry mode and problems of adaptation or standardization are pointed out as important in most studies on this subject. The aim of this chapter is to examine, through consideration of Carrefour in Taiwan, some issues of how foreign retailers enter local markets and how their behaviour affects local distribution systems. Taiwan is considered because it has operated a more open-market policy for sixteen years, after the deregulation in 1986 of the policy of limiting foreign investment in the service industry. Since 1986, various types of retail formats brought from developed countries have become established. The impacts of hypermarkets on Taiwan's traditional distribution system are illustrated with the case of Carrefour, the major hypermarket company in Taiwan.

The hypermarket sector in Taiwan

Following the establishment of an open market policy, the leading companies of
several major retail formats entered Taiwan. Department stores (Tsuchiya 2000)
and convenience stores have entered from Japan, supermarkets from Hong Kong,
and the hypermarket and discount store from France, the Netherlands and USA.
The formats have competed intensely with each other in the past fifteen years.
'Simultaneous frequent occurrence and the compulsory innovation' (Davies and
Yahagi 2001: 337) have characterized foreign retailing.

Table 2.1 shows the entry dates of the major foreign and domestic hypermarkets in Taiwan. In 1989, Carrefour opened its first branch in Taiwan. In the same
year, Makro opened its first store in Taoyuan, in the northern part of Taiwan.
After that, domestic firms followed and began to enter the hypermarket business.
Sternquist (1998: 8–10) suggested that licensing, joint venture and wholly owned
subsidiary are the main entry modes in the process of internationalization of
retailing. Table 2.1 shows that in Taiwan most foreign firms adopted joint ventures as their entry mode. Since the deregulation in 1986 was only partial, the
Taiwanese market did not open completely. The Taiwanese government, although
allowing foreign investment in retailing, still prohibited the foreign retailers from

Table 2.1 Entry of major foreign hypermarkets and discount stores

Year	Retailer	Taiwanese investor	Foreign investor	Form of enterprise	Related firm
1989	Carrefour	Uni-President Enterprise Corp. (49%)	Carrefour group (France 51%)	Joint venture	7-Eleven Uni-President Bread Franchise store
1989	Makro	Holmsgreen group (35%)	SHV (the Netherlands 55%) Charoen Pokphand (Thailand 10%)	Joint venture	LaiLai OK Convenience store
1993	Hyper-fee	Far Eastern group (70%)	Promodès (France 30%)	Joint venture	Far Eastern Department store Far Eastern Aimai
1997	Costco	President Department store (49%)	Price Costco (USA 51%)	Joint venture	President Department store
2000	Jéant	Far Eastern Department store (50%)	Géant-Casino (France 50%)	Joint venture	Far Eastern Department store
2000	RT-MART	RT-MART (33%)	Auchan (France 67%)	Joint venture	

Sources: Wealth Magazine 1998(3): 257 and Distribution News 2001(2): 10.

Table 2.2 The number of stores and sales of major hypermarket firms in 2000

Store	Number of stores	Sales NT$100 million
Carrefour	26	430
Makro	8	138
Géant	10	131
Fuyuan	12	74
Asia Pacific Development	3	70
RT-MART	8	54.1
Save & Safe	3	53.8
KAOMART	8	40
Wanjiafu	4	37.3
TUNIEX MART	1	21.1

Source: Distribution News 2001(5): 14.

holding majority ownership. In a second stage of deregulation complete foreign ownership was allowed subsequently. In mid-2002, there were fifteen firms operating a total of approximately hundred hypermarkets in Taiwan. Their gross sales, in 2000, amounted to approximately NT$150 billion, which is about 5 per cent of the total retail trade (Ministry of Economic Affairs 2001).

Table 2.2 shows the number of stores and the amount of sales of the major firms operating hypermarkets, in 2000. The top three companies are all foreign firms: the French Carrefour, the Dutch Makro and the French Jéant. They account for 47 per cent of the total sales of the hypermarket sector. In this highly competitive market, Carrefour has an overwhelming lead: its sales are three times as much as that of Makro, and it accounts for 35 per cent of the total sales of the hypermarket business.

The phenomenon of the gross sales of general merchandise stores or discount stores exceeding that of department stores is considered as an index that marks a turning point for the distribution system in a country. For instance, in 1921 J. C. Penny, a clothing chain store exceeded the sales of Macy's, which is one of the largest traditional department stores in USA. In Japan, the gross sales of general merchandise stores exceeded the sales of department stores in 1972. In the same year, the gross sales of Daiei, the largest general merchandise store, exceeded those of Mitsukoshi, the largest department store (Sato 1974: 29–30). When this index is applied to Taiwan, department stores still exceeded hypermarkets in gross sales in 2000, as is shown in Figure 2.1.

While the position of department stores in Taiwan is still strong, the sales of hypermarkets have been increasing at a faster rate. If this trend continues, it is just a matter of time before hypermarket sales exceed those of department stores. On the other hand, in 1993, the sales of Carrefour already exceeded that of Pacific Sogo group, which was the largest department store group at that time. The position as the largest department store company changed from Pacific Sogo group to Kong Mitsukoshi group in 1998. Figure 2.2 shows the change in number of stores

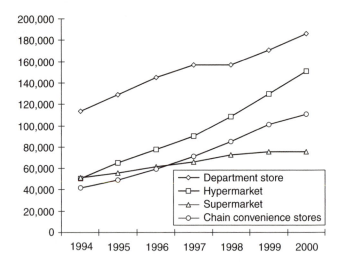

Figure 2.1 Sales by the main formats in Taiwan.

Source: Ministry of Economic Affairs (2001): 6.

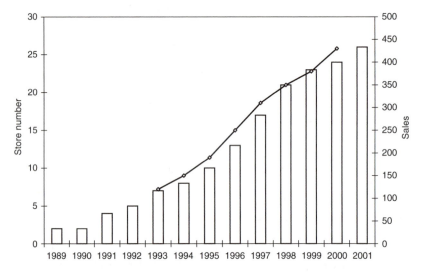

Figure 2.2 The number of stores and sales of Carrefour (NT$100 million).

Source: Taiwan chain stores and franchise association.

and sales for Carrefour. After opening its seventh store in 1993, Carrefour's annual sales reached NT$12 billion and exceeded Pacific Sogo's NT$9.6 billion. In 2002, Carrefour is Taiwan's second largest retail company after 7-Eleven Taiwan, PEC group.

Merger and acquisition activity by foreign firms often exerts a big influence on Taiwanese firms who develop a business partnership with the foreign firms. An example is the acquisition of Promodès by Carrefour at the end of 1999. As Table 2.1 shows the Far Eastern group developed a hypermarket named hyper-fee by forming a joint venture with Promodès in 1993. However, when Carrefour merged with Promodès in 1999, the Far Eastern group suddenly lost its business partner. Consequently, the Far Eastern group had to search for a new business partner and established a contract with Géant (Casino) in 2000. They changed their store name to Jéant, and established a new firm to include their related firms. This indicates the inevitable risks for firms that introduce a new type of business by forming joint ventures with foreign enterprises.

Factors contributing to the success of Carrefour

The operation of Carrefour in Taiwan has been regarded as a success and this success has been due to three reasons. First, the economic situation in Taiwan had resulted in the hypermarket business being underdeveloped so providing Carrefour with little competition. Second, its local business partner is the largest food company, which at the same time is the largest retailing group in Taiwan. Third, the distribution system in Taiwan was particularly suited to the hypermarket's business style.

Ideal market

The first reason, for success of Carrefour in Taiwan, concerns the economic environment. In the late 1980s, the Taiwanese economy entered a period of rapid economic growth. It was at this time that Carrefour entered the market. Figure 2.3 shows the change in per capita GNP in Taiwan. In 1989, per capita GNP exceeded US$7,600; in the next decade, it almost doubled. In the 1990s, Taiwan experienced the emergence of mass consumption under the rapid economic growth.

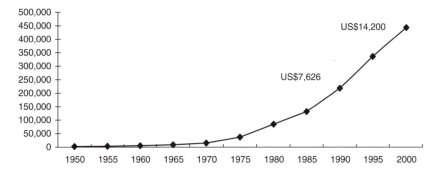

Figure 2.3 The change of per capita GNP in NT$.

Source: Taiwan Statistical Data Book (2001).

Table 2.3 Comparison of GNP per capita Taiwan and selected Asian
countries, 2000

Country	GNP per capita (US$)	Population (million)	Number of stores of Carrefour
Japan	37,945	126.87	3
Singapore	22,953	4.02	1
Taiwan	14,216	22.22	26
Korea	9,628	47.28	21
Malaysia	3,670	22.71	6
Thailand	2,160	61.81	14
China	775	1,253.60	27
Indonesia	640	209.26	7

Source: Economic Statistics Indicators of Major Countries 2001,
www.Carrefour.com

We see from Table 2.3 that Taiwan was a strong market compared with other
Asian countries. Taiwan is large enough for substantial chain operation unlike
Singapore; at the same time Taiwan's per capita GNP is higher than that of many
other Asian countries. This meant that Taiwan was an ideal market for Carrefour
to enter and provided substantial opportunities for growth.

Underdevelopment of hypermarket

The distribution system in Taiwan was underdeveloped before the deregulation of
foreign investment policy in 1986. There were some typical non-traditional retailing formats such as department store, small supermarket and convenience store
alongside the traditional markets. Only the department store constituted large-
scale retailing. Although some supermarket chains existed, most of them were
small or medium-sized businesses. In this situation, when Carrefour entered the
Taiwanese market, there were no major local rivals and the hypermarket was
accepted as an entirely new, large-scale retail format which brought about a distribution revolution. Davies and Yahagi (2000) have shown parallels with
Carrefour's success in the underdeveloped retail markets in Central Europe. The
main competitor to Carrefour in Taiwan was Makro, a Dutch retailer that also
opened its first branch in the same year as Carrefour. Intra-type competition
became limited to foreign firms.

Local business partner

When Carrefour entered Taiwan, it had to adopt the joint venture mode due to
governmental regulation. One of the key factors for Carrefour's success was
closely related to its local business partner. This partner was Uni-President
Enterprise Corp (UPE). UPE is the largest food company in Taiwan; it had
several subsidiaries including some leading companies in the service industries

such as 7-Eleven Taiwan, Starbucks Taiwan and President Transnet Corporation. The partnership with UPE and its subsidiaries created advantages for Carrefour.

The first advantage was the capital power. The hypermarket cannot achieve success through scale economies of buying and provision of low prices if it is not able to develop a number of owned stores. So, increasing the number of branches rapidly is one of the most important criteria for success in an underdeveloped market where there are no competitors. This rapid growth, however, can cause financial stress to the firm, even though the cost of hypermarket development is relatively low compared with that of department stores. In the case of Carrefour in Taiwan, because of the substantial capital power of its local partner, Carrefour was able to increase its branch network rapidly.

The other advantage was the political connections of the local partner. It can be difficult for foreign companies to get real estate at good locations if they have to deal directly with government. UPE's political influence helped Carrefour to get excellent real estate smoothly. This illustrates the importance of the careful selection of a local business partner in the process of internationalization of retailing.

The local distribution system

The third factor of Carrefour's success concerned the local distribution system. Table 2.4 shows the wholesale/retail sales ratio in Taiwan from 1994 to 2000 for various commodity groups. Although the numerical value of some industrial goods such as chemical products and building materials is high, most of the consumer goods show extremely low values.

One of the reasons why the sales volume of wholesaling is less than retailing relates to business customs in Taiwan, where direct deals between the manufacturers and retailers are preferred. Except for deals with foreign traders, there is a general tendency to eliminate the middleman. For example, with agricultural goods, it is common that farmers sell their products in the wholesale market themselves. Most retailers, in a similar way to suppliers, are small and they can buy goods directly from manufacturers. As both sides (manufacturer and retailer) are small to middle sized, the distribution system is kept in balance. A further reason why the role of wholesaling is insignificant is Taiwan's small size. This small size enables the direct links between producer and retailer.

Thus, the traditional distribution channel system of Taiwan works in favour of the development of Carrefour, who purchase merchandise directly from manufacturers. Carrefour was able to purchase from many manufacturers (including its business partner UPE) directly and to develop in Taiwan without any great challenge from the traditional distribution system. From this point of view, the situation was completely different from its entry into the Japanese market, where many strong wholesalers exist and new foreign entrants are prevented by various business customs from direct purchasing.

Other characteristics of the distribution system in Taiwan have facilitated hypermarket growth. It is often observed that manufacturers have expanded their business into retailing in order to have direct access to consumers. For example,

Table 2.4 The wholesale/retail ratio in Taiwan from 1994 to 2000

	1994	1995	1996	1997	1998	1999	2000
Total	0.66	0.65	0.67	0.65	0.62	0.60	0.61
Agricultural and aquatic products, food products and groceries	0.86	0.92	0.94	0.95	0.93	0.92	0.95
Fabrics, clothes and apparel accessories	1.38	1.35	1.24	1.22	1.23	1.30	1.30
Furniture and fixture	0.53	0.54	0.52	0.53	0.53	0.54	0.54
Hardware articles and household utensils	0.98	1.04	1.03	1.09	1.06	1.06	1.04
Chemical products	1.83	1.91	2.06	1.96	1.98	1.88	1.85
Drugs and cosmetics	1.08	1.09	1.15	1.11	1.10	1.05	1.07
Educational and entertainment articles	1.04	1.08	1.14	1.14	1.10	1.12	1.10
Watch, clocks and spectacles	0.24	0.24	0.25	0.22	0.21	0.22	0.22
Building materials	1.38	1.46	1.43	1.40	1.39	1.47	1.63
Fuel products	0.07	0.08	0.09	0.09	0.10	0.09	0.09
Machinery and equipment	1.00	1.00	0.98	0.98	0.88	0.76	0.73
Vehicles and parts supplies	0.36	0.31	0.33	0.30	0.28	0.28	0.30
Jewelery and precious materials	0.54	0.53	0.58	0.56	0.53	0.53	0.49

Source: Ministry of Economic Affairs (2001).

most department stores originated from firms in the spinning industry or construction industry, which then diversified into retailing. Similarly, most firms which have developed convenience stores were major food production and processing companies. UPE, which diversified into 7-Eleven is an example. The same situation is observed in the household electrical products sector. Tsan Kuen multinational group and E-life, both of which were medium-sized manufacturers originally, diversified into retailing and have created substantial businesses in electric appliance discount stores. The reason why they expanded their roles from manufacturers to front-line sellers is not only for the investment of excess capital but also to gain better distribution. While they continued to increase their manufacturing productivity, the traditional retailers were not able to sell sufficient products due to their small size. To solve these problems, Tsan Kuen and E-Life adopted the strategy of expanding into retailing and being engaged in controlling the channel themselves.

The effects on the local distribution system

Carrefour has become the most influential firm in the retail industry in Taiwan. This influence is seen in many areas but particularly in the evolution of relationships between retailers and manufacturers.

The vertical influence in distribution system

One of the influences of large-scale retailers is the power to shift the initiative in the distribution system from manufacturer to retailer. The appearance of large-scale retailers like hypermarkets has caused the power position to shift from manufacturers to retailers. Thus, the new distribution system in Taiwan is characterized by retailer-controlled channels due to the advantages of their strong buying power.

Carrefour's overwhelming position in hypermarket business can be seen from the amount of sales and the number of stores. Moreover, its business attitude towards suppliers, most of whom are small- and middle-sized manufacturers, has gradually become more aggressive. For instance, its contract with suppliers is about twelve pages, compared with other hypermarkets which have only one or two pages, with many details of the transaction agreements specified. The suppliers are required to pay various costs, and the amount and rate are dependent on the scale of the supplier and their merchandise. The main terms of contract are as the following.

Service fee. The service fee is one of the several expenses that are attached to transactions with Carrefour. This is the so-called slotting allowance and is calculated on every item and the number of stores. It is a monthly charge. For example, when company X sells merchandise α and merchandise β in the stores of Carrefour, and if the slotting allowances of the merchandise are NT$500 (merchandise α) and NT$450 (merchandise β), respectively, the total amount will be NT$950 per month. This total amount is multiplied by 26, the number of Carrefour stores. Consequently, the total slotting allowances that company X has to pay is NT$24,700 per month. Carrefour requires suppliers to pay this service fee every year, while other hypermarket firms demand such a fee only once.

Rebates. From 1 to 6 per cent of the annual or monthly total sales amounts are paid as rebates. Generally, some profit of the retailer from sales promotion and price maintenance of the manufacturer's product are paid back to the manufacturer under the conditions of a manufacturer-controlled channel. This is typical in automobiles sales channel. But, now the position is reversed and suppliers have to pay the retailer for maintaining the business with the large-scale retailer.

Festival promotional fees. There are, in Taiwan, some traditional events called Four Seasonal Festivals, for example, The Chinese New Year, Dragon-boat Festival,

Ghost Month and Mid-Autumn Festival. Retailers including department stores, convenience stores, hypermarkets have sales promotions at theses times. Carrefour is no exception. Suppliers are required to pay about NT$1,000–10,000 (depending on the company) per store as promotional fees for the sales promotions at each festival. In addition to these, some promotional fees are required at other special promotions, for example, National Day and the Inauguration Day of President (May 2000).

Other allowances. In addition to the fees mentioned above, Carrefour demands several other kinds of payments. For example, display fees, advertisement-inserting fees, fees for advertising on TV and in newspapers. Moreover, supplier contributions for new store opening, store remodelling and reopening, allowances for inventory loss of stolen or damage goods, communication fees for using computer networks, bank service charges, plastic bags fees, tasting fees and cleaning fees, etc. are all paid by suppliers.

As mentioned above, suppliers are levied expenses for various reasons. These expenses are a transparent part of the transaction cost. However, some other expenses are not so clearly specified, for example, it is claimed that informal payments are made for keeping good relationships with the store manager. Carrefour initially adopted a decentralized purchasing system in which each manager merchandised directly from suppliers. This was the position until 1997. With the merchandising power concentrated in just one person's hands (usually the manager), the potential for these informal payments was considerable so the decentralized purchasing system was changed to a concentrated purchasing system after strong requests from the supplier side in 1997. There is also one more intangible expense called 'secret fee' that can be paid as a percentage (depending on company) of total transaction amounts at the end of year.

With these arrangements for allowances, rebates and payments Carrefour has changed the nature of the retailer–supplier relationship in the Taiwan grocery sector. Carrefour succeeded in transferring to suppliers some costs which retailers usually have to shoulder, for example, display fee, advertisement fee, inventory loss, stolen or damage goods, etc. Demands by Carrefour became greater after it developed its ninth store in 1995. Its demands were growing more severe year by year (Commercial Times 1997c). Under such a situation, small- and middle-sized suppliers were forced to accept serious financial burdens in their dealings with Carrefour to the extent that they were not able to make any profit from doing business with Carrefour. As an example, a middle-sized food manufacturer could have been faced with expenses on service fees, rebates, festival promotional fees, national anniversary fee amounting to 26 per cent of its total trade with Carrefour, and in addition, the hidden expenses such as informal payments were another 18 per cent. In sum, this food company had to pay about 44 per cent of the total deal as additional fees. In addition they sometimes sold their products below cost and because more of their products sold, a considerable loss was incurred. But, it is true that the presence of Carrefour provided a huge marketing channel that fascinated small- and middle-sized manufacturers. Giving up their business with Carrefour means the loss of a huge market for them but a market on which they make little, if any, profit.

Therefore, most of these manufacturers secured their profit by normal price transactions with established wholesalers or the small- and medium-sized retailers. But it is easy to see that the number of these smaller sized retailers will eventually decline under these circumstances as they lose their price competitiveness. This has been the experience in some developed countries. Although the total number of retail stores in Taiwan is still increasing because of the increase in the overall size of the market, the small- and middle-sized retailers, who cannot compete on price, are already beginning to be weeded out. Concentration in the marketing field in Taiwan has been increasing rapidly, following the pattern experienced by developed countries.

The precedent of developed countries suggests that manufacturers will change their price strategy under this unfavourable situation. To secure their profit, products will be priced taking account of all the expenses imposed by large-scale retailers, and the supplier's price will increase to the same level as the wholesaler's price (Shafter 1991). This example suggests that the pursuit of short-term price competition will damage consumer welfare from the long-term point of view.

Dispute between Carrefour and suppliers

The behaviour of Carrefour has caused friction with suppliers for several years (Commercial Times 1997a). The dispute with some manufacturers over the content of annual contracts in 1997 provides an example. At that time, several food manufacturers tried, as a group, to resist the requests of Carrefour because the amount of expenses, such as service fees, increased substantially compared with the previous year. The increase was not negotiated but imposed unilaterally (Economy Daily Times 1997). Carrefour argued that the contents of the contract for this year had not changed compared with the previous year, and the view of suppliers was not true. Consequently, New Zealand Milk Products (Far East) Ltd, which supplied dairy products to Carrefour decided to withdraw its products from Carrefour completely. According to New Zealand Milk Products Ltd, although its sales to Carrefour was a high proportion of its total sales, the various fees demanded were too high to allow it to make a profit. Therefore they made a decision to stop doing business with Carrefour. Other food manufacturers, for example, King Car group which has a strong national brand of coffee called Mr Brown, Vedan enterprise corporation, Tait Group and Standard Foods also announced withdrawal of some of their products. King Car, Vedan enterprise corporation, Tait Group and Standard Foods, are major companies in Taiwan and are ranked in the top 20 suppliers: Tait Group is 8th, Vedan is 9th, King Car group is 12th, Standard Foods is 16th (Distribution News 2001). Unlike P&G and other global firms that have international brands and can keep their own position against large-scale retailing, the local major companies lack power for negotiation and have to accept the conditions required by Carrefour (Commercial Times 1997b). The problem is that most manufacturers in Taiwan are too weak to negotiate with large-scale foreign retailing.

The introduction of new systems by Carrefour in 1998 (Commercial Times 1998) also caused problems for suppliers. Carrefour notified all of its suppliers that they had to use the newly developed electronic payment system. Carrefour insisted on the use of this new system enabling suppliers to download detailed accounts every month from the network, to respond instantly when some problems occurred, and to receive fast payment. However, the major issue for suppliers was not in the use of the new system, but its fees. Carrefour demanded 0.3–0.9 per cent of the annual deal amounts as a fee, and also issued a notification that if suppliers did not agree with the introduction of this new system, Carrefour would not issue the detailed account. Supposing that the charge was calculated at 0.3 per cent, Carrefour would receive new revenue of about NT$52 million on the assumption of NT$175 billion of total purchases at that time. Many suppliers considered this demand to be unreasonable and therefore resisted. At the same time, they requested that the Fair Trade Commission look at the situation. Originally, the detailed account should be provided to a business or nominee as the duty of contract. Therefore, the dissatisfaction was over why suppliers had to pay the costs of issuing the detailed account that they should be able to get as a right of contract. In response to the request, the Fair Trade Commission undertook a survey about the potential abuse of a preferential position by Carrefour because of its 35 per cent or more market share. This problem is still unresolved in 2002.

Carrefour also came into conflict with a wholesaler who is one of its suppliers. Carrefour signed a one-year contract with Ming-Chen, a wholesaler, from January to December 1997, and levied NT$800,000 as a service fee. However, Carrefour built up direct buying channels from some manufacturers in respect of several kinds of goods in which Ming-Chen dealt. Carrefour, in October of that year, began to sell at lower prices than the purchase price from Ming-Chen. After that, the sales planning of Ming-Chen was disrupted and it faced a management crisis due to Carrefour's unexpected changes. Finally, Ming-Chen reported Carrefour to the Fair Trade Commission seeking damages incurred in the violation of the contract. The result of the investigation was that the Commission first mentioned the gap of power due to the difference in size at that time between Carrefour (NT$24 billion) and Ming-Chen (NT$30 million). The Commission, then found Carrefour guilty of violating Article 24 of the Antitrust Laws for the following reasons: Carrefour did not inform Ming-Chen of the possibility of cancellation in the contract; this was completely unexpected for Ming-Chen (United Daily News 1998a). It is normal for Carrefour to try to eliminate the middle-man, but this case was a judicial precedent which pointed out a violation of the contract and an abuse of its superior position in market.

Thus, Carrefour has caused some problems and conflicts with suppliers over transactions. The Fair Trade Commission considered these situations to be serious, and began to investigate in more detail the fees, for example, as Service Fees, Festival Promotional Fees, etc. The investigation highlighted the prevailing conditions, such as large demand, the redundancy levy, tight finance of suppliers, and came to the conclusion that Carrefour was disturbing the smooth order of transactions in the market by abusing its superior market position. This inquiry was the first concerning regulation of the demands for 'unfair costs' to retailers after the Antitrust Law was amended. The Commission fined Carrefour NT$4 million on 19 October 2000 (Economy Daily Times 2000). This was an insignificant amount of money, however, compared with the total rebate income of Carrefour which was estimated at NT$200 million. After the fine, Carrefour has taken an even more aggressive attitude, than before, in its negotiations with suppliers.

Implications

The open-market policy in Taiwan was synonymous with the coming of an age of retailer-controlled channels. At the same time, aggressive business practices arrived associated with the huge buying power of large-scale retailing, often associated with international retailers. In particular, the arrival of the hypermarket generated the reform of the original distribution system, notably in respect of the relationships between the manufacturer and retailer. The tendency of large-scale retailers to demand extra fees from suppliers as part of the relationship has been observed in the developed countries. But, in many developed countries, strict rules associated with antitrust law and competition policy govern the nature of these relationships and curb potential abuses of market power. Under such rules it is doubtful if retailers such as Carrefour could have behaved in the way they did in Taiwan.

Although in this chapter the focus has been on some potential negative aspects of corporate behaviour during the internationalization of retailing, it should be remembered that there are many positive aspects in this process. The large international retailers generate modernization of the retail business sector including the improvement of customer service, the introduction of new technologies and equipment. Consumers enjoy shopping at the new retail formats because they have more choice and a larger range of products. Nonetheless, while there is acceptance of foreign retailing and its benefits, some rules are needed to ensure a business environment where fair transactions are workable. The case of Taiwan suggests that an open-market policy for accepting large-scale foreign retailers and the absences of rules of competition policy can cause unfair competition. This means that the need for strict domestic antitrust policies has become more important for ensuring fair trade for developing countries that are preparing to open their service industry to foreign retailers under the recommendation of free trade by WTO.

A possible extension of this study would be to study these relationships in the development of retail business in China and explore the extent to which the experience of Taiwan is being replicated in China. As was indicated earlier, merger, acquisition and joint ventures involving foreign retailers have a big influence on the host country for example in the case of Carrefour and Promodès and the impact on Taiwan. In the case of the merger of RT-MART by Auchan, this was undertaken with some expectation of gaining from the experiences of RT-MART in China rather than in Taiwan. There are also potentially important issues in the transfer of human resources as well as the capital between Taiwan and China.

Already many Taiwanese are headhunted for their retail managerial experience and skill gained from their training in Taiwan and are employed in retail business as executives in China. Recent trends suggest that foreign retailers will use their experience in Taiwanese retailing as a means of entering the market of China, following from China joining the WTO. A study of the transfers of knowledge, skill and expertise from Taiwan to China would be an interesting area for further study. There remain many subjects to be researched before there is a clear understanding of the nature of international retailing in this part of Asia.

References

Commercial Times (1997a) 'Carrefour taking a firm line, foodstuffs companies protesting vigorously', *Commercial Times*, 16 January: 30.

Commercial Times (1997b) 'P&G take no notice to Carrefour: other suppliers follow P&G', *Commercial Times*, 1 February: 10.

Commercial Times (1997c) 'The competition between suppliers gets fierce', *Commercial Times*, 28 October: 33.

Commercial Times (1998) 'Carrefour facing strong protest: suppliers charging to Fair Trade Commission for exposure', *Commercial Times*, 30 March: 34.

Davies, R. and Yahagi, T. (eds) (2001) *Asian Global Retailing Competition*. Tokyo: Nihon Keizai Shimbun, Inc.

Distribution News (2001) 'Top suppliers ranking 2000 in Taiwan', *Distribution News*, 10 June: 16.

Economy Daily Times (1997) 'Carrefour complete signing of year contract with suppliers', *Economy Daily Times*, 12 March: 26.

Economy Daily Times (2000) 'Carrefour against The Antitrust Law: four million New Taiwan dollar penalty', *Economy Daily Times*, 20 October: 37.

Ministry of Economic Affairs (2001), *Commercial Monthly Statistics*, March: 4–5.

Sato, H. (1974) *Japanese Distribution System*, Tokyo: Yuhikaku.

Shafter, G. (1991) 'Slotting allowances and resale price maintenance: a comparison of facilitating practices', *RAND Journal of Economics*, 22(1): 120–35.

Sternquist, B. (1998) *International Retailing*. New York: Fairchild.

Tsuchiya, H. (2000) 'Internationalization of Japanese department store'. In: Yoshitada Kato, Yasuyuki Sasaki, Kazuyosi Manabe and Hitoshi Tsuchiya (eds) *The Development of the Japanese Distribution System*, Tokyo: Zeimukeirikyukai, pp. 207–225.

United Daily News (1998a) 'Carrefour falling into disorder with suppliers over transaction: Fair Trade Commission preparing for intervention', *United Daily News*, 31 March: 24.

United Daily News (1998b) 'Carrefour break law in the process of buying from suppliers', *United Daily News*, 9 April: 24.

3 Moves into the Korean market by global retailers and the response of local retailers

Lessons for the Japanese retailing sector?

Sang Chul Choi

Introduction

In the last few years, the entry into the Japanese market by Western global retailers has been cited as one of the main factors that has caused an upheaval in the Japanese distribution system. But if you look more closely, you can see that the moves into the Japanese sector are not that great in reality. It may be because of the prolonged recession in Japan, but global retailers seem to be showing a cautious approach. This does not mean that global retailers are looking at the Japanese market less seriously. If the Japanese economy improves, by coming out of its deflationary condition, then it is the common view that global retailers will move fully into Japan, which is still the world's second biggest consumer market. The news announced in March 2002, that the world's biggest retailer Wal-Mart would come to Japan in a tie-up with the Seiyu Ltd is evidence of the high interest still shown towards the Japanese market by global retailers.

What is of particular interest is that global retailers, who are developing operations on a global scale in order to win in the rapidly heating up global competition, are preparing to invest into the Asian market the business resources that they have prepared for the Japanese market. This investment is showing a good rate of return. The Korean market, which is on the rise, having overcome the IMF crisis, is one of the target markets for these moves. In contrast to Japan where the large retailing companies, such as General Merchandise Store (GMS) and department stores, are performing poorly in the market, the desire of global retailers to move into Korea is growing strongly. One reason for this is the overall strong growth of the Korean market. Already, global retailers such as the French Carrefour, US Wal-Mart, Costco and UK Tesco have moved into urban areas in Korea and it has been reported that there will be increased aggressive policies for opening stores in the next few years.

In this chapter, the situation of the special discount store market in Korea will be analysed. In this market there will be an unavoidable major battle between the global retailers and local retailers. The discount store sector, called *Harin* stores in Korean, whilst going beyond the boundaries of retailing types such as discount stores, supercentres, hypermarkets and GMS, are regarded as within the same retail group because they are thought to provide low prices and a comprehensive range of goods to the Korean consumer.

This retail format is becoming a particular Korean-style Discount Store, hereafter KDS, developed by the Korean local retailers and also by the strong global retailers. In this chapter, the structural characteristics of the KDS market will be considered, using some local data sources, observation and interviews by the author. The history and evolution of this type of retailing will also be considered. In addition to arguing that the competition between local retailers and global retailers has generated the growth of the KDS market, it is also argued that rapid growth in the end brings the fear that such growth will speed up the movement of the KDS market to a mature phase. Finally, looking at the major reforms in the Korean retail market centred on the KDS market and the strategic response of the local KDS in Korea, which fought against the global retailers, the possible implications for the Japanese large-scale retailing companies will be discussed. There may be lessons from the Korean experience that are of value in Japan as global retailers move strongly into the Japanese market on the back of continued economic decline.

Historical developments in the Korean retailing system

Before discussing recent market trends in Korea by local retailers and global retailers, it is useful to start with an explanation of the Korean retailing system. The complex and dynamic structure involving a pre-modern style versus a contemporary style and also rivalry between the foreign retailing companies and local retailers is very different from the structures found in Japan and other developed countries. In order to understand the particular nature of the Korean situation it is necessary to have some historical knowledge about the Korean retailing system.

Until the mid-1950s: the continuation of pre-modern retailing and distribution

To the middle of the twentieth century retailing activities on the Korean peninsula were carried out according to a pre-modern system. Broadly speaking, there was a retailing system based on five-day markets in the regions and retailing arcades consisting of groups of specialized shops in large cities such as Seoul.

With the establishment of the Mitsukoshi clothing store in 1906, which was the Seoul outlet of the Japanese Mitsukoshi, modern retailing was introduced into Korea. The Mitsukoshi Seoul outlet was changed to the Seoul branch in 1929, at the middle of the period of Japanese occupation, and in 1930, on the site of the present Shinsegae department store, a large building was erected consisting of one basement and four upper floors. The Mitsukoshi store operated with a fixed-pricing system and a goods-return system and it changed the trading customs of stores at that time. It can be seen as the pioneer in the Korean department store sector. In addition to the Mitsukoshi store there were other department stores run by the Japanese. The Dongwha department store, which opened in 1937, was the first department store operated by a local retailer. In 1954, the Midopa department store opened and in 1955 what had been the Hwashin department store before the war reopened as the Shinshin department store. The advent of department stores had a big influence on retailing history in Korea. However, retailing and distribution in this era was supported mainly by conventional markets and small wholesalers and retailers.

The 1960s: the start of modern distribution

After the establishment of the Korean state in 1945, the Mitsukoshi department store became the Dongwha department store which was run by employee representatives, but after the Korean War it was not possible to continue to run it as a direct concern and it became leased retail space. This situation continued until 1962, when it was taken over by Dongbang Insurance. In 1963, Dongbang Insurance was incorporated into the Samsung group, the Dongwa department store became a subsidiary of the Samsung group and changed its trade name to Shinsegae. This marked the birth of the revolutionary Shinsegae department store in the Korean retail industry.

The Shinsegae department store stopped the leasing system and, in 1969, declared that it would restart as a directly controlled department store (actually 85 per cent direct control). The department store contributed greatly to the modernization of Korean distribution by being able to push through distribution innovations such as developing store brand products, setting up a pricing system, implementing free return of goods and bargain sales, hiring students and housewives on a part-time basis and introducing credit cards (An and Cho 2000: 53).

Companies such as the Midopa department store, which was stimulated by the direct control used by the Shinsegae department store, soon changed to direct control themselves. This shows that department stores played a leading role in the modernization of the distribution system. However, although the department stores were entrusted with the role of modernizing the distribution system, they represented no more than a minor part of the distribution system as a whole. During this period, the main players in retailing and distribution still continued to be the existing markets and small wholesalers and retailers.

1970s: substantial activity by department stores and the advent of supermarkets

The characteristics of the retail system in this period were that the directly controlled department stores grew quickly and the existing leased department stores withered. The period also marks the start of the decline of the regional five-day markets. Also of note is that after the arrival, in 1971, of the Saemaul Super-chain, supermarkets became a major factor in the retailing system in Korea. The supermarket chains, which started as one of the policies of the Korean government for modernizing the distribution system, grew rapidly in the 1970s, and by 1979, there were 30 companies operating 1,131 stores (Baek 2000).

This period saw continued moves into the retail sector by big corporations. In particular, moves into the business of department stores and supermarket chains by Zaibatsu groups were conspicuous. For example, in the department store sector, the Lotte group opened the Lotte Department Store No.1 in 1979 in Seoul where already the Samsung Shinsegae department store and the Midopa department store of Daenong Corporation were operating. These three Zaibatsu companies dominated the department store market. Other Zaibatsu companies began to start operating in the supermarket sector.

During this period, consumer trends were divided into two major groups. The rich people in Seoul and other major cities used department stores and supermarkets, and throughout the rest of the country the general public used the existing markets.

1980s: expansion of department stores and the weakening of traditional retailing

In the 1980s, with the increase in population and the rapid rise in urbanization, large consumer markets emerged. The government revised their industrial policies based on manufacturing as a priority and accordingly created a support system for the distribution sector which then entered a period of strong growth.

In this period, the department store sector strengthened its position even further as the leader of the distribution industry. The department stores had virtually monopolized the needs of the middle class. The supermarkets were finding it difficult to gain competitive dominance over the existing markets and therefore could not establish themselves in many places.

In the first half of the 1980s, the three Zaibatsu companies of Shinsegae, Midopa and Lotte, all with stores in Seoul, had split the department store market into three. But, by the middle of the 1980s, in the urban areas surrounding Seoul, construction companies and real estate companies and even the Zaibatsu company Hyundai had moved into the department store sector. In response to this, the three Zaibatsu companies with existing stores started to open new stores in these areas outside Seoul. There began, therefore, a period of expansion of department store numbers.

The supermarkets, which where supported by the government, could not find opportunities for growth because they were beset with problems such as lack of know-how in chain operations, lack of ability in merchandising and continuing small store in size. In contrast, new retailers such as convenience stores and catalogue sales entered the retail sector. As a result, the regionally based small and medium supermarkets and local retailer markets began to weaken.

1990s: arrival of KDS and moves by Western-funded distribution groups

Until it was faced with the IMF economic crisis, the growth of the Korean economy was seen as moving the country into a mature phase of economic development. There was a rise in the numbers of middle-income consumers, the needs of consumers were diversified and consumption started to become strongly individualized. However, what brought a huge shift in the Korean distribution sector in this period was the complete opening up of the distribution market and great activity in the KDS sector.

With the total opening of the distribution market on the 1 January 1996, the regulations on floor space and number of shops were abandoned. The Korean distribution sector feared entry by global retailers. Carrefour, who had been waiting for the de-regulation of the distribution sector, entered, followed by Makro in a joint venture. Since then global retailers have been speeding up their plans to move into Korea.

Furthermore, because the Korean retail market in this period was predominantly small scale, with only the department stores being modern, there was a need to develop retailing with the capability to compete against these global retailers. The opening of the first E-mart store by Shinsegae department store group, in March 1993, was important. Shinsegae group decided to develop a new business format to compete with the moves by global retailers after the opening up of the distribution market. As discussed at the beginning of this chapter, we will call both local discount stores like E-mart and Korea-located stores developed by global retailers such as Wal-Mart and Carrefour, KDS. These KDS have only a short history but have grown to be one of the most important distribution formats.

In 1997, Korea entered the 'IMF period'. It was unavoidable to enter a period of reduced personal incomes and a price war in distribution, but this brought a huge change to the structure of the retail sector that had been led by the department stores until that time. The consumer pattern changed dramatically from an age of high-priced consumerism based on the department stores to an age of large-scale and diversified consumerism based on the department stores and KDS. The department stores opened in the regional cities and hurried to increase the number of stores in order to increase in size and capture scale economies. As a reflection of the more diversified and mature consumer needs, the diversification of retailing formats went ahead at a rapid pace.

2000 and beyond: saturation of the KDS market and entry to the second distribution revolution

After emerging from the short period of the IMF crisis, the polarization of consumer spending in Korea widened. The high-income consumers extended their consumption of high-quality merchandise, but the lower- and middle-income consumers did not revert to their earlier behaviour patterns. Overall, the consumer pattern of low price, high quality and high service was established.

It is clear that KDS now form the core of retail distribution in Korea. It is likely that the competition between local and global retailers will become fiercer in the future. At present, the market is expanding with competition between the KDS to open stores, and they are rapidly approaching the department stores in overall market size. Furthermore, because the competition to have many stores is increasing, it is being said that by 2003, the KDS market might reach saturation point. The global retailers, however, are planning a second attack which will see a rapid opening of new stores. In response to this, the local KDS are continuing to open stores and are also looking to move into the Asian market. The whole KDS sector is moving along the path of shifting away from price wars to service competition, high quality brands and increasing in size.

It is now expected that the Korean retail sector will go into a full-scale second distribution revolution. Generally speaking, the first distribution revolution was when the KDS pioneered the lowering of retail prices around the time of the IMF crisis. Following this, there is now evidence of the second distribution revolution with the rapid growth in new retailing forms. The two extremes of the Department Store and the KDS will continue but there may also soon be a realignment of the distribution system with the introduction of Internet and TV shopping. While the trend will be towards a decrease in wholesalers, small and medium supermarkets and conventional markets, there is the possibility that contemporary super supermarkets (SSM) led by the Zaibatsu companies will form the core of the market. Convenience stores are increasing in number. The distribution system is undergoing a period of rapid change with the growth in the open-price system, a reduction of long and complicated distribution stages, changes from competition between manufacturers and distributors to alliances or partnerships between them, and an increase in the supply of private brand (PB) merchandise. The result is likely to be a further decline in traditional small-scale distribution companies and conventional markets.

An analysis of the KDS sector

Birth of the KDS

At present in Korea there is a fierce fight underway to open stores in the KDS market. The fight is between global retailers such as Carrefour and Wal-Mart, local retailers such as Shinsegae E-mart and Lotte Magnet (Lotte Mart since 2002), and joint companies such as Samsung Tesco. KDS is a sector unique to Korea. These KDS companies are leading the way in the Korean retailing sector (Oh 1998).

Since the comprehensive de-regulation of the distribution market, the size of the market has grown with the entry of influential companies from both inside and outside of Korea. The market continues to show high growth above 30 per cent each year. How has the KDS managed such a high level of growth and become so strong? There is a need to consider the developments since the start of the 'E-mart' by Shinsegae in order to answer these questions.

The Shinsegae department store was a pioneer in the history of the contemporary Korean retailing. The company felt that as an existing department store it could not win in the emerging domestic competition, which was becoming globalized, and so tried to develop a new form of diversified business. This department store carried out benchmarking against the US discount stores, French hypermarkets and Japanese GMS store operations. Although they carried out benchmarking on operations with low cost structures in the developed countries, they created a retail format which suited the conditions in the Korean market. Stimulated by the good start of the first E-mart shop in Chandong area of Seoul, they speeded up the opening of new E-mart stores at the time that the other influential domestic companies were moving into the KDS sector. Shinsegae sought first-mover advantage.

Local KDS companies, while keeping one eye on the efforts of E-mart, felt confident they could compete with global retailers who were moving into the Korean market such as the Makro, Carrefour and Costco.[1] In 1998, Wal-Mart decided to move into the Korean market by acquiring the four Makro stores, which were suffering because of their massive start-up investment. At this time there were widespread predictions that the appearance of the world's biggest retailing company would have a major impact on the local retailers. Nonetheless, the defensive strategies of local retailers were successful and noted as positive competitive responses both inside and outside of Korea.

The KDS market went through a period of high growth in a short period of time through the aggressive opening of stores by innovative retailers from inside and outside Korea. The KDS sector was able to achieve high growth despite the slump in the economy brought on by the IMF crisis. Consumer purchasing suffered badly with the reduction in incomes. KDS, however, continued to prosper by responding to the new consumer conditions.

What are KDS?

It is necessary to explain a little more about the definition of KDS. KDS in Korean are called *Harin* stores and are related to but not the same as discount stores such as those developed in America. Table 3.1 shows that KDS, as recognized generally in Korea, is a collective idea that includes discount stores, supercentres, hypermarkets, even wholesale clubs and outlet malls. Accordingly, KDS is not classified as a separate retail format as set down in traditional retail theory. KDS are grouped to include several formats which make them an interesting case. This new form of retailer called KDS is not a retail mix or something which has a common technical base, rather it should be thought of as a retailing form which provides 'low cost, high service, and a comprehensive range of goods simultaneously', which the existing retailers such as department stores and traditional retailers cannot provide.

Table 3.1 Categorization of KDS by type

Category	Company name
Discount store (DS)	Wal-Mart, some E-mart and Magnet stores
Supercentres (SC)	E-mart, Magnet, LG Mart, Megamart, Top Mart, Kim's Club, Samsung Tesco (Home Plus), Wal-Mart Super Center
Hypermarkets (HM)	Carrefour, Aram Mart
Wholesale clubs (MWC)	Hanaro Club, Costco
Discount store and outlet (DS & OC)	Grand Mart, 2001 Outlet

In Korea, because of the policy set out by the Korean government for growth based on the manufacturing companies, the main manufacturing companies have power in the distribution channel. Because of this, the KDS were welcomed by the Korean people as innovators who broke down established patterns of retail pricing. Of course, they needed to have large-scale stores to enable them to buy in large quantities and so give them buying power. In addition to this, simply for the statistical convenience, the KDS generally are shops with a floor space of above 3,000 m². This definition is provided by the *Distribution Industry Development Law* of the basic law for Korean distribution. In respect of their operating characteristics, they have a chain management organization including such features as large-scale buying, large displays, low margins, high turnover and self service.

However, these definitions of KDS are no different to the low-cost retail styles in the USA or the large retail shops which are regulated in Japan's Large-Scale Retail Store (Location) Law (Daiten Ho before 2001; Daiten Richi Ho since 2001). The KDS, however, are recognized as distinct by the Korean consumer. As already discussed above, the KDS market, of which E-mart is typical, while having a low-price orientation like those found in the developed countries such as the USA and Japan, was introduced to fit the comprehensive opening up of the Korean distribution market, and started with a format that suited Korean consumers. The KDS are aimed at a wide target market that is the middle class (particularly middle-class housewives). This is the group to which most Koreans think they belong. KDS make it possible to do one-stop shopping by dealing in both daily goods and clothes while focusing on foodstuffs. They are comprehensive high-class discount stores which respond to the shopping styles and buying styles of the Korean people, by bringing out a feeling of high quality and high service and not just a low price (Chung 2001).

KDS, as well as being a group concept which over-arches the low cost trends, is also a concept that represents the birth of a new retail format. We can say that it is a new unifying concept that promotes the changes of retailing from the perspective of the consumer rather than being a classification of the retail sector from the point of the distribution services such as simply low price or the logistic technologies.

Furthermore, the retail format of global retailers can be regarded as not simply discount stores but KDS by the fact that there will be an adaptation of their business model from the point of view of the Korean consumer, in order to meet the Korean consumer behaviour.[2] In order to avoid confusion in the following discussion the KDS, which are developed by global retailers in the Korean market, will be called 'global KDS' and the KDS funded by Korean capital will be termed 'local KDS'.

Characteristics of the KDS market

Large size of sales

What structural features does the KDS market have? According to a survey by the Korean Chamber of Commerce (2001) that took data from the 123 shops of the representative global and local KDS, the average annual turnover for KDS was 84.9 billion Won (approximately US$71 million). If we exclude the department stores (169.3 billion Won or US$141 million) then it is well above all other formats in the retailing sector. In the case of E-mart, for the 40 stores for which annual data were available for 2001, 19 stores exceeded 100 billion Won leaving other companies far behind. Although a late starter, Lotte Magnet (Lotte Mart since 2002), second in the sector for number of stores opened, had 3 stores that exceeded 100 billion Won in 2001.

The company attracting the most attention because of its efficiency is the third placed Samsung Tesco.[3] This company which has been rated highly for succeeding in Korea among the foreign investment retail companies had 12 stores out of 14 that exceeded a turnover of 400 million Won (approximately US$0.3 million) in a single day. The store that is located in Daegu the third biggest city in Korea exceeded a turnover of 243.7 billion Won (US$200 million) in 2001 and ranked as the number one store among the main four companies. However, Carrefour, which ranked in fourth place, only had 3 stores out of 22 that exceeded 100 billion Won.

High ratio for foodstuffs

The high percentage of food in the total turnover is a significant characteristic for KDS. The percentage of sales in food is close to 60 per cent (see Table 3.2). Furthermore, when the breakdown of food is considered, the percentage of fresh foods (primary foodstuffs) is above 26 per cent which is a very high level (Korean Chamber of Commerce 2001: 65). It is possible to forecast that the percentage will be high for food (particularly fresh foods) in KDS because of the consumer trend of Korean consumers generally to spend heavily on food items. In retail shops in Korea, in the fresh food area it is not unusual to see the motto 'Korean people should eat food produced in Korea for the health of body and mind'. This shows how the Korean people's eating habits especially for fresh foods tend towards choosing Korean food. For the Global KDS which have the ability

Table 3.2 Sales and category mix of KDS

Category	1999		2000	
	Category mix (%)	*Sales (billion Won)*	*Category mix (%)*	*Sales (billion Won)*
Clothing	9.5	713.6	10.8	1,139.5
Foodstuffs	57.6	4,326.4	58.6	6,183.1
General	32.9	2,471.1	30.6	3,228.7
Total	100.0	7,511.1	100.0	10,551.3

Source: Korean Chamber of Commerce (2001: 65).

Note
The result is based on the survey of 123 low-priced KDS shops with a floor space of more than 3,000 m² for as of at the end of 2000.

to globally source products this is a disadvantage for them in their Korean operations.

Low rate of profits

The large volume of foods has the result that it works negatively for business efficiency because of low profit rates. Table 3.3 shows that KDS, compared to other sectors have a lower gross margin and lower percentage operating profit. Other productivity measures are better in the KDS, for example, the stock rotation is higher at 21.7 times (Korean Chamber of Commerce 2001: 71–2).

Increase in the percentage of PB products

In order to overcome the problem of low profits, the development of PB products is an unavoidable choice for KDS who need to emphasize low pricing and low costs. Because of this, partnerships with manufacturers are sought. Table 3.4 shows the situation of the main KDS in respect of PB products. E-mart, the top operator in the sector, has PB products for each main product line including 'E-plus' (fresh foods), 'E-basics' (fashion, lifestyle products), 'Schema' (clothes) and 'Myclo' (American style casual clothing). E-mart has PB products in the

Table 3.3 Profitability in Korean retail sector by format

Format	Gross margin (%)		Operating profit (%)	
	1999	*2000*	*1999*	*2000*
Department stores	21.5	22.0	5.6	5.2
KDS	15.1	14.8	0.4	0.3
Supermarkets	13.4	15.1	6.2	6.7
Convenience stores	29.8	29.2	4.2	8.3
Home sales	60.3	66.4	5.4	7.6
Catalogue sales	32.3	32.5	3.0	−1.0

Source: Korean Chamber of Commerce (2001: 14).

Table 3.4 Number of stock keeping units (SKU) and market share of PB product in the main KDS

	1998	*1999*	*2000*	*2001*
E-Mart	n.a.	300 (13%)	1,500 (14%)	3,000 (17%)
Magnet	n.a.	68 (1.5%)	144 (2.5%)	200 (3.5%)
Home Plus	n.a.	120 (n.a.)	286 (3.0%)	430 (4.6%)
Kims Club	160 (2.1%)	192 (4.7%)	328 (6.3%)	n.a.

Source: *Discount Merchandiser Monthly* (2001), August: 27.

Notes
The figures for 2001 are target values.
n.a. – not applicable.

home electronics sector which is a difficult sector because of the presence of a powerful oligopoly of manufacturers. In the case of E-Mart, 14 per cent of the total sales in 2000 were accounted for by PB products and internally they have decided to raise this figure to 40 per cent. The number of products sold in the E-Mart shops is around 35,000 items (Sku base) which is 10,000 items more than other companies and within this figure around 3,000 items are PB products (Chung 2001).

Price competition ability

The reason that KDS, that have shops with large buying volumes and standardization and offer efficient operation through chain operation, are attractive to the consumer is because of the low prices. In the case of the biggest E-mart their competitive power on prices is unrivalled. Approximately 60 per cent of items are cheaper compared with other KDS including global retailers, 20 per cent are around the same level with the remaining 20 per cent at less competitive price (Lee 2002). The confidence in their price competition is shown in their 'Guarantee of double the difference in price system' in which if the same item is bought from a nearby shop they will guarantee to refund double the difference in price.

However, while the KDS are changing to large-scale high quality routes, it is not certain that they will have an absolute dominance in pricing. In the case of home electronics that are among the most appealing products to consumers, the department stores and agent shops are virtually the same price. When compared to new channels such as Internet shopping malls, KDS prices are higher for home electronics goods (e.g. refer to the homepage of the Korea Consumer Protection Board). The KDS, worried about low profit rates, are showing signs that they have to move away from simple low pricing in their business strategies and adopt new approaches.

The fight between local and global retailers in the KDS market

The rapid growth of the KDS market

The number of both local and global shops of KDS in Korea was 95 at the end of 1998, 123 the following year surpassing the number of department stores (99 in 1998, 91 in 1999), and at the end of 2001 stood at 192 stores. In 2000, the total sales were 10.5 trillion Won around 70 per cent that of department stores, but in 2002, the figure rose to 13.6 trillion Won (9.2 per cent of the retail market as whole) and in 2003, it is expected to be 22.4 trillion Won (an estimated 13.5 per cent share of the whole market). In 2003, sales of KDS are expected to exceed those of department stores (estimated at 21 trillion Won) (Han 2002: 33–42). The most important of the reasons that the KDS market has grown so fast in a short period of time is that the consumer psychology of the middle class in Korea has changed due to the IMF crisis. Also, governmental policies have been a life raft for the KDS.

Even though innovators such as E-Mart created the KDS market, there was a lot of resistance from the large retailers such as department stores and manufacturing companies with the KDS being seen as an upstart in the market when looked at from the traditional ways of doing business. However, the government of the time which was grappling with the issue of chronic inflation had a positive attitude towards the advent of discount stores who would help control the situation, and the Korea Fair Trading Commission required the opposing factions not to engage in unfair trading practices with KDS. The government of the time decided that the price stability and consumer growth in income were a plus and made it clear that they would provide financial and tax support to companies moving into the discount store market, so that large-scale corporations including Zaibatsu moved positively into the KDS market.

It is certain that the growth of KDS market, before and after the mid 1990s, led to a price-cutting syndrome. This not only brought about price stabilization and an increase in incomes but also raised economic productivity from the various points of view. Examples are

- the operation rate of production lines that had suffered from the IMF crisis was increased, and this contributed to a stimulus for the domestic economy;
- channel leaders such as Zaibatsu or large manufacturing companies could not respond fully to the needs of KDS for low prices and so partnerships were struck with small- and middle-sized companies;
- an improvement in the international competitiveness of Korean manufacturers because they had to respond to global sourcing of the global retailers.

As a result of the deliberations on the 'Distribution Industry Development Law' by the Korean government's 'Regulatory Revision Committee' in December 2001, the establishment of large stores with a floor space of over $990\,m^2$ will be made easier. Previously such stores were subject to a procedure whereby the regional local authority had to give approval, but this has been revised to simply a notification that a store will be opened. This will be implemented from the end of 2002, so that we can see that the decision was taken from a positive view of the economic effects of KDS.

The favourable public opinion towards low-price retailers such as KDS is not just limited to local KDS. The strength of local KDS is a result of what they learnt from global KDS, and therefore even though Korea has been a strongly nationalistic country we can see that the trend towards a strong resistance to foreign investment has started to relax visibly. The global KDS have gained a substantial place in Korea.

The hard fight by the global retailers

In the KDS market the oligopoly of the large companies is already becoming a problem. The big four of E-Mart and Lotte Magnet as local retailers, the foreign Carrefour and the hybrid Samsung Tesco represent 67 per cent of the total market. This oligopoly by these four companies is likely to deepen in the future.

Of the big four in the KDS sector, as far as stores and total sales in 2001 are concerned, E-mart (42 stores and 4.8 trillion Won) and Magnet (24 stores and 1.65 trillion Won) are first and second, respectively. Carrefour as the world's second largest retailer and the pioneer in the Korean market was in second place in 2000, but fell to third place, in 2001, in terms of store numbers (22 stores) and was no more than fourth largest in estimated sales (1.51 trillion Won). Samsung Tesco, the UK–Korean joint corporation (14 stores and 1.54 trillion Won sales) was the third largest in sales in 2001. Wal-Mart has gone on the offensive opening three stores, in 2001, but is ranked in sixth place (estimated sales of 650 billion Won) after Kim's Club, a local KDS. Wal-Mart has yet to make any real profits after three years in the Korean market.

The global retailers that are operating in Korea now are those that moved into the Korean market around the time that Korea fell into the IMF crisis. At that time there was little resistance from the Korean government which saw the influx of overseas capital as a way to overcome the IMF crisis. There was also little resistance from consumers who rated positively the stability in pricing. Despite this, from an objective point of view, the battle between the local and global retailers has gone in favour of the local retailers. It is difficult to conclude that the global retailers have succeeded in Korea. So, why is it that they have not been able to gain a better position against the local retailers who have less experience in this type of retailing?

Some reasons for this can be found by examining the example of E-Mart (Business Week 2002: 21). It can be argued that the success of E-Mart in 'holding off the Wal-Marts of the World' was helped by the IMF crisis which gave E-Mart the 'wings to fly'. More than this however, first, E-Mart has gained considerable business know-how through tie-ups with Shinsegae department store and Costco, and second, they have developed a format that fits the needs of the Korean consumer. The vitality of local Korean KDS such as E-Mart is due to

- response to environmental factors (changes in consumer behaviour and government measures as a result of the IMF crisis);
- learning distribution know-how from global retailers, but, most of all;
- success in developing their own retail formats to suit Korean consumers.

It may be assumed that the first two factors were not necessarily more favourable to local retailers compared to global retailers. It is the third factor that is critical. The Korean local retailers learnt a lot from the systems of low-priced retailing of the developed countries, but that was not just about copying discount stores, rather they created the *Harin* stores as a new retail format to suit the Korean situation. In all probability global retailers such as Carrefour and Wal-Mart were constrained by their global mode of operation and were late in developing formats to fit the Korean consumer, and therefore found that they had difficulty competing in Korea.

In the competition between the local and global retailers the local retailers are in the ascendant position. The local KDS have the pricing power in all products from foodstuffs through to home electronics, because they could continue the numerous deep relationships with Korean local manufacturers. In the case of E-Mart they are selling clothing and home electronics at 30 per cent lower price than that of other retailers such as department stores. There is also a big difference in the atmosphere in the stores of local KDS compared with foreign ones. For example, in the case of Wal-Mart it is usual that they pile goods up to the high ceilings and in order to save on costs they have concrete flooring. Korean consumers feel closed in by this. The Korean local KDS, on the other hand, have merchandising displays built to match the average height and eye-level of the Korean consumer and that suits the Korean consumers' desire to feel the goods (Chung 2001). As a result local KDS have created a store atmosphere that has some of the feel of a department store (Business Week 2002: 21).

In contrast to the local KDS, which are strongly tied to the regional and local companies, the trend of the global retailers is to stress that they globally source their products. This indication of global sourcing has a negative effect with the Korean consumers who have a strong nationalistic outlook. Also, the global KDS, particularly Wal-Mart and Carrefour with their alleged unfair practices in dealing with local suppliers, and the repeated interventions of the Korea Fair Trading Commission, continue to give a negative image. The actions of the global retailers who cause conflicts with their suppliers by ignoring the customs of Korean society have been criticized as showing the companies' lack of ability to handle local conditions. This increases the Korean consumers' perceptions of them being overbearing foreign companies.

The fightback by the global retailers

In 2002, it is too early to say that the local KDS retailers are going to win the fight, in the long term, with the global retailers. The global KDS have more resources than the local retailers, including the abilities to secure funding, to source globally and to develop PB products. In the future they will surely use these resources and try to overcome their biggest problem which is their strategic response to the local situation.

On this point, while it is a joint venture, the strategy of Samsung Tesco is worth looking at closely. Korean consumers perceive this KDS to be like a local retailer. Table 3.5 gives a comparison of two stores. These are the Carrefour and Samsung Tesco stores in Pusan, the second biggest city in Korea. These two stores are located on the same street where the competition to attract customers is fierce. The business style and performance of the two stores is very different. Samsung Tesco is a joint venture but it is seen by the Korean consumer as a local KDS. On the other hand, Carrefour as the pure global retailer is operating the store using global strategies. Compared to the Samsung Tesco store which is running the store on local lines and has achieved citizenship as a local store, Carrefour is beset with problems.

It is apparent that recently global KDS operations are learning from the local KDS and experimenting with strategies to deal with the local situation. There are

Table 3.5 A comparison of the Carrefour and Samsung Tesco stores

	Carrefour Sasan store	*Samsung Tesco West-Pusan store*
Overview		
Opened	June 1996 (first foreign-owned store in Pusan)	February 1999 (originally the second Home Plus store Samsung owned)
Space	9,240 m^2	8,039 m^2
Opening times	10.00–24.00	10.00–24.00
Sales	About 100 million Won per day	About 350 million Won per day
Store manager history	From Carrefour headquarters	After changing jobs from a large Korean distribution company, chosen from Samsung Trading Co.
Staff recruitment	Core staff with language ability (French or English) Full-time staff are recruited from Carrefour Korea	Core staff are distribution experts In recruiting full-time staff, priority is given to local university graduates
Localization strategies	No shuttle bus Mainly global sourcing Advertising by Seoul HQ	Shuttle bus provided until June 2001 Partnerships with local suppliers Emphasize local community activities
Store atmosphere	Stresses French atmosphere	Run on Korean lines, although a joint venture between Tesco and Samsung
Format standardization with other stores	Emphasis on strict format standardization	Emphasis on format adaption to fit local culture and consumers

Source: Author interview (held on 6 October 2001).

probably many points they have learnt from the success of the Samsung Tesco (Home Plus) strategy. Carrefour who received a lot of attention by coming into Korea early has been criticized for adopting a hard-line global strategy and not taking into account the Korean culture. But, Carrefour has recently tried to reduce the friction with the local society by increasingly adopting policies from the Korean management and local shop manager. Wal-Mart who uses its own business strategies has focused on out-of-city stores but recently it has looked at opening stores in city areas. Furthermore, the global KDS have been gaining praise for their strategies such as raising the amount of fresh foods they handle in their range, stressing a softer image in their store furnishings, which are liked by Korean women, increasing the amount of goods purchased from local suppliers and hiring local staff.

The maturity of the KDS market and the intentions of the global retailers

The global KDS that have been stimulated by the success of the local retailers such as E-Mart and Samsung Tesco (Home Plus) as the hybrid KDS are trying different new approaches, but they must reform their global formats into local ones so that it will be accepted by the Korean consumers. By doing this the global retailers are being seen as 'Global KDS' who are making efforts to deal with localization and not just seen as 'Global Discount Stores'. Global KDS and local KDS have increased their customer bases by both fierce price and non-price competition. So, it cannot be expected that the local KDS will continue in the way it has so far within the total KDS market. Undoubtedly, localization is the key for global retailers but if they go too far they can loose their identity which may result in them confronting the so-called 'global dilemma' (Mukoyama 1996). Leaving aside Samsung Tesco, global retailers such as Wal-Mart and Carrefour are unlikely to fall into the trap of the global dilemma. They are surely looking hard at the Korean KDS market and formulating policies. They have competitive power that far outweighs that of the local KDS, so what strategies are they planning?

In Korea, the current view is that the KDS market, at the earliest, will reach maturity in 2003. At this time the market will be close to saturation and the current emerging oligopoly will increase. For example, it has been reported that if Wal-Mart takes over any failing company then in one stroke the market structure will be changed. Carrefour among others might take a similar path. As has been seen in the moves into other countries, global retailers like to move to a large scale through acquisition strategies when there is a mature market. In this respect the trends in Korea are no exception.

Conclusion: some implications for Japan

According to the Japan Chain Store and Japan Department Stores Associations, the total sales for GMS and department stores in 2001, compared to the previous year, fell by 5.2 and 0.4 per cent (current store base). This in part was due to the fall in base prices caused by deflation. As a result of this the two mainstays of retailing have fallen on hard times, with annual decreases of total sales for the last five years in a row.

Retail distribution in other Asian countries, however, where global retailers are entering continually is full of activity (Kawabata 2000). The dynamism of Korean retailing is of particular note and contrasts strongly with Japan. The department stores and KDS in Korea continue to post good results and the rapid growth of the KDS market built by the global and local retailers is of particular note.

Korea, which is still historically a young country in the field of contemporary retail systems, has learnt a lot from and has been influenced by Japan. Despite this, why is it that the Korean retail system, while seeing the hardships faced by the Japanese system, has been able to grow from year to year and now thinks about moving into other Asian markets? The answer is quite simple. The Korean retailers while having to deal with the moves by global retailers have learnt from the retail formats of Western countries and Japan and have developed the innovative KDS format using the advantages available to them. Many of the global retailers have also generated retail formats that meet the needs of the Korean market. As a result and as we have repeatedly stated in this chapter, the local KDS and hybrid KDS as well as the global KDS have expanded the whole KDS market through competition and this is having positive effects on the whole of the Korean retailing industry.

Japanese retailers, who have been protected by distribution policies such as the Large-Scale Retail Store Law (Daiten Ho) and have experienced only local competition in a very stable market, will have to face the age of real global competition from now on. Many analysts think that the Japanese retailers, who are already facing hard times, will face greater difficulties. However, they could learn from the battles fought by the local KDS of Korea.

The competitive position is very dynamic. The modest performance of the global retailers in Korea should not be interpreted as major strategic mistakes. The managers of Carrefour do not think that their strategy in Korea is a mistake at all (Daily Economic Newspaper 18 Jan. 2002). Within the global portfolio strategy of the French Company, rather than the Korean situation being a 'visible fight' over a short period in terms of numbers of stores and turnover, they give precedence to a view of a 'step-by-step war' aimed at building profits over the long term in a specific country, using their business resources in multiple countries.

What should be stressed is that this stance of global retailers for a long-term strategy in Asia is linked closely to movements in Japan. They have had moderate success in the growing Korean market, but most probably the Korean market is a 'training ground for the Japanese market' (Yamanashi 2000). One of the aims of moving into the Korean market can easily be seen as providing a bridgehead for entry into the Japanese market which is ten times bigger than the Korean market. The global retailers have opportunities to learn about the Korean market which is somewhat similar to the Japanese market in terms of its cultural and social aspects. The global retailers may be flexing their muscles in the Korean market in preparation for moves into the huge Japanese market.

Notes

1 Shinsegae department store and Costco merged in October 1994 and opened the first wholesale 'Price Club'. In 1998, when US Price Costco recognized the opportunities in the Korean market, they revoked the merger and in January 1999 restarted with 'Costco Wholesale'.

2 The analysis of Western global retailers changing their hypermarket formats to suit the country into which they were moving is referred to in Dawson and Henley (1999).

3 In May 1999, the Samsung Trading Co. of the Samsung group received US$2,500 million from Tesco and started a new company (the shares held by Tesco and Samsung were 81 and 19 per cent, respectively). This was the birth of Samsung Tesco but the 'Home Plus' store brand given by Samsung originally was continued because of the potentially negative feelings of Koreans towards foreign companies. For Koreans it was seen as a global retailer but did not have the connotations of being a foreign company.

References

An, G. H. and Cho, J. Y. (2000) *The Principle of Distribution*. Seoul: Hakhyounsa (in Korean).

Baek, I. S. (2000) 'The emergence of mass-consumption market and change of retail business: the case of Korea', *Keieishigaku*, 34(3): 49–75 (in Japanese).

Business Week (2002) 'Holding off the Wal-Marts of the world', *Business Week*, January 21: 21.

Cho, Y. H. and Han, H. C. (2001) 'Toward high quality and low price: PB strategy of Korean discount stores', *Monthly Discount Merchandiser*, August: 24–33 (in Korean).

Chung, Y. S. (2001) *The Current View and Growth Strategy of Korean Discount Stores*. Seoul: Samsung Economic Research Institute (in Korean).

Dawson, J. A. and Henley, J. S. (1999) 'Internationalisation of hypermarket retailing in Poland: West European investment and its implications', *Journal of East-West Business*, 5(4): 37–52.

Han, H. C. (2002) 'The performance of Korean discount stores in 2001 and short-term prospects', *Monthly Discount Merchandiser*, January: 33–42 (in Korean).

Kawabata, M. (2000) *The Internationalization of Japanese Retailers: Locations and Strategies*. Tokyo: Sinhyoron (in Japanese).

Korea Chamber of Commerce (2001) *The Analysis of Management of Korean Retailers*. Seoul: Korea Chamber of Commerce (in Korean).

Lee, G. S. (2002) 'The myth of E-Mart's success', *Weekly Chosun*, February 7: 25–31 (in Korean).

Mukoyama, M. (1996) *Entering the Pure Global Strategy by Japanese Retailers*. Tokyo: Chikurashobo (in Japanese).

Oh, S. (1998) *The Management of Korean Discount Stores*. Seoul: Bakyoungsa (in Korean).

Yamanashi, H. (2000) 'Whole aspect of Seoul as the training ground for the Japanese market for Carrefour, Wal-Mart and Costco', *Shokuhin Shogyo*, September: 32–67 (in Japanese).

4 Structural changes in the retail industry

The Korean government's industrial policy subsequent to opening the domestic market

Seong Mu Suh

Introduction

The Korean retail industry experienced a new stage of development when Korea agreed to join the World Trade Organization (WTO) in 1996. WTO demanded that service industries such as finance, retail, business services and education be open to foreign investors. Many Koreans considered these industries were too important or culturally bounded, to be controlled by foreign companies. In reality, the competitiveness of the domestic service industries was far behind that of the leading countries. For example, productivity of Korean retail workers is a third of that of American retailers. Many believed that foreign companies would take control of the service sector once the industries become liberalized. Nevertheless, the market was opened to worldwide competition and Korean retailers had to face the global challenge.

In the meantime, the Korean economy continued to enjoy a healthy growing rate since the 1988 Seoul Olympic Games. Per capita income increased to US$10,300 in 1997 from US$4,300 in 1988. The gross domestic product (GDP) was increasing on average 7.5 per cent per year. The stock market and the real estate industries were experiencing their best years in decades. Naturally, the retail industry benefited from the growing consumer expenditure. The industry's growth rate was ahead of the GDP growth recording annual growth rate of 12 per cent on average during 1992 through 1997. Many economists and even government officials seemed to have forgotten the days when they were apprehensive of the imminent inroad of the foreign capital. They erroneously believed that the Korean economy was strong enough to get along with foreign investment. Local retailers started to expand their store networks aggressively. Kim's Club, for example, was so aggressive that the debt to capital ratio was almost 545 per cent, when it eventually collapsed in 1998. Many retailers could not survive the Korean financial crisis that started in November 1997 continuing through 1998 when foreign institutions suddenly withdrew capital from Korea.

The Korean economy showed some resilience by recovering from the worst economic shock. In 1999, the economy grew at 10.9 per cent and in 2000 at 8.8 per cent to regain the 1997 level. Accordingly, consumers were changing.

Consumers demanded quality and services in shopping. Korean consumers' lifestyles became more diverse as in the leading countries. Many of them were not satisfied with their shopping experiences. The retail industry was ready to face a new stage inviting different types of retail formats in Korea.

In retrospect, opening the Korean economy and the subsequent financial collapse in 1997 were important landmarks in Korea's economic development history. It signalled the beginning of the new era in a dramatic way. People learned that they live in a borderless world and that they must acquire skills to survive in the global market and adapt to the global standard. Local businesses realized that they had to change their business paradigms to be successful; profitability is just as important as sales growth. They also understood that financial strategies should be more conservative than in the past. Most importantly, Korean executives accepted that they had to keep up with changes in the business environment and learn new business models.

This chapter reviews the changes in the retail industry since the free trade agreement in Korea. The review will focus on the responses of a local retailer and the Korean government's industrial policy in the new environment. The chapter begins with the characteristics of the Korean retailing industry, followed by the reviews on the major retail institutions. Finally, the Korean government's industrial policy for the retail industry will be introduced.

Characteristics of the Korean retail industry

Retailing and wholesaling constitute approximately 10 per cent of GDP and about 19 per cent of employment in Korea. The retail industry employs as many people as the manufacturing sectors although the contribution to GDP is half that of manufacturing. As of 1998, the number of stores per ten thousand people in Korea is 186. This is three times as many as in the USA and one-and-a-half times as many in Japan. Less than four people are employed in 92 per cent of the stores. The average annual sales volume per store is US$127,000, approximately 9 per cent of the USA and 21 per cent of Japan. In short, the Korean retail industry is very fragmented and unproductive.

Table 4.1 Percentage of retail sales by store type

	1995 (%)	1996 (%)	1997 (%)	1998 (%)	1999		
					(%)	Billion Won	Full-time employees ('000)
Department stores	11.7	11.9	11.4	10.7	13.3	10.0	29
SCs	0.8	2.2	3.4	5.6	7.7	5.8	14
Supermarkets	6.4	6.3	6.3	6.6	4.6	3.5	32
Convenience stores	1.0	1.0	1.0	1.0	1.0	0.8	4
Other stores	79.9	78.3	77.5	75.8	73.4	55.4	1,233

Source: Internal report of the Ministry of Industry and Resources, Korea, 2000.

Table 4.1 shows the structure of the retail industry with their relative positions in terms of sales volume. Department stores, supercentres (SCs), supermarkets and convenience stores are incorporated retailers. The number and importance of the department stores and SCs are steadily increasing.

As of 1999, over 70 per cent of the sales in the retail industry are from small retailers that are mostly not incorporated. Many of them are in traditional shopping districts where facilities are outdated and usually not clean. Since the traditional markets comprise property owners, merchants and street vendors, there are no strong management entities to govern each group's individualistic behaviour and to pursue a unified strategy. Therefore, it is not surprising that many consumers find unpleasant shopping experiences in the traditional markets.

New types of retail business

As early as 1990, some local retailers were convinced that they would inevitably be facing global retailers such as Wal-Mart and Carrefour in the near future. One such local company was Shinsegae Department Stores Co. Shinsegae opened as the Seoul branch of Japan's Mitsukoshi Department Stores, in 1930, when Korea was under Japanese government. After the Second World War, Samsung Group took over the store and changed its store name. Eventually, Shinsegae was separated from Samsung in 1997. The store established its reputation as a high-quality department store. Other premium department stores in Korea are Lotte and Hyundai. These three stores dominated the department store business. They have been busy catching up the rising consumers' demand for quality shopping since the 1980s.

In the meantime, the executives in the Korean department stores became shopping mall developers, not the genuine retailers who do much of merchandising to meet customer demands. As in Japan the three department stores' prime strategy is to secure good locations and to manage tenant mixes. They do not care much about developing products, sourcing and managing inventories that can significantly improve their profit margins. Such merchandising function was left to the individual tenant in the department store. The tenants performed market research, planned product mixes and sold the products.

The leased department strategy of Korean department stores was successful when the demand for upscale shopping facilities grew faster than the supply of such malls. The upper-class consumers and growing economy rewarded them with handsome revenues and appreciation of the real estate values. Management's prime concern was securing locations and managing tenants. Department stores were patronized mainly by upper-class consumers who paid less attention to prices than service. However, such a strategy is not effective to compete with low cost retail operators such as Wal-Mart. A real retailer was needed to meet the demands of increasing numbers of middle-class consumers.

Merchandising is the essence of retailing business because it involves identifying the right products, buying them in the right quantities at the right times, and selling them in a right way. In other words, a retailer's job includes buying and presenting products, managing inventories and promoting their products at their own risk. In the process, the retailer can differentiate its brand and products from its competitors and demand a higher price. In this sense, Korean department stores are not retailers.

E-mart was the first of the large retailers in Korea that did their own merchandising. In November 1993, it opened its first store, as a division of Shinsegae, at a residential area in the northern suburbs of Seoul. The opening ceremony generated much public attention because Shinsegae declared that they would compete against the global retailers that were to penetrate the domestic market. Stimulating patriotic enthusiasm was a fad among local companies at that time because many people erroneously believed that foreign companies might take control of the Korean service industries. Patriotism was a perfect fit for the situation. Many believed that Koreans should patronize local stores to respond to the foreign threats.

This first E-mart store was a success. Consumers were satisfied with the competitive prices of the products and their shopping experiences at the store. The shopping facilities, including a large parking area, were as good as the department stores. The E-mart management gained confidence and launched an aggressive rollout strategy across the country. Their goal was to strengthen their positions before the global companies entered the market. Figure 4.1 shows the number of new stores opened and cumulative selling space of E-mart. They set up four new stores in 1998, even when the Korean economy was experiencing a 7 per cent decline.

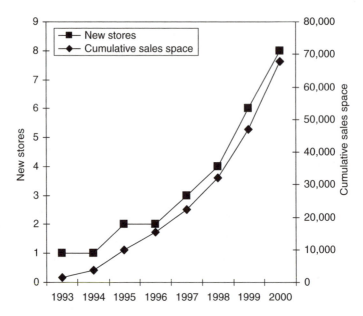

Figure 4.1 E-mart – new stores and cumulative selling space.

The year 1996 is remembered as a special point in the history of Korean retailing. The largest two global retailers, Carrefour and Wal-Mart launched their stores in Korea. They would compete with E-mart in the same market segment. The locations, shopping facilities and product mix strategies of the three companies were very similar but new to most Korean consumers. The new business type will be called supercentres or SCs in this chapter. An SC is typically about 3,000 pyung (1,000 m²) and is located in the vicinity of a large residential area. The trade area has a radius of about 5–10 km and contains approximately 100,000 middle-class consumers. A typical SC handles over 30,000 stock-keeping units.

Carrefour opened three SCs with a total sales space of 10,800 pyung (3,300 m²). Wal-Mart opened two stores totalling 7,300 pyung (2,200 m²). The two foreign retailers alone contributed about 42 per cent of the newly added sales space of SCs in 1996. Figure 4.2 shows that the cumulative sales space of SCs takes off in 1996. Another global retailer, Tesco, joined the group by taking over 81 per cent of the capital of a local SC in 1997. Tesco named its stores Homeplus. Lotte Shopping, established in 1970 and owned by a Korean–Japanese retailer, entered the SC market in 1998. They named the new division Lotte Magnet. Lotte considered Shinsegae's E-Mart as a major competitor to their business. As of August 2001, the five companies are major players in the SC category. Three of them are global retailers, one of them is a localized Japanese retailer and E-mart is the one originating in Korea.

E-mart stressed fresh food and snack corners while their foreign competitors merchandised to their strengths in home appliances and commodities. In terms of organizational structure, E-mart is flat; they have only eight executive offices to run a business with US$2 billion sales. E-mart's efforts seem to be working.

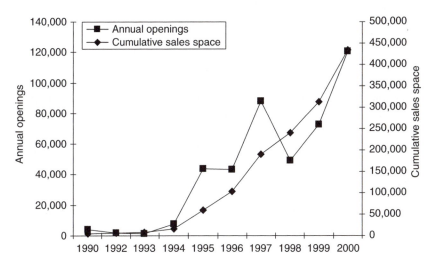

Figure 4.2 Annual openings space and cumulative space in SCs (pyungs).

Table 4.2 Financial indicators of major SC firms

	E-mart	Carrefour	Samsung-Tesco	Wal-Mart
Sales (100 million Won)	23,564	10,392	5,626	4,027
Expenses (100 million Won)	2,832	1,859	1,174	517
Expenses as % of sales	12.0	17.9	20.9	12.8
Operating income (100 million Won)	882	324	−367	70
Stockturn	35.7	15.1	14.0	16.7

Source: Hankook kyungjae, 13 July 2001.

Table 4.2 shows that E-mart is outperforming global players on several financial measures. Their sales-to-inventory ratio is extremely high compared to their competitors. The operating expenses are also the lowest. They expect sales to reach US$3 billion in 2001.

Industry observers expect that SCs will continue to grow until the total number reaches around 400 in 2005, which is the saturation point based on 1 store per 100,000 residents. The global major retailers are expected to maintain an aggressive position. For example, Tesco announced that they would continue to invest annually about US$600 million until 2005, when they expect to have 55 SCs in Korea. Tesco's management are much encouraged by the successful opening of new stores. New stores keep breaking the first day sales records in Korea and even among the Tesco stores around the world. The average daily sales of the seven Tesco stores are over US$400,000. E-mart, Wal-Mart and Carrefour are strong competitors to Tesco's aggressive strategies. The coming several years will see fierce competition among major SC retailers in Korea.

Other types of retailing

The rapid growth of SCs is a threat to the traditional department stores since SCs provide competitive shopping experiences to department stores. The major difference is product mix, with department stores being stronger in fashion goods. Many consumers are satisfied at the SC's one-stop shopping facilities. They are also content with the value for money of SCs. The recent forecasts show that SCs will outsell department stores in 2003, when the total sales of SCs reach over US$17 billion. The total number of SCs will reach 400 by 2005, with total sales of approximately US$20 billion. If the Korean economy slows down as many economists predict, the department stores will feel the impact of slowdown sooner than SCs.

Because the department stores cannot compete with the SCs on price, they plan to handle more premium fashion brands, such as Versace and Prada. They also emphasize their excellent customer services to differentiate themselves from SCs. However, a major challenge for department stores is that they do not have much bargaining power with the premium brands to demand lower prices when SCs' competition increases. In order to bargain for good prices with premium brands, it is important for the Korean department stores to build their store reputation.

Supermarkets grew fast in the 1980s when per capita income in Korea increased from US$1,000 in 1980 to US$4,300 at the time of the 1988 Seoul Olympics. A typical supermarket run by a major firm is around 140 pyung (450 m^2), and, in 1999, had sales of about 200 million Won (US$1.6 million). The supermarket industry's share of the total retail industry was maintained at about 6 per cent until a sudden decline in 1999. SCs are attracting consumers away from supermarkets because most SCs are handling food and convenience goods. These two categories account for about 67 per cent of sales of a typical SC. As SCs are located in residential areas, they greatly affect local supermarkets. In order to compete with SCs, the supermarket companies are increasing selling space and providing better customer service. As of 2001, no foreign companies are involved in the Korean supermarket industry.

The share of other types of retailing in Korea is negligible, compared to the three major types of retailers explained above. For example, convenience stores such as 7-Eleven took only about 1 per cent of the total retailing business in 1999.

On the other hand, Cable TV retailing deserves some attention. The leader, LG Home-Shopping Channel, established in 1995, is expected to have over US$900 million of revenue in 2001. Their arch rival 39Shopping expects to sell only a little less than LG. The industry will grow fast in the next few years because the Korean government allowed three more companies to compete.

The government policy towards the industry

The massive investment in SCs by leading companies after Korea's joining WTO changed the Korean retailing industry. On the positive side, most Korean consumers in the metropolitan areas improved their shopping experience in the new shopping facilities. The SCs provide higher customer satisfaction with better quality shopping. Importantly with the growth of SCs, Korean retailers were able to acquire a more sophisticated knowledge base from heavy investment in a scientific management system and training programmes. The leading retailers' efforts had a spillover effect on small retailers and suppliers. Suppliers were able to improve management skills with retailers' joint efforts to streamline product flows. In addition, suppliers and retailers could better understand consumer behaviour by analysing the Point of Sale (POS) data. This was quite a change for suppliers since they could not obtain such a specific sales record in the past.

However, liberalizing the retailing industry has had some side effects. Traditional shopping districts in particular, were endangered by losing customers to SCs that provided low prices and a wide variety of products. To make matters worse, the aggressive promotion campaigns of SCs and their free shuttle bus services further exacerbated local retailer's distress.

Another side effect was the conflict that arose between SCs and local suppliers. SC's strong bargaining power forced local suppliers to adhere to the trading conditions requested by the SC firms. As the trade volume increased, SCs demanded lower prices and more contributions to their promotional campaigns. In some cases, the conflict was taken to court. Carrefour, for example, had been involved in legal conflicts with local suppliers due to promotional expenses that were considered unreasonable. Many believe that the global retailer's business practices in a unique Korean business culture have caused such trouble. Instead of adjusting to the local business practices, Carrefour and Wal-Mart attempt to maintain their business style and culture by directly sending managers from global headquarters.

To manage the changes in the retailing environment, the policy makers in the Korean government attempt to achieve three short-term objectives:

- to support the traditional small merchants in coping with the changes;
- to encourage investments in the most developed retail practices, and;
- to preserve fair competition in the retail industry.

Modernizing traditional shopping districts

Considering the fact that traditional shopping districts are a major employment source, their sudden fall became a political issue in Korea. Accordingly, the government planned the following:

- The government rewards traditional shopping districts by providing financial subsidies based upon the business plan prepared by the merchant associations of the districts. The local association's determination to change and the viability of the plan are major factors in evaluation.
- A special law is proposed to simplify the remodelling and renovation procedures. The new law allows retailers to build larger stores for any given land than is permitted by the present law.
- A business centre is made available to provide merchants with business services. The services include business consulting and training.
- The government supports small retailers to develop joint distribution systems for themselves.
- The government attempts to minimize regulations in franchise operations.

Promoting new information technology

The government recognized the importance of the information technology in the retailing industry and took the following actions. Some have been implemented while some are still in process.

- The government created Korea Supply Chain Management Committee in order to promote information technology in the retailing industry. The committee comprises forty university professors and businessmen with the deputy minister being the head.
- The committee discussed the four important issues for a sound information infrastructure: Bar Code, POS System, Electronic Data Interchange (EDI) and electronic catalogue.

- The committee prepares a scorecard to measure the industry's progress in Supply Chain Management (SCM) development. The scorecard will minimize the trial and errors of individual company that implements SCM for the first time.
- The committee supervises a database-building project that will list product information on over 100,000 items. The electronic catalogue from this project is considered a necessity for successful business-to-business transactions.
- The government wishes to standardize freight containers, boxes and equipment in order to improve logistics systems. For example, the government decided on twenty-six different kinds of packaging modules to streamline the flow of the packages from factories to stores. Every package will be identified by a Universal Bar Code.
- The government plans to conduct a survey of approximately 13,000 small stores over the country. The results will be available in a database and will be used to evaluate industrial policies.
- The government will provide loans for companies that wish to modernize their distribution systems. The Distribution System Modernization Fund, a specific fund for such purpose, was set up under the Ministry's supervision.

Revising the legal system

The government wishes to revise the legal systems that deal with various problems in the retailing industry. Being concerned about the large retailers' monopolistic behaviour against local retailers and suppliers, the government has shown some legislative effort towards alleviating such problem.

The Ministry consulted with the Fair Trade Committee on whether free shuttle bus services of large retailers should be allowed. The Fair Trade Committee decided that the government should ban free shuttle bus services due to its unfair practice against small merchants and the city transportation business as well. Subsequently, the government banned free shuttle bus services in Korea.

The government attempts to delegate more power to the Local Trade Arbitration Committee. The government believes that the Local Trade Arbitration Committee will better arbitrate conflicts between large retailers and local merchants. Without doubt, the government will remain strict on regulating large retailer's excessive promotions practices, notably those involving gifts or contests.

Conclusion

In retrospect, opening the retail industry to foreign investors, in 1996, posed a major challenge to Korean retailers. The local retail industry leaders responded by attempting new types of retailing to compete with the global players. E-mart, in particular, is the leader in this venture. E-mart was astute enough to anticipate the change in the retail industry and aggressively open new stores before global retailers became established in the new market. As a result, E-mart has the highest sales level and store numbers, more than Wal-Mart, Carrefour and Tesco as of August 2001. Industry experts believe that the real competition is yet to come when the retail giants begin to use their worldwide supplier networks.

As of August 2001, there were 175 SCs in Korea. The development has been impressive considering that the first SC was opened by E-mart in 1993. Investments in SCs in a short period have changed the Korean retail industry structure. The combined sales volume of the new retailing is expected to surpass that of the department stores by 2003.

Amid the dramatic change in the retailing environment, consumers are the major beneficiaries. Consumers are able to enjoy pleasant shopping experiences at SCs that were once only possible in department stores. Consumers also have shopping choices due to new retailing formats such as home shopping TV channels, and larger supermarkets that provide high-quality service.

In addition, the opening of the Korean retail market and subsequent large investments in opening the SCs contributed to developing management skills by Korean retailers. Sophisticated information systems were installed in large retailers to handle complex merchandising systems and store operations. Accordingly, a large number of retailing managers were trained as store managers, merchandisers, information engineers and retail experts.

Despite these gains from the liberalization, the traditional shopping districts suffered from losing customers to the new retailing outlets. Their limited resources and skills have put them in difficulty to compete with SC's low-priced, variety-product mixes. They have had to renovate their stores and find a niche in the market to survive in the industry.

Other victims from Korea's retailing liberalization are local suppliers. With SC's strong bargaining power from high volume sales, SCs demanded lower prices and more services that were seemingly unreasonable for local suppliers. Even a prestigious brand in the domestic market is known to have major conflicts with SCs over the terms of transactions. Some executives believe that global retailers will gradually shift away from local suppliers to foreign suppliers once the retailers are settled down in Korea. In such case, local suppliers will soon be facing global competition as well.

The short-term objectives of the Korean government's industrial policy can be summarized as follows: to subsidize local merchants to adjust to the new retailing environment, to provide new information technologies to improve the distribution systems in Korea, and to ensure fair trades and balanced developments in the retailing industry.

References

Hankook Kyungjae (2001) 'Localized service beats foreign discount stores', *Hankook Kyungjae*, July 13: 10.

Korea Superchain Association (2001) *Retail Business Yearbook*, Seoul: Korean Superchain Association.

Ministry of Industry and Resources (2000) *Report on Helping Local Small Merchants*, Internal Report, Department of Public Relations, November.

Ministry of Industry and Resources of Korea (2001) *Recent Changes in the Retail Industry and Directions for Industrial Policies*, Internal Report.

Shinsegae Department Store (2000) *The Album for the 70th Anniversary of Shinsegae*, Seoul: Shinsegae Department Store.

5 The impact of World Class Distributors on the retail industry in Thailand

Jirapar Tosonboon

There are three main parties in the distribution system, consumers, distributors and suppliers and/or producers. The distribution system functions after bargaining between suppliers and distributors. Each supplier must compete within the market by improving efficiencies. To improve efficiency, the successful supplier must be able to sell the right quality of product at the right time and at the right place. Suppliers must use appropriate technical support and have good relations with both distributors and the consumer. For the distributor to compete successfully with others, they also must improve their efficiency. The key to success in the distribution system is acceptance by the customer. 'World Class Distributors' who have experience in many countries, have access to large amounts of capital, have knowledge of customers, are likely to win over the potential customer's mind very easily. In this way they gain success in the market. This chapter considers the emergence and growing power in Thailand of these World Class Distributors.

Four stages of distribution in Thailand

Within the past fifty years, the distribution system for consumer products in Thailand has changed greatly. This change can be divided into four stages (Figure 5.1).

First stage (1944–1957): power in the hands of the wholesaler

After the Second World War, America the leader of the world's economy at that time, used Thailand as their army base and hoped that by strengthening the Thai economy, they could reduce the communist power in Asia. During this time, America contributed substantial funds to the Thai government. These funds enabled growth in Thailand's economy. With this growing economy, many international companies who were both producers and suppliers such as Unilever, Berli Jucker, Colgate Palmolive, etc., opened subsidiaries in Bangkok. Also, two Japanese companies, Kao Commercial Co. Ltd and Lion Co. Ltd joined Thailand's consumer market. The expansion of the consumer market changed the local distribution system from one based on hawker formats to one based around the grocery store.

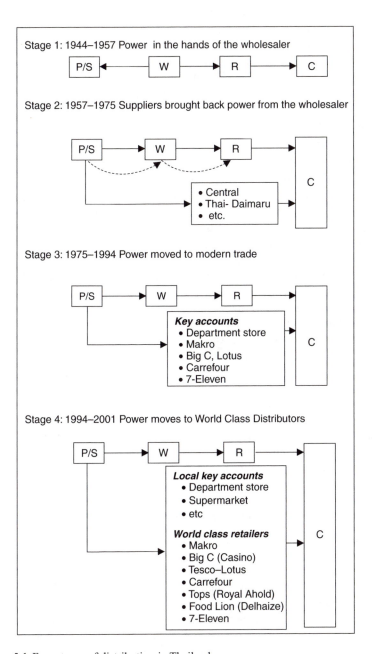

Figure 5.1 Four stages of distribution in Thailand.

Though, demand for consumer products spread through the country, there was limited infrastructure, and producers had to sell their products through wholesalers. Most of the powerful wholesalers were located at 'Sampeng'. Sampeng was traditionally a Chinese settlement, and was the centre of traditional trade for consumer products. In 1952–1958 Sampeng had an approximately 80 per cent market share in the wholesaler trade in Thailand.

Second stage (1957–1975): suppliers brought back power from wholesalers

At the end of the first stage, Central Department Store changed their business model from that of the small grocery store to the department store and opened their first branch in 1956. Central, the oldest and the largest department store, positioned itself for the medium- to upper-income market. During this stage, Central opened four more branches. Additional to Central, Thai-Daimaru, the first foreign department store in Thailand, opened its first branch in November 1964. Many small- and medium-sized department stores opened at this time. These modern stores encouraged a change in consumer behaviour and about 40 per cent of Bangkok's population quickly got familiar with shopping at the new convenient department store.

During the second stage, there was a strong competition among suppliers and an increase in the power of the wholesalers. To further control the market, suppliers re-organised their sales system. For example, Unilever introduced the 'Stockist System'. This system limited the role of the wholesaler and forced them to be an expert only in stock management. For sales, Unilever sent their salesmen to work closely with the stockist and sell to the retailer directly. The stockists earned their income on a commission basis, from the amount of total sales made by each salesman. The stockist system saved Unilever from having to construct depots across the country. Unilever earned loyalty from their stockists since these wholesalers sold only the company product. Also, Unilever had a close relationship with their retailers who had important consumer information.

Third stage (1975–1994): power moved to modern trade

In the second stage, there were only Central, Thai-Daimaru and some small- and medium-sized department stores. Competition among these department stores was not aggressive, until direct competitors to Central emerged in the form of Robinson's and The Mall Department Store that opened in 1979. Robinson's was opened and operated by a young management group. Robinson's used extensive marketing activities and to remain innovative, moved from a position as 'the department store for a young generation' to 'fast' and 'class', meaning fast service and high-quality image of product. For the Mall, the founder started his business in a cinema, changed to the entertainment business and then opened The Mall Department Store. The Mall positioned itself as a *shopping centre and an entertainment complex* which was a unique concept. The Mall developed a one-stop shopping centre that included a department store, movie theatre, food mall, hypermarket, play land and exhibition hall.

However, the real competitor for Central was Makro, the first cash and carry store in Thailand. Makro was a joint project between CP Group (Chalern Porkapam Group), the biggest group in agricultural products and telecommunication in Thailand, and SHV Holdings N.V. The first Makro branch opened in Bangkok in 1989. Makro's total sales increased from TB1,000 million in 1989 to TB19,300 million in 1994, which was almost equal to those of Central who had forty-two years of experience.

In the third stage, power changed from being held by suppliers to being held by modern trade. Suppliers considered each unit of the modern trade firms to be a key account. Therefore, they sent a special team to work closely with each key account.

Fourth stage (1994–2001): power moves to World Class Distributors

The success of Makro indicated that the behaviour of the Thai consumer was changing. With the expansion of community facilities in the suburbs, the expansion of higher education, the higher income of consumers and pressures on consumers' time, consumers especially in the middle classes and lower-income brackets were looking for a reasonable product with a reasonable price. They tended to have less brand loyalty, less regard for store displays, but a strong response to price. The cash and carry, discount store, supercentre and hypermarket became more attractive.

To cope with this change, Central opened Big C, the first supercentre in Thailand, in 1994. Big C was a joint venture between Central and local investors. Big C aimed at the middle- to low-income Group (B–C class) who worked or lived within 3–4 kilometres of the store. Central also invited Carrefour France to open Carrefour Thailand in 1996. Central hoped to use the Carrefour hypermarket as a fighting brand to compete against Makro.

The CP Group, in the same year that they opened Makro, also opened 7-Eleven. The shopping life style of the Thai people was changed by 7-Eleven from the local grocery store to the modern convenience grocery store. The first store opened in June 1989. In November 1995, CP Group opened Lotus supercentre. Their main target for Lotus was the medium-income market who lacked brand loyalty but needed a quality product at a lower price.

In this fourth stage, modern trade had tremendous power. For a supplier to lose one of these key accounts was to lose a large amount of market share. The power of these key accounts further increased when Thailand faced its economic crisis which started in 1998. Due to rapid expansion and heavy debt repayments forced by the devaluation of the Thai Baht, most Thai partners had to sell their shares to World Class Distributors.

World Class Distributors in Thailand

World Class Distributor means a distributor that is in the top rank of total sales and is an expanding trans-national business. Table 5.1 shows details of the retailers in the world's top 100 in 1998 and that have some relationship to the Thai retail business.

Table 5.1 The representation of the biggest 100 retailers in 1998 in Thailand

Retailer (by rank, home country: primary line of trade)	1998 Sales (US$ million)	Number of stores	Number of countries	% of sales outside home country
(1) Wal-Mart Stores, Inc (USA: Discount store)	130,523	3,599	9	9.4
(5) Royal Ahold (The Netherlands: Supermarkets)	37,070	3,927	16	70.9
(7) Promodès Group (France: diversified)	36,204	5,978	16	38.1
(8) Carrefour SA (France: Hypermarkets, Supercentres)	36,020	1,661	20	43.6
(18) Tesco Plc. (United Kingdom: Supermarkets)	28,436	821	8	7.8
(21) Auchan Group (France: Hypermarkets, Supercentres)	25,087	1,269	11	38.1
(27) Jusco Co. Ltd (Japan: General merchandise superstores with food)	18,825	2,355	9	8.4
(33) Casino Group (France: Hypermarkets, Supercentres)	15,130	4,799	7	17.7
(34) Delhaize 'Le Lion' Group (Belgium: Supermarkets)	14,346	1,926	10	77.5
(38) Marks & Spencer Plc. (United Kingdom: General merchandise superstores with food)	13,630	683	36	19.7
(58) The Office Depot (USA: Hard lines Specialty stores)	8,998	789	19	11.6
(71) The Boots Company, Plc. (United Kingdom: Drugstores)	7,442	2,018	4	4.9

Source: Pricewaterhouse Coopers Global Retail Intelligence System, 1998.

Within Table 5.1, there are six world class retailers that have had a strong influence in the Thai retail industry. They are Wal-Mart Stores Inc., Tesco Plc., Carrefour SA, Casino Group, Royal Ahold and Delhaize 'Le Lion' Group.

Wal-Mart Stores Inc. (United States: discount store)

Wal-Mart Stores Inc. was known to all modern traders in Thailand. Thai businessmen wanted to know the secrets that had brought success to Wal-Mart, however, they were afraid that Wal-Mart would enter Thailand. Before the Lotus supercentre opened in November 1995, Lotus invited a consultant team from Wal-Mart to give advice on superstore operations. However, bearing in mind the different culture, Lotus finished the contract and asked Elwin L. Johnson, a top executive from Wal-Mart to work with the Lotus supercentre (KooKang ThuraKit 1996). Possibly related to this move, Central and Robinson's agreed to merge under the name of CRC or Central Retail Group Corporation in 1995. This merger brought together two chains and led to a near virtual monopoly of the department store business in Thailand at that time (PrachaChat ThuraKit 1995).

Tesco Plc. (United Kingdom: supermarkets)

Tesco Plc. is a supermarket in the United Kingdom. In 1998, Tesco Plc. was ranked 18 in the top 100 retailers, with total sales of US$28,436 million from 821 stores in eight countries (Table 5.1). Tesco Plc. came to Thailand in 1995 at the invitation of CP Group. At that time Thailand's economic crisis had started. CP and Tesco Plc. opened a new company called Tesco Thailand Co. Ltd. CP Group held 51 per cent of the shares and Tesco Plc. held 49 per cent. CP then allowed Tesco Thailand Co. Ltd to hold 75 per cent shares of the Ekchai Distribution System Co. Ltd, the company that owned Lotus supercentre. Therefore, CP became a minor shareholder of Lotus supercentre, holding only 10.71 per cent at the beginning of 2000 (PrachaChat ThuraKit 1998).

Carrefour SA (France: hypermarkets, supermarkets)

Carrefour was a pioneer in hypermarket retailing in France, opening their first store in 1963. Carrefour's original principles continue to underpin the company: one-stop shopping, self service, discount prices, quality products and free car parking. Carrefour's international expansion started in the late 1960s in Europe. Its most successful foreign operations were in Spain and Brazil. Carrefour entered and then withdrew from the United Kingdom, Belgium and Switzerland due to lack of expansion space and from the United States, where results were poor. Carrefour was looking for partners in the Asia-Pacific region and went to Taiwan in 1989.

In late 1993, during a short trip to Thailand, the French Embassy's Trade Promotion Department informed Carrefour's new CEO for Asia, that Central Group's top management was trying to contact Carrefour. A few days after that,

Thai representatives flew to Taiwan to visit local Carrefour operations and a joint venture was quickly arranged. Since majority ownership had to be Thai, the ownership structure was: Carrefour 40 per cent, Central 40 per cent and a local holding company 20 per cent (Courbon and Lassere 1994).

At the end of 1997, Carrefour had seven branches with satisfactory sales. However, with strong competition from other World Class Distributors, Carrefour decided to increase their investment from TB800 million to TB4,800 million. With the economic crisis it was quite impossible for Central and the other local investors to remain players so they allowed Carrefour France to take over Carrefour Thailand (Tharn SethaKit 1998).

Casino Group (France: hypermarkets, supercentres)

Casino started business in 1889 as a small grocery store in France. Casino changed its business to supermarket operation in 1960, opened the Geant hypermarket in 1970 and went into the international market in the same year. Alongside the hypermarket business, the Casino Group also runs chains of supermarkets under the name of Casino, Franprix and Leader Price. The Casino Group has 2,300 convenience stores, in the names of, Petit Casino, Spar and Vival. The Casino Group also operates other businesses including restaurants, auto service, food processing and wine bottle manufacture.

In 1998, Big C supercentre, one of the main businesses of CRC faced financial problems. Big C had to stop expanding and tried to negotiate with Lotus, Wal-Mart and Carrefour but could not find a solution. In 1999, CRC and other local investors decided to sell their shares of 66 per cent in Big C to Casino.

Royal Ahold (the Netherlands: supermarkets)

Royal Ahold is a top ten supermarket in the United States and the main supermarket in the Netherlands where it has 3,600 branches. Royal Ahold also runs other types of retail business, including hypermarkets and discount stores in America, Poland, Belgium and Portugal.

In 1995, Central and Robinson's Department Stores merged under the name of CRC. Since CRC was not keen to be involved in the supermarket business, they asked Royal Ahold to create a new company called CRC Ahold and allowed Royal Ahold to have 49 per cent of their shares in Top's supermarket. Top's supermarket became very popular in a short period of time. However, during the economic crisis in 1998, CRC had to mortgage 50 per cent of their shares and sell another 1 per cent of shares in CRC Ahold to Royal Ahold.

Delhaize 'Le Lion' Group (Belgium: supermarkets)

From Table 5.1 we can see that, in 1998, Delhaize's total sales volume from 1,926 stores across 10 countries was US$14,346 million and 77.5 per cent of these sales came from outside the home country. In October 2000, Food Lion had 62 branches in Asian markets – 19 branches in Thailand, 27 in Singapore and 16 in Indonesia.

Delhaize Le Lion came to Thailand with the encouragement of The Mall Department Store. Delhaize Le Lion and The Mall set up Bel-Thai Supermarket Co. Ltd to run the Food Lion Supermarkets in Thailand in 1998. Food Lion planned to operate supermarkets close to consumers' homes. It sought to replace the traditional market, and focused on the middle to lower group, who could walk or use public transport to visit the store. Delhaize 'Le Lion' Group had aggressive strategies. They aimed to have 100 outlets of Food Lion in Thailand within five years. As part of this programme, Food Lion bought and renovated seven Sunny Supermarkets from CP Group. This huge investment over-stretched the domestic partners, including The Mall, who then had to sell their shares to Delhaize Le Lion (PrachaChat ThuraKit 2000).

Factors influencing World Class Distributors in Thailand

There are three main factors influencing the activity and performance of World Class Distributors in Thailand:

- strong market potential;
- lack of strong competitors;
- Alien Business Operations Act 1999.

Strong market potential

Before facing the economic crisis, Thailand had a period of very strong economic growth. Within fifteen years (1980–1995), GNP per capita increased from TB14,065 to TB69,047 and GDP increased from TB662,482 million to TB4,188,929 million. The average monthly income per household increased about three times, from TB3,631 in 1986 to TB10,179 in 1996 and average monthly expenditure increased from TB3,783 to TB9,190 over the same period (Table 5.2).

Table 5.2 Average household size, monthly income and monthly expenditures: 1986–1996

	1986	1988	1990	1992	1994	1996
Average household size (person)	4.3	4.0	4.1	3.9	3.8	3.7
Average monthly income (Baht)	3,631	4,106	5,625	7,062	8,262	10,779
In %	100	113	155	194	228	293
Average monthly expenditure (Baht)	3,783	4,161	5,437	6,529	7,567	9,190
In %	100	110	144	173	200	243

Source: National Statistical Office (1996).

Table 5.3 Population of Thailand by age group percentages

Age group	1980	1985	1990	1995	2000	2005	2010	2015
0–14	40.01	36.21	32.68	29.38	26.64	4.63	23.15	21.78
15–59	54.58	58.14	61.12	63.70	65.56	66.82	67.27	66.96
over 60	5.41	5.65	6.20	6.82	7.79	8.54	9.58	11.26
Total (%)	100.00	100.00	100.00	100.00	100.00	100.00	100.00	100.00
Total (1,000)	46,718	51,581	56,033	60,198	64,071	67,722	71,017	73,819

Source: National Statistical Office (1996).

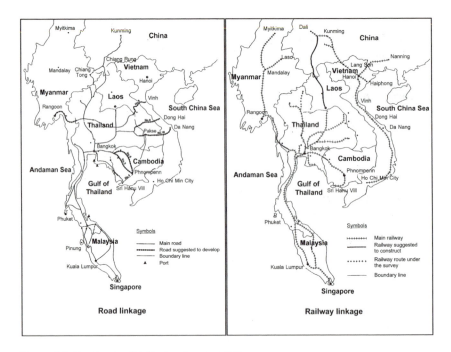

Figure 5.2 Road and rail infrastructure in 1995.

Source: Thai Engineering Construction Co., Ltd, Frederic R. Harris BV and Upham International Corporation, *Master Plan of Maritime Industry*, August 1999.

Not only has per capita wealth increased but also the total number of population increased by almost 20 million over twenty years. The proportion of the population in the working age group has increased substantially (Table 5.3).

Thailand has been developing a multi-model transport infrastructure with its neighbours in recent years. As seen in Figure 5.2 Thailand has become the base for market potential across several countries that collectively had 1,722 million people in 1996.

Within South-east Asia, China remains the most challenging market, since China has about 70 per cent of the total regional population. Entry to the Chinese market is very difficult but is helped by the close relationship between Thailand and China, over many years. Most of the distributors in Thailand originally migrated from China. Among them was Mr Jia Exchore, father of Mr Dhanin Cheavanont, Chairman and Chief Executive of CP Group. Mr Jia was the biggest distributor of seeds in Indochina. He opened a store selling seeds in Bangkok named 'JiaTai', the first business of the CP Group.

CP went to China immediately after the country opened its markets in 1979. They entered with several joint-venture manufacturing activities including Continental Grain from United States, Honda Motorcycles from Japan and Boon Rawd Brewery from Thailand. In 1996, CP made a major move by opening the Makro cash and carry wholesale business in Guangzhou and further opened Lotus supercentre in Shanghai in 1997. CP spent about a year obtaining approval. The Lotus store had a selling area of $24,000\,m^2$ and 10,000 product items. On the opening day more than 200,000 people came to the store. The most popular products were microwave ovens and Sony Trinitron televisions. Given this record of this success CP did not have difficulty in gaining agreement from Tesco Plc. to be their partner in 1998 (SubPiboon 2001).

Lack of strong competitors

Most Thai distributors grew up alongside the small grocery store and used their own experience in running their businesses. Their children, the second generation were able to receive an MBA background but lacked the special talent needed to run this kind of business with flair. So, when CP invited World Class Distributors, Makro, 7-Eleven and Wal-Mart to help them run the business, CP got acceptance from Thai consumers in the short term who could run their business with strength and efficiency. The success of CP Group in running cash and carry, convenience stores and the supercentre made other World Class Distributors confident in investing money in Thailand's market.

Alien Business Operations Act (1999)

During the economic crisis in 1999, in order to attract foreign investors to Thailand, Mr Chuan Leekpai, the Prime Minister at that time revised the law on alien business operations. This Act permits aliens to operate in all kinds of retailing and wholesaling, with a total minimum capital of more than TB100 million or a minimum capital for each retail store of more than TB20 million (TB100 million for wholesaling). Mr Chuan Leekpai also changed the law on ownership to allow aliens to hold more than 49 per cent of shares and having the right to buy land, condominiums and rent property. These Alien Business Operations Acts contributed to the decline of the local distribution system. From Table 5.4, we can see that in less than two years of joining with the foreign investors, all the main retail businesses, including Big C, Lotus, Carrefour, Tops and Food Lion, were controlled by World Class Distributors.

Table 5.4 Retail business before and after the involvement of world class retailers

Business	Before crisis			After crisis		
	Shareholder	%	Number of outlets (year)	Shareholder	%	Target outlets at the end of 2000
Lotus	CP	100	13 (1998)	CP	10.71	24
				Tesco	89.29	
Big C	Central	32.63	20 (1999)	Central	13	25
	Robinson's	14.55		Casino	66	
	Land and House	0.80		Small		
	Small shareholder	42.02		shareholder	21	
Carrefour	Central	40	7 (1998)	SSCP Holding	60	12
	Carrefour France	40		Carrefour		
	SSCP Holding	20		France	40	
Tops	Central Retail	51	41 (Q1, 1998)	Royal Ahold	100	45
	Royal Ahold	49				
Food Lion	The Mall	45	5 (1998)	Delhaize Group	49	21
	Delhaize Group	45		Food Lion Inc.	51	
	Sahaphat	10				

Source: PrachaChat ThuraKit (2000).

The impact of World Class Distributors

The arrival in Thailand of World Class Distributors had several direct impacts on the whole distribution system. These impacts involve all participants in the channel of distribution.

Impacts on local retailers

From Table 5.5 we can see that between the year 2000 and 2001 about half of the department stores in Thailand closed. Most of the department stores that remained open belonged to the CRC Group, The Mall Department Store and the leading department store firms in each province. The larger and stronger firms were able to survive. Not only the department stores but half of the supermarkets also closed. Again the smaller weaker stores closed with the most active and competitive supermarkets being Tops (Royal Ahold, the Netherlands) and Food Lion (Delhaize 'Le Lion' Group from Belgium). The decrease over a single year is dramatic.

Impact on the distribution of power

Makro had a major influence on changes in consumer behaviour in Thailand. However, this change became more marked when Lotus, Big C and Carrefour

Table 5.5 Number of retail stores in Thailand

	2000	2001[a]
Modern trade		
Hypermarket/Supercentre[b]	77	99
Department store[c]	473	236
Supermarket	473	211
Convenience store	3,100	3,350
Others	626	635
Total	4,276	4,531
Traditional trade		
Grocery store	253,010	227,979
Others	3,724	3,352
Total	256,734	231,331
Total retail stores	261,010	235,862

Source: Investment Strategy, Nation Group, 29 July 2001.

Notes
a Estimated number.
b Including Big C, Lotus, Carrefour and Makro.
c Including Provincial department stores.

proved to the consumer that they could get what they wanted at a lower price. So the distribution of power shifted from the department store to the four World Class Distributors, Big C (Casino), Lotus (Tesco), Carrefour and Makro. The attraction, over the department store, was one of price. However, for the supermarket the situation was different. Tops supermarket educated their customers in what the excellent supermarket should look like in terms of price and service. Food Lion attracted the middle- and the lower-income group in Bangkok and the provinces nearby, with consumers moving away, at least in part from shopping in the traditional market. While price was important other service factors started to become important.

It is estimated that at the end of 2002, the hypermarket and the supercentre, with only ninety-nine branches, will have 43 per cent of total sales. If we combine total sales of the hypermarket, supercentre and supermarket together it is estimated that, at the end of 2002, half of the modern trade sales will be in the hands of the World Class Distributors. We also estimate that in 2002, more than a quarter of the retail distribution of consumer products in Thailand is under the control of foreign distributors (Table 5.6). From Table 5.6 it can also be seen that the proportion of modern trade was more than that of traditional trade for the first time, by 2001.

Impact on consumer behaviour

Impact on the shopping place. The figures in Table 5.6 show that consumer's tended to shop more in the hypermarket and in the supercentre than the department store. The reason was that, to gain market acceptance all of these

Table 5.6 Estimated sales and market share of retail stores (2001)

Type	Number of stores		Total sales	
	Branches	*%*	*TB million*	*%*
Modern trade				
Hypermarket/Supercentre[a]	99	0.04	122,015	22.78
Department store[b]	236	0.10	97,400	18.19
Supermarket	211	0.09	22,785	4.25
Convenience store	3,350	1.42	34,175	6.38
Others	635	0.27	8,545	1.89
Total	4,531	1.92	284,920	53.19
Traditional trade				
Grocery store	227,979	96.65	221,595	41.38
Other	3,352	1.42	29,035	5.43
Total	231,331	68.07	250,630	46.81
Total retail stores	235,862	100.00	535,550	100.00

Source: Investment Strategy, Nation Group, 29 July 2001.

Notes
a Including Big C, Lotus, Carrefour and Makro.
b Including Provincial department stores.

Table 5.7 Advertising spending of retail stores from January–
June 2000 and 2001

Type	January–June 2000		January–June 2001	
	TB million	*%*	*TB million*	*%*
Total	97.97	100	149.10	100
Tesco–Lotus	19.84	20	52.27	33
Tops	28.48	29	44.09	30
Big C	14.89	15	21.76	15
Carrefour	15.92	16	17.66	12
Foodland	7.16	7	5.91	4
FoodLion	2.97	3	1.18	—
Makro	0.96	1	—	—

Source: PrachaChat ThuraKit (2001), 30 July–August.

World Class Distributors used aggressive marketing strategies including price
wars, increased numbers of stock keeping units (SKUs), opened large stores and
provided extra services. These approaches proved to be attractive to consumers.
Tesco–Lotus at Klong Toey and Carrefour at Ratchada are good examples.

Tesco–Lotus Klong Toey: In April 2000, Tesco–Lotus open their twentieth
store at Klong Toey, Bangkok. This store was not the traditional stand-alone store
format. Included was Watson's personal care, A–Z and U-F-O apparel, Adidas

and Nike shops, a City Chain Watch shop, Au Bon Pain restaurant and ENC food supplement shop. The store is 31,000 m², with more than 100,000 product items including imports. The store is open 24 hours.

Carrefour Rachada. Carrefour, opened its thirteenth branch on Ratchada Road, Bangkok, in July 2001. The store is sandwiched between the Japanese-Thai owned supermarket Jusco and the Thai-owned Robinson's Department Store, all of which are only a few blocks away from Tesco–Lotus. The operator of Carrefour store said that, the pre-opening in early July 2001 drew, at least 10,000 visitors to the store every day.

To gain market share, Top's supermarket located in Robinson's launched a 'buy one get one free' campaign. Tops offered lower prices at its food court by TB5 per item to compete with Carrefour's food centre that charges only TB15 (half of the usual price). Tesco–Lotus boasted a new lower price campaign, reducing by 8 per cent the prices on some 1,000 items and launched a 'buy two get one free' campaign for more items.

Changing purchasing discipline. To encourage more frequent buying and to increase the amount of spending per visit, these World Class Distributors gave special credit cards to the medium- and lower-income Group. For example Tesco–Lotus joined with GE Capital, the international financial firm and the world leader of private label credit cards. They offered 'The Tesco–Lotus Card' for the individual who is at least 20 years old, and has an income over 10,000 TB/month (Bangkok) or 7,000 TB/month (outside Bangkok) and has been in employment for over one year. Member's of the Tesco–Lotus Card also receive an extra credit line of fifty days interest free credit, with easy repayment terms (as little as 5 per cent). Tesco–Lotus also launched another card for members of the public who have an income of more than 5,000 TB/month, with minimum repayment of 5 per cent. The members have to pay 12 per cent interest per year and a fee for using their credit card of 2 per cent per month. To compete with the Tesco–Lotus Card, Carrefour introduced the 'Simple Credit Card' for the individual aged 20–65 years old, in employment, but with no threshold on income. This card can be used for any product item which is priced at 3,000 TB and above. Repayments will start from 400 TB/month over a forty-eight-month period. All of these credit cards have the potential to seriously damage the purchasing discipline of the medium- to lower-income Group.

Changing consumer brand loyalty. World Class Distributors tried to change customer's brand loyalty from the suppliers' product brand name to the store's brand name. They increased their advertising in all kinds of media, for example, newspaper, radio, cinema and outdoor billboards. Table 5.7 shows the media expenses for January–June in the years 2000 and 2001. From the table we can see that together Tesco–Lotus and Tops jointly spent more than 60 per cent of the total advertising expenditure of the major groups in 2001.

However, we have to keep in mind that the main part of this money came from suppliers who were willing to sell their products into these channels. Even though the customer began to change their buying habits from being attracted by low prices to being attracted to the stores' external promotional strategies. Only, Makro, who positioned, itself as a wholesaler did not use this tactic but tried to use in-store promotions instead (see Table 5.7).

Impact on the supplier

Declining loyalty in supplier's brand. It was a common practice for all well known and powerful distributors to have their own product, selling in their own channel. These products were called 'house brands' or 'distributors own brand'. For Thailand, Makro, pioneered the house brand, using them as *loss leaders* to win market acceptance. Makro lowered the price of its own brands for food items by 5–20 per cent and non-foods items by 15–35 per cent. In 1997, with total sales of TB32,700 million, only 4 per cent came from house brands and they hoped to increase this to 10 per cent in 1999. The Thai-owned department stores, Central, Robinson's, The Mall, also had their own house brands but across a limited product range.

At the beginning most of the house brands were commodity products such as sugar, soya sauce, rice, paper tissue, cotton buds and drinking water etc. The house brand that shocked the market was Tesco-Cola. The packaging looked like Coca-Cola yet was 23 per cent lower in price. The success of Tesco-Cola illustrates the decline of brand loyalty in the supplier brand.

Decline of small and medium suppliers. The World Class Distributors used each countries speciality suppliers to produce competitive products for their house brand. At the beginning of the year 2001 Tesco–Lotus announced that, any manufacturer who wanted to produce items to sell under the 'Supersave' logo, their house brand for food items, must have achieved the ISO 9002 certificate. Tesco–Lotus used the British Retail Consortium (BRC) Technical Standard, the production management system which is popular in England and Europe. To meet BRC requirements, most suppliers need to spend at least TB100,000 to improve their manufacturing processes. With the economic crisis it was, quite impossible for the medium- and small-sized suppliers to comply.

Possible ways to save Thailand's retail industry

From my point of view, blame cannot be attached to the World Class Distributors for coming to Thailand and using their marketing strategies to stimulate the market as they had in their own countries. It was Thailand who invited the investors to the market in an effort to solve economic problems, and gave rights to foreign investors without establishing regulations to control the outcome. With the WTO agreement and the economic crisis, Thailand now cannot amend the Alien Business Operation Acts or introduce new acts to limit foreign investors. However, in my opinion, a number of actions may possibly save Thailand's retail industry:

1   *Credit card restriction*: There should be more stringent controls on credit card application, to avoid a build-up of bad debt in the lower-income groups.

2   *Close supervision from the government*: The government should increase their efforts to improve the efficiency of the small and medium suppliers, until these firms are able to meet the higher standard requirements. Also the government must be the agency to bargain with World Class Distributors to give adequate access to the retail market for local products possibly with special offers on rental agreements for specialist retailers.

3   *Build up member trust within the local distribution channel*: Thailand's investors must try to co-operate, especially regarding the sharing of facilities to reduce their costs. To help small grocery stores they must form 'buying groups' and let local, large corporations help them with logistic management. Also, if possible the concept of 'Co-op' must be renewed within the small community.

4   *Strengthen the unique position*: For the department store and the local supermarket, to survive in this competitive market, they must strengthen their unique position.

5   *Using direct marketing*: Since distributing products through the modern trade system costs about one-third of the retail price, producers and suppliers can use this margin as their budget for direct marketing.

References

Courbon, P. and Lasserre, P. (1994) *Carrefour in Asia, (B): The Expansion in Asia.* Fontainebleau: INSEAD-EAC.

Industrial Finance Corporation of Thailand (1996) Annual Report.

KooKang ThuraKit (1996) 'Wal Mart gave advice to Lotus', *KooKang ThuraKit*, 29 January–4 February.

National Statistical Office (1996) *Report of the Household Socio Economic Survey, Whole Kingdom.* Bangkok: Office of the Prime Minister.

PrachaChat ThuraKit (1995) 'Wal Mart and Lotus Supercenter', *PrachaChat ThuraKit*, 18–21 May.

PrachaChat ThuraKit (1998) 'Tesco Plc and CP Group title', *PrachaChat ThuraKit*, 2–5 July.

PrachaChat ThuraKit (2000) 'Delhaize Le Lion', *PrachaChat ThuraKit*, 30 October– 1 November.

SubPiboon, Athiwat (2001) *Case Study of Mr. Dhanin Cheavanont.* Bangkok: Second Education Public Company Ltd.

Thai Engineering Construction Co., Ltd, Federic R. Harris BV and Upham International Corporation (1999) *Master Plan of Maritime Industry*, August. Bangkok.

Tharn SethaKit (1998) 'Carrefour France took over Carrefour Thailand', *Tharn SethaKit*, 16–18 July.

6 Globalising retailing in Singapore

Cultural commodification and economic change

Victor R. Savage

Introduction

Globalisation, defined by Joseph Nye (2001: 2) as 'networks of interdependence at worldwide distances', is viewed as a 'chaotic concept' (Jessop 1999: 19) that has become a catch-all phrase in almost all economic, political, cultural and social areas of discussion. Keniche Ohmae's (1990) view of a borderless world, best captured in such unfortunate circumstance as the 1997 financial crisis when Southeast Asian currencies were used as commodities, is a true reflection of economic globalisation. Many countries, especially in Asia, experienced for the first time, the real impact of globalisation. This fluid economic system has become a focus of two contending schools, with each school having its own academic and political adherents.

The anti-globalisation school has played itself out in violent demostrations in the USA, Switzerland, Italy, Australia and Thailand at World Bank, WTO and global economic forums. Globalisation is seen as the scourge for many people in the developed and developing countries. Specifically, globalisation is seen as creating unemployment and shifting industries and economic services to cheaper labour markets. For the developing countries, led by its most visible critique Dr Mahathir (Prime Minister of Malaysia), the full impact of globalisation is seen as creating economic chaos amongst poor, developing countries. The central argument is that small, developing countries do not have the financial muscle to withstand the onslaught of large developed countries, financial power brokers or transnational corporations (TNCs) representing the interests of the developed economies.

On the other hand, the pro-globalisation school sees globalisation as an inevitable process that all countries, governments and private sector organisations must confront and accept as the new order of the day. The World Bank and the Singapore government are very strong pro-globalisation advocates. Much pressure from Singapore's leaders has been levied on Singapore banks and private sector corporations to embrace globalisation. This recognition has been translated into the merger of local banks into bigger banks and hence, currently, there are only three major banks (DBS-POSB; UOB-OUB; OCBC-Keppel-Tat Lee) in Singapore. The buying of companies overseas, the open-door policy to foreign talent and the divestments of government involvement in many commercial enterprises are all aspects of Singapore's globalisation operation. Singapore's retail sector is also severely affected by globalisation and this chapter develops several themes with regard to the impact of globalisation on Singapore's retail sector.

Singapore's retail sector

Retailing in Singapore has remained a historically embedded economic activity. Established as an entrepot, Singapore, since its founding in 1819, was an attractive free port for wholesale and retail goods. Indeed, over the decades, downtown Singapore has become a city of shops, shopkeepers and shoppers. As an international port of call, Singapore's retail industry has traditionally represented goods and services that reflect two broad areas:

- Asian goods and services that reflected very much Singapore's multi-racial society and in particular, its Chinese, Malay, Indian and Eurasian populations as well as Asian religious beliefs – Hinduism, Buddhism and Islam.
- International goods and services that first catered to the British colonial population and was later supplanted by a local population craving for international brand name products and services.

After the Second World War, Singapore's retail distribution followed the traditional spatial concentration as found in many cities of similar development. The spatial concentrations of retail activities were as follows: the automobile industry along Orchard Road; bookshops along the Bras Basah Road; shoe shops along Middle Road and South Bridge Road; jewellery shops in High Street; stationery shops along Chulia Street and Upper Cross Street; Indian money lenders among Market Street; and textile shops along Arab Street.

In order to deal with the globalisation of Singapore retail business, we need to estimate the overall development and structure of that sector. Singapore's retail sector in 1998 comprised 18,751 establishments. This was a 5.4 per cent drop from 19,818 establishments in 1997. There were 82,103 persons employed in the retail sector in 1998. The retail sector in 1998 accounted for S$21.4 billion which was 6.5 per cent of Singapore's total commerce sector. Though retail trade seems to be a small sector of Singapore's total economic pie, it is an important foreign exchange earner. In 2000, 58 per cent of the S$11 million spent by tourists in Singapore was associated with shopping. Currently there are 16,300 retailers, but 96 per cent of them are now located in the public housing HDB heartlands (*The Straits Times*, 8 March 2001: H1).

Like many countries, the retail sector is one of the most sensitive barometers of the state of the national economy, Singapore's retail sector figures between 1997 and 1998 demonstrate clearly that the financial crisis hit the retail sector severely, with a drop of 4.9 per cent in employment and a drop of 9.6 per cent in turnover per establishment.

Basic determinants of Singapore's retail landscape

The major internal factors that have conditioned the structure of Singapore's retail sector can be summarised as follows:

- Singapore's free port and open economy;
- the multi-racial population; and
- the changing living standards of Singaporeans.

Free port and open economy

Since its founding in 1819, by Sir Stamford Raffles, Singapore has remained an entrepot. As a free port, it has been involved in the wholesaling and retailing of commodities from around the world and thus wholesale and retail shops are embedded in Singapore's landscapes. Singapore has been, for over a century, basically a trading and mercantilist society. Throughout its history, Singapore made its money from shipping, trading and processing goods for re-export. The British colony was the major emporium of Southeast Asia and thus retailing has always been an integral part of Singapore's business culture.

Until the 1970s, much of Singapore's retailing sector was housed in two- and three-storey shophouses that dominated the city centre landscape. In his study, Bellett (1969) noted that there was a 70 per cent increase in the number of retail establishments, between 1953 and 1963, in the Central Area. Traditionally, Singaporeans shopped in the Central Area in Chinatown, High Street, North Bridge Road, Middle Road, New Bridge Road and South Bridge Road. These roads and areas were, to a large extent, the major retail shopping belts of Singapore in the 1960s and 1970s. By the 1980s, the Central Area including Orchard Road still dominated the retail landscape, accounting for 36 per cent of retail trade, 35 per cent of restaurants and 70 per cent of hotel locations (Yeung 1991/1992: 94).

Singapore's retail sector was transformed in two areas from the 1970s. First, the government's public housing programme led to the development of satellite town centres and neighbourhood shops that drastically decentralised retailing in Singapore. Second, the retail sector was transformed in the central city area as a result of urban renewal programmes with the demolition of shophouses and other old buildings. New shopping centres were developed and department stores and small retail shops began to operate in shopping malls and shopping centres. Beginning with Lucky Plaza in 1977, shopping centres began to be established in the Orchard Road area, which has subsequently led to the current major retail 'highway' of Singapore.

Multi-racial Singapore

Since its inception as a British colony in 1819, Singapore has always been a poly-glot society. Singapore's population represented a diversity of ethnic groups that came from East Asia (China, Hong Kong, Taiwan and Japan), South Asia (India,

Pakistan and Sri Lanka); West Asia (Arabs, Armenians and Jews) and Southeast Asia (mainly Malaysia, Indonesia and Myanmar). This vastly diverse population together with Americans and Europeans, created a vibrant, multi-cultural landscape. Since each group was confined to its own ethnic areas, retailing was ethnic and community based, and concentrated in five major districts. The heart of the Chinese retail sector was Chinatown or the 'old' Chinatown (as opposed to the 'new' Chinatown). For the Indians, it was Little India; and for the Malays and Muslim population, it was the Kampung Glam and North Bridge Road areas as well as the Geylang Serai area. The Eurasian and the Nyonya Babas shopped around Katong and Joo Chiat where they congregated as a population. The European shopping area was mainly concentrated in the Raffles Place area with three department shops that catered to the resident British population and the 'White' population. The three major department stores in Raffles Place were Robinsons, John Little and Whitaways. Raffles Place was the central commercial area for the 'firm-centred economy' (Geertz 1963: 28), where all the major banks, insurance companies and European trading houses were located.

Given these ethnic enclaves, Singapore's retail sector was extremely diverse because, apart from the Raffles Place department stores, retailing was carried out in small family shops where the typical form of buying and selling was based on 'bargaining'. Except for the department stores and supermarkets, 90 per cent of Singapore's retail sector up to the 1960s was not based on fixed prices. Besides the retail shops, the retailing of foodstuff was carried out in the 'bazaar' economy (Geertz 1963: 28) of wet markets that were located in various populated areas around the island. As satellite towns were built and public housing estates were constructed, wet markets were also developed to cater to the local populations living in these large public housing estates.

As Singapore was a British colony and a cosmopolitan trading port with British, American and European nationalities residing in the colonial city, Singapore's retail sector had an early exposure to First World, Western shopping traditions. To cater to the 'White' population, Singapore had large fixed-price department stores as well as supermarkets. The two earliest supermarkets to cater to the 'White' population in colonial Singapore were Cold Storage and Fitzpatricks. Department stores and supermarkets tended to sell goods that came from the West or products that suited the Western palate (e.g. lettuce, cheese, wine, fresh milk).

Changing living standards: from 'bazaar' to 'firm-centred' economy

The retail sector is perhaps one of the best parameters of the changing standards of living of any society. In Singapore, per capita incomes have changed radically from about US$400 per capita GDP in 1959 to over US$24,000 per capita GDP today (2001). For example, private consumption expenditure almost doubled between 1956 and 1968 at a compound annual average growth rate of 5.7 per cent (Yeung 1973: 100). This dramatic increase in per capita income has obviously meant an upgrading move of Singapore from Third World to First World status, which was best captured in modern Singapore's founding father, Lee Kuan Yew's (2000) book. That change has meant not only more disposable income, but also changing values and tastes, and a much more global orientation in consumer behaviour. It is thus no surprise that over the last forty years, Singapore's retail sector has gone through major changes both in terms of its form and structure as well as its commodities.

Soon after the Second World War, Singapore's retail sector remained a 'bazaar' type, informal system characterised by itinerant hawkers, wet-markets, night markets and shophouse retail shops. The informal retail sector as dominated by hawkers and street vendors represented 33 per cent (or 28,000 street vendors) of the retail labour force between 1957 and 1966 (Yeung 1973: 103). Of the 25,000 licensed and unlicensed hawkers in 1969, 80 per cent comprised those selling market produce and cooked food (Yeung 1973: 95). Of the hawkers in the 1960s, 30 per cent operated within the Central Area (Yeung 1973: 95). Arising from the urban renewal programme, environmental and health concerns and Singaporeans' changing food habits, the government became the 'great reorganizer' of itinerant hawkers and 'pined down' and controlled them in government-built, covered markets and hawker centres (De Koninck 1992: 112). Hawker centres have become a norm for Singaporeans, especially after these centres increased from 31 in 1969 to 106 in 1989 (De Koninck 1992: 112). In Newton Circus Hawker Centre, a popular food place for both tourists and Singaporeans, the merger of the informal and formal economy is evident by the availability of credit card facilities by some of the sea-food hawker stalls.

The ethnic character of Singapore's retail sector remains still embedded in the locations that have been defined historically. Today, the First World shopping system is best defined in the shopping malls and shopping centres of Orchard Road and in shopping malls in the town centres of public housing satellite towns. Given Singapore's affluence, bargaining and the 'bazaar' economy have become shopping habits of the past. Today, the bulk of Singaporeans prefer to shop in fixed-price department stores, retail outlets, as well as supermarkets. Even in eating habits, Singaporeans have ditched the traditional *Kopitiams* (traditional coffee shops) for fast food outlets, Starbucks and restaurants.

Based on a survey of the most visited places by adult Singaporeans, it is evident that retail behaviour is based on 'firm-centred' establishments, with 87.7 per cent frequenting supermarkets, 61.3 per cent minimarts (fixed-price small supermarkets), 60 per cent fast food outlets and 51 per cent Central Area shopping centres (See Table 6.1). Among the top five, only going to fast food outlets is classed as 'non-shopping'. Shopping in supermarkets and suburban shops were both listed by over 80 per cent of the population as among their most-visited places. Minimarts and city shops also enjoy high patronage. The overall results show that shopping is still one of Singaporeans' most-loved activities.

Singapore's growing affluence has also led to greater numbers of Singaporeans travelling overseas for pleasure, business or education. Given the strong Singapore dollar, many Singaporeans tend to go overseas on shopping sprees. The result is that the retail business has lost many local customers. In 1997, for example,

Table 6.1 Top most-visited places (2000 Media index, all adults)

Supermarkets (%)	Suburban shops (%)	Minimarts (%)	Fast food outlets (%)	City shopping areas (%)
87.7	84.5	61.3	59.8	51.1

Source: *The Straits Times*, 14 May 2001: 20.

Singaporeans spent a whopping S$7.3 billion at shops abroad (*The Straits Times*, 8 March 2001: H1).

Globalising retailing: retailing global commodities

'The city-state of Singapore itself, which has grown from fewer than 300,000 people in 1900 to four million today, also represents a dramatic characteristic of the global culture' (Swerdlow 1999: 5). Defined by Anthony Giddens (1990: 64), as the 'intensification of worldwide social relations which link distant localities in such a way that local happenings are shared by events occurring miles away and vice versa', globalisation has not only economic outcomes but also political, social, cultural, demographic, environmental and religious manifestations as well. This section of the chapter explores the major operational mechanisms of globalisation affecting Singapore's retail industry.

Three blanket statements can be made about globalisation and the retail sector. First, is that globalisation helps to provide quality control and standardisation of products, which are of benefit to consumers. For example, if all mobile or cellular telephones had the same bandwidths, it could be convenient for all regular travellers. Second, globalisation has helped to empower consumers *vis-à-vis* the manufacturers of commodities. Today customers can influence manufacturers by boycotting goods if they are not up to standard. The Weber Shandwick survey on customer priorities clearly demonstrates the point that the number one consideration that customers want from any manufacturer of a commodity is for the company to 'make good, reliable products' (see Table 6.2) (*The Straits Times*, 28 March 2001: H5). The most positive outcome of this is the national endorsements of eco-friendly products. Green retailing has international endorsement, with various countries adopting green labels to identify environmental friendly products: Taiwan (Green Mark), Germany (Blue Angel), Scandinavia (White Swan), Canada (Environmental Choice), United States (Green Seal) and Singapore (Green Leaf). In the international survey of consumer priorities, it is evident that Australians, Europeans and even Singaporeans place a high priority on buying goods that help to 'protect the environment' (see Table 6.2) (*The Straits Times*, 28 March 2001: 5). Third, globalisation has provided a catalyst for an infinite number of new commodities resulting from cross-cultural exchanges and the use of best practices and patents across national boundaries. Indeed, what is surprising about the international consumer survey is that people are least concerned that the product they buy should come from 'a local company' (see Table 6.2) (*The Straits Times*, 28 March 2001: 5).

Table 6.2 Consumer priorities

How important are the following to you when buying a company's product? It must:	Singapore	Australia	Belgium	Britain	France	Germany	Italy	Spain	USA
Make good, reliable products	1	1	1	1	1	1	1	1	1
Keep prices low	2	5	4	2	4	4	5	7	2
Protect the environment	3	2	3	4	3	3	2	3	4
Help charities and good causes	4	7	6	6	6	5	6	7	6
Work for benefit of local community	5	6	5	5	7	7	4	5	5
Be good to its employees	6	3	2	3	2	2	3	2	3
Be a local company	7	4	7	7	5	6	7	4	7

Source: Weber Shandwick Worldwide (*The Straits Times*, 28 March 2001: H5).

It is possible to identify seven major themes that have affected the globalisation of the Singapore retail sector:

- mass tourism
- popular culture
- global franchise and global brands
- e-commerce
- global labour force
- global department shops
- cross-cultural issues.

Mass tourism

With rising standards of living not only in Singapore but also in the Asia-Pacific region, mass tourism has become a major industry in the region and the world. In the 1960s, Singapore was invaded by American and European tourists; in the 1970s, it was the Japanese and Australians; in the 1980s, Southeast Asians, Koreans, Taiwanese and Hong Kongers; and in the 1990s, it was the South Asians and Chinese. Today, nearly 70 per cent of Singapore's tourists come from Asia.

Given its small size and lack of natural resources, Singapore has always maintained a diversified economy in which the service sector has played an important role. Tourism is a big industry in Singapore, and accounted for over S$11 billion (US$6.37 billion) in tourist expenditure in 2000; up from US$5.21 billion in 1996, the year before the 1997 financial crisis (*The Straits Times*, 19 August

1998: 34). The tourist sector has traditionally been a very important contributor in maintaining Singapore's service and retail sectors. Given that 58 per cent of total tourist expenditure in 2000 was spent on shopping clearly indicates the importance of tourism to Singapore's retail sector.

While the tourist-orientated, specialised shopping of Asian Arts and Crafts was concentrated in the 1960s and 1970s in four areas (Stamford Road area, Raffles Place, Orchard Road and Tanglin Road), (De Koninck 1970) today it is more decentralised. The new locations of Asian Arts and Crafts are in Holland Village, Tanglin Shopping Centre, Chinatown, Kampung Glam and the Dempsey Road areas.

Shops in Singapore have maintained a comparative advantage for tourists' expenditure because of two major reasons:

1   Different tourists are enticed by different ranges of goods that are sold in Singapore. For example, Singapore appeals to many Japanese and rich tourists from the region because of the variety of Western branded goods, especially in the apparel trade. Japanese tourists, for example, are known to buy Louis Vuitton suitcases of all types. Nearly every major fashion house in clothes, shoes, perfumes and women's accessories has a retail outlet in Singapore. Currently, for the Southeast Asian, Australian and South Asian tourists, Singapore is seen as a mecca of high-tech and New Age commodities. Shopping centres like Sim Lim Square and Funan IT Mall are known for their portable music players, digital cameras, laptop computers, software and hand-held organisers (*The Straits Times*, 17 April 2001: 10).

2   Singapore has been able to attract tourists' expenditure for its goods and commodities because nearly all the countries in the region have very high domestic taxes on foreign imported and branded goods. Hence, travellers and tourists from Thailand, Indonesia, Malaysia, the Philippines, India and Australia come to Singapore principally to buy branded goods that are 20 per cent to 40 per cent cheaper than they are in their home countries. If Singapore does not maintain its free port status, or if its surrounding countries disband their import duties and taxes, Singapore will not be an attractive mecca for the shopping of branded goods. Hence, despite the high rentals and labour charges in Singapore, Singapore's tax-free imported goods remain favourable commodities for tourists.

Popular culture

'Popular culture is concerned with the everyday practices, experiences and beliefs of what have been called the "common people" – that overwhelming proportion of society that does not occupy positions of wealth and power' (Burgess and Gold 1985: 3). Popular and 'pop' cultures are important expressions of capitalism and one of the most important outcomes of globalisation. This is a cultural force that transcends cultural boundaries and national borders. The heart of popular culture lies with youths around the world. This is a young population that shares and upholds the true effervescence of global culture. The rise of global popular culture has, to a large extent, been endorsed by several key influences: popular music, fashions, sporting fads, fast foods, computer games, snooker parlours, video arcades, discos, cinemas and recreational activities. Popular culture has essentially commodified and globalised consumer behaviour, products and services. Singapore, as a global city, is at the forefront of consumerism of popular and 'pop' culture products. Indeed, over the last few years, 'pop' culture influences have come from East Asia – Hong Kong, Taiwan, Japan (J-culture) and, most recently, Korean pop culture. In the Mandarin 'pop' culture market, several countries seem to be vying for a stake in the industry of music, TV dramas and cinema. The industry was initially anchored by Hong Kong and Taiwan, but is now being challenged by Singapore, Malaysia and China (Chua 2001).

The powerful expressions and manifestation of popular culture endorsed by various commodities and activities have opened a floodgate of retail activities. The *McDonaldisation* and *Coca-Colaisation* of global youth underscore the power and pervasiveness of popular culture. This is a cultural tradition that is totally commodity-oriented and where mass participation becomes an important testimony of being 'in-sync' with youths worldwide. Whether it is the choice of hairstyle, clothes, shoes, dance craze or food, youths in Singapore engage in consumer behaviour as a badge of honour.

Essentially, popular culture is fed by peer pressure within the young population. What popular culture does is that it provides a sense of community amongst youths through the act of consumption. For example, the most powerful expression of this is music consumption. As Storey (1996: 102) argues, music consumption is used as a sign 'by which the young judge and are judged by others. To be a part of a youth subculture is to display one's musical taste and to claim that its consumption is an act of communal creation'. This line of thinking recalls Marcuse's (1968) argument that the ideology of consumerism works as a form of social control in the sense that people recognise themselves in their commodities and find their 'soul' in their cars, hi-fi sets, clothes, television sets and the shoes they wear. Unfortunately, popular culture creates a consumerism of false needs and desires. Popular culture is not about consumption related to daily needs but rather a consumption of people trying to develop a sense of identity either individually or as part of a larger group. Given the multi-cultural dimensions of popular culture, it is difficult to say that the spread of pop culture and customer goods is the 'triumph of western civilization' because Huntington (1996: 58) believes this 'trivializes western culture'.

And since popular culture is the 'cosmopolitan culture' of the youth, it is best reflected in Singapore in the Orchard Road landscape. Often, tourists wonder where Singapore's old population live because all they see on Orchard Road is a very young and youthful population who hang out in fast food outlets, street cafes, restaurants, computer game arcades, shopping centres and department stores. The indoctrination of 'pop' culture in youths in Singapore has to do with the widespread exposure to the mass media (television, magazines, radio), its effective bilingual population (English and Malay; English and Mandarin; and English and Tamil) and its growing affluence.

Popular and 'pop' cultures, however, are not static phenomena. They are dynamic and so provide a constant catalyst for the retail industry. Fashions, fads, 'events', music trends, dance crazes and lifestyle changes all help to constantly revitalise the retail business. Indeed, screen and music stars change as quickly as a new generation enters the youth market, that it is difficult to sustain 'pop' commodities even for two years. This is the reason why Planet Hollywood has lost its shine. The movie stars of five years ago who owned the franchise, no longer have the same star quality appeal for a new generation of teenagers. In short, each generation of teenagers 'invents' its own 'pop' and movie icons and symbols.

Within the context of popular culture is another new wave of consumer activities and products called 'New Age Capitalism' that is defined by Eastern ideology and culture (Lau 2000). As in other developed cities, Singaporeans have caught on to aromatherapy, macrobiotic, vegetarian and organic foods, yoga, t'ai chi, Indian Ayurvedic practices, traditional body massages, Chinese herbal medicine, reflexology and the like.

Global markets, global franchise and global brands

The current era is one where global brands have become part of our consumer landscape. This issue of global branding of products has become a heavily debated issue in terms of its pros and cons for influencing consumer behaviour. Global branding of goods and services covers three key areas:

- international fast food chains, restaurants and coffee cafes chains;
- high value commodities in the fashion industry; and
- household products.

In an era of globalisation, it seems inevitable that consumer behaviour will be increasingly determined by brand names.

In post-modern societies like Singapore, consumption of goods has come into the realm of public and personal psychology (Bocock 1993: 14). People buy goods for a whole range of reasons but many now do so for 'symbolic' desires and needs. As Bocock (1993: 110) argues, not being able to consume 'in the post-modern sense, becomes a source of deep discontent'. This is partly because consumption of goods and participation in activities has a lot to do with forging personal identities. Consumption experiences can change, shatter or reform identities of individuals and groups. Hence, companies tend to capitalise on 'identity' imaging of their products in the marketing and advertising of their commodities and services.

Given the numerous brands that flood the market for each particular commodity, it is inevitable that consumers will be guided by the awareness of and trust that they have with particular brand names. Indeed, branding has a powerful impact for both manufacturer and customer. Good brand names that are associated with reliability, superior technology and environmentally friendly manufacturing processes and would require little advertising in order to sell their products. Hence, manufacturers will take great pains to not only ensure and uphold a good commodity, but also to maintain the customer's expectations and confidence *vis-à-vis* their products. For example, in Singapore, Sony has a good reputation for being an innovative and reliable company and hence, consumers are willing to pay a premium for Sony products. Sony is indeed the top preferred brand in Singapore in a recent 2001 survey (*The Straits Times*, 18 September 2001: H7). Branding has clearly internationalised customer-shopping preferences amongst Singaporeans. In a recent customer survey, Japanese brands (4 out of 10) were the most popular of the ten most-preferred brands, followed by US brands (3 out of 10) and European brands (2 out of 10). Two brands (Samsung and Hyundai) from Korea were the least preferred. (See Tables 6.3 and 6.4) (*The Straits Times*, 18 September 2001: 7).

Given the nature of global demand for very similar products such as television sets, washing machines, rice cookers, microwave ovens and vacuum cleaners, companies have to deal with the branding of global goods. Such global goods transcend national and cultural boundaries and become cheaper for the consumer if the company manufactures on a large scale. Hence, many companies are able to sell products easily if they have established a certain trust with consumers at a price that is sensitive to local demands. For example, in Singapore, while Korean products are not viewed favourably, Korean-made refrigerators such as Samsung have taken the Singapore market by storm. Cheaper than the Japanese brands, and

Table 6.3 Most preferred brands in Singapore

Brands	Percentage
Sony	30
Nike	12
National	11
Toshiba	11
Panasonic	10
Nokia	10
Philips	8
Levis	5
Giordano	5
Coca-Cola	4

Source: *The Straits Times*, 18 September 2001: H7.

Table 6.4 Least preferred brands in Singapore

Brands	Percentage
Samsung	10
Philips	6
Hyundai	5

Source: *The Straits Times*, 18 September 2001: H7.

as aesthetically pleasing in design as the American models, the Samsung refrigerators are so popular that one often has to wait 3–6 months in order to obtain some of their refrigerator models.

Due to the globalisation of taste and the commodification of services, international franchise of the retail sector has become a major influence in the retail sector. Today, there are many American fast food franchises – McDonalds, Burger King, Kentucky Fried Chicken, Pizza Hut; Coffee Cafes – Starbucks, Coffee Bean and Tea Leaf, Spinelli, Banoffi, Gloria Jean's; convenience stores – Seven-Eleven; and restaurants – Denny's, Swensen's, Delifrance, Hard Rock Café, Planet Hollywood and A & W.

International franchises are the future for global retailing. One of the most highly visible and successful international franchise names is McDonalds, which currently has 28,000 fast food restaurants worldwide. And the giant company has been quick to engage in new consumer trends by starting McCafe (first adopted in 1993 in Melbourne). There are now 300 McCafes worldwide to compete with Starbucks' 3,300 global outlets (*The Straits Times*, 1 May 2001: 18). International franchises have both a positive and negative effect on the Singapore retail landscape. On the one hand, international franchised outlets have helped to upgrade the retail sector by providing some level of professionalism. On the other hand, such franchises have undermined local services and commodities.

In Singapore, like in other newly rich countries of Asia, a new 'leisure class', as defined by Thorstern Veblen, has developed, and with it has come 'conspicuous consumption'. This consumption pattern that is meant to provide an overt show of wealth through consumption, has been a major stimulant for Singapore's brand name retail sector. The best example of this is the car market: Singaporeans love to drive branded cars like Mercedes-Benz, BMW, Volvo and Jaguar. And so do most Asian executives, as reflected in a survey where 40 per cent of executives in Asia were 'label-mad', with the Rolex watch topping their shopping list. Filipinos lead this list with 67 per cent compared to Australians with 29 per cent (see Table 6.5).

Table 6.5 Percentage of population desiring to own a Rolex watch

Filipinos	67
Indonesians	50
Malaysians	50
South Koreans	49
Hong Kongers	45
Singaporeans	42
Taiwanese	38
Thais	38
Japanese	31
Australians	29

Source: *Far East Economic Review*, 2000: 74.

The other important aspect of branding and franchising of products and services in the age of globalisation has been the implementation of copyright laws. Since the Singapore government enforces copyright laws very strictly, fake and imitation products have been almost eradicated in the retail sector. The side effect of copyright laws is that law-abiding citizens will seek to purchase branded goods rather than goods without brands.

As Singapore moves into global city status with similar consumer behaviour like that in other First World cities, the fixed-priced, firm-centred economic system will increasingly become the accepted norm for Singapore's retail sector. The youth of Singapore who have grown up in this environment are no longer equipped to make judgement calls on the quality of products and certainly have lost their 'bazaar' economic 'bargaining' skills. For example, many Singaporeans find that if they were to bargain for an electronic product in one of the retail shops in Lucky Plaza (Orchard Road), they will probably end up paying more for the product than if they had shopped for it in a fixed-priced department store like C K Tang's (Orchard Road/Scotts Road).

Information technology: e-commerce

The expansion of information technology (IT), in the 1990s, has had three major impacts on the retail sector in Singapore and globally. First, IT has created a whole new range of retail products from hardware (computers) to software (data programs on CD Rom). The amount of personal computers, for example, has increased tremendously in Asia, with Japan (39.2 per cent) leading the highest percentage in Asia followed by a rapidly gaining China (20.2 per cent), South Korea (8.8 per cent) and Australia (8.7 per cent) (see Table 6.6). However, if we take per capita ownership of personal computers, Singapore leads in Asia followed by Hong Kong, Malaysia and Thailand (see Table 6.7). IT is big business because it has universal applications for diverse activities, whether in the office, factory, educational institutions or at home. It has software that can be used for schools, office work, personal inventories, sports and entertainment. The information revolution that has taken the world by storm has created in its wake a whole lot

Table 6.6 Personal computers in Asia – percentage of total by country

Country	Percentage
Japan	39.2
China	20.2
South Korea	8.8
Australia	8.7
Taiwan	4.9
India	4.5

Source: *Asia Week*, 29 June 2001: 49.

Table 6.7 Personal computers and telephone lines per 1,000 population

	Personal computers	*Telephone lines*
Singapore	485.3	486.6
Hong Kong	346.1	578.7
Malaysia	104.7	210.3
Thailand	23.5	83.2
Philippines	19.6	39.7
China	16.1	121.1
India	4.6	32.3

Source: *Asia Week*, 29 June 2001: 49.

of billionaires around the world, with Bill Gates leading the world's richest person's list.

Second, the spin-off from IT has had a profound effect on all aspects of the global economy. Resulting from IT, we have academics and politicians talking increasingly about the 'New Economy' and the Knowledge-Based Economy (KBE). These concepts signal nothing really new because knowledge, ideas and innovation have always been a defining characteristic of human intelligence. But what is new is that no company or organisation has now the monopoly over ideas and innovations. Today, the transparency that IT has brought about, has allowed a more level-playing field for people with new ideas to become entrepreneurs. Hence, in Singapore, Sim Wong Hoo developed the application of using sounds in computers (sound blaster) and *voilá*, he has become a local icon of innovation and entrepreneurship.

What IT has done is that it has presented numerous opportunities to apply its use in various activities and products. IT has revolutionised the whole toy, video games and entertainment industry. The list of new products arising from IT is just endless and continues to expand. IT has in fact been a major catalyst of the global economy since the mid-1980s.

Third, IT has led to a new way of marketing, advertising and trading products and services between retail outlets and customers through e-commerce. E-commerce was a US$200 billion (S$332.4 billion) global industry in 1998, and is projected to hit US$1 trillion in turnover by 2002. In Asia, e-commerce generated US$700 million (S$1.2 billion) in turnover in 1998 and is forecasted to top US$30 billion (S$49.7 billion) in 2003 (*The Straits Times*, 8 January 2000: 72).

Of all the countries in Asia, Singapore is the most ready to capitalise on the commercial potential of the Internet, based on a survey of sixty countries by the Economist Intelligence Unit (*The Straits Times*, 11 May 2001: S13). Singapore has a 7.87 out of 10 e-readiness score (based on telecom infrastructure, security of credit card transactions, computer literacy), which places it seventh in the world and first in Asia (see Table 6.8). Despite this, only 1 in 20 small retailers have e-commerce capabilities. The Singapore Productivity and Standards Board

Table 6.8 Top ten countries with highest e-readiness score

Country	e-readiness score – maximum 10
1 US	8.73
2 Australia	8.29
3 Britain	8.10
4 Canada	8.09
5 Norway	8.07
6 Sweden	7.98
7 Singapore	7.87
8 Finland	7.83
9 Denmark	7.70
10 The Netherlands	7.69

Source: *The Straits Times*, 11 May 2001: S13.

(PSB) hopes to improve that to 1 in 8 by 2003 (*The Straits Times*, 29 September 2001: H1). The Board has set aside S$6 million to jumpstart e-retail which will be used to provide subsidies of up to 50 per cent or a maximum of S$20,000 for each small retailing firm that wants to engage in e-retailing (*The Straits Times*, 29 September 2001: H1). The e-retail scheme provides benefits not only for shops, but also for restaurants. For example, Pacific Breeze Restaurant notes that after giving its waiters palmtop computers to take orders, it has reduced its labour costs, increased customer orders per waiter, reduced the time diners get their food and increased turnover by 30–40 per cent (*The Straits Times*, 29 September 2001: H1).

Global labour force

Given its small size and limited population, Singapore has been opening the lid to the entry of foreign labour since the 1970s. However, when the country began to increase its standard of living, foreign labour inputs increased dramatically for construction workers and maids in the 1980s. The foreign labour inputs in the 1990s, arising from globalisation and the move towards a KBE, has been targeted at higher and professional and skilled workers. For Singapore, attracting 'foreign talent' is an integral part of the government's acceptance of the processes of globalisation.

Singapore's population reached 4 million in 2000 but over 25 per cent of the population is 'foreign'. In short, one in four 'Singapore' residents is a foreigner. This high foreign population has led to greater variety of consumer demands for Singapore's retail business. Indeed, with the large numbers of foreign labour and domestic maids, Singapore has seen a rise in shops within shopping centres catering to an ethnic-based clientele. Hence, Filipino maids tend to cluster on weekends at Lucky Plaza (Orchard Road), male Myanmar workers congregate at Peninsula Plaza (North Bridge Road), Thai construction workers meet at the Beach Road Shopping Centre (Beach Road) and Indian and Bangladeshi workers mill around Little India (Serangoon Road). Foreign workers have brought in a whole new retail sector to cater to their own culture groups. Despite the ups and downs in the economy, Little India has been booming because the retail outlets have catered to the large South Asian labour force and the growing South Asian tourist inflows. Little India is a specialised niche market for everything 'Indian' and the business has even led to many Chinese goldsmith shops with Chinese salespersons speaking fluent Tamil.

Global retail organisations

Since the mid-1970s, major department store chains have opened branches in Singapore. Yaohan pioneered the first wave of Japanese department stores/ supermarkets to establish itself in Singapore. Yaohan brought a very successful system of supermarket cum family shopping experience in Singapore. Following in its footsteps, other Japanese department stores opened branches in Singapore (Isetan, Seiyu, Daimaru, Sogo and Takashimaya). Other European, US and Hong Kong department stores joined the fray in the 1980s – Printemps, Galleries Lafayette, Toys R Us, Lane Crawford. However, the shake-up in the late 1980s and early 1990s led to the closure of many of these department stores.

Given the global city clientele comprising of both Singaporeans and tourists, the norm for shopping in Orchard Road and regional town centres has been large department stores and shopping centres since the 1980s. The global retail experience now seems to be based on a 'one stop' shopping experience. Singaporean customers today want three qualities for their shopping experience: air-conditioned environment and a good shopping ambiance; a wide range of commodities to choose from in one location; and multiple convenience under one roof for shopping and tending to other services – supermarket, hair-dressers, boutiques, watch shops, bank facilities, cafes, restaurants and retail outlets.

Cross-cultural issues

'One of the most striking aspects of modern capitalist societies, not often marked, is the degree to which the commodity has become integral with culture: language, music, dance, visual arts and literature. This culminates in advertising, film, comic books and highbrow pop art'. (MacCannell 1999: 21–2). As more people live in cities and as more cities become 'global cities', the issue of commodities and services targeted at cosmopolitan societies is revolutionising the marketing and advertising industry. The publication of a 'dictionary of global culture' (Appiah and Gates 1997) is indicative of the cross-cultural global issues we are all exposed to today.

The retail and service industry has to respond to two major influences. The first is the 'homogenisation' of global cultures that allows products to be sold across national borders and that transcends cultural and religious differences. By and large, the fast food products and 'pop' music have had the most universal appeal globally. McDonalds, Starbucks, Kentucky Fried Chicken, 'pop' and movie stars like Arnold Schwarzenegger, Madonna and Michael Jackson are icons amongst youths the world over. Global culture means in some ways, a common acceptance of taste, aesthetics and lifestyles.

On the other hand, globalisation has helped to universalise cultural traditions of particular societies. The best example is the rapid rise of karaoke bars and karaoke home entertainment in the 1980s. Here, we see a traditional form of Japanese entertainment being globalised. In many forms of 'pop' culture, commodities and entertainment, the local ethnic/national cultural elements surface through 'global culture' experiences. For example, popular Khmer rock bands in America play 'pop' music to traditional Khmer rhythms of the *roam vuan, roam kback* and *saravan*. In Singapore, the traditional Chinese geomantic principles of *feng shui* (wind and water) governing the propitious locations of offices, houses, factories and graveyards have now been adopted by many non-Chinese. The American Club in Singapore, for example, has been planned according to *feng shui* principles and many European banks are located likewise based on *feng shui*.

In a global market, it is often difficult to even find 'names' of companies or products that are cross-culturally acceptable. For example, the Datsun car, 'Bluebird' could not sell very well in Singapore because the term 'bluebird' when translated into Hokkien (the major dialect group in Singapore) means 'penis'. In Brazil, the name of the Ford car 'Pinto' when translated into Portuguese, refers to 'small penis'.

In looking at Singapore's cross-cultural global influences, two important factors need to be considered. First is that Singapore's multi-racial society creates an 'instant Asia' ballast for many fusion goods and services (fusion food). Singapore's retail sector remains diverse because it services a multi-racial and multi-religious consumer base. This means that retail commodities have to pander to a wide range of cultural-based preferences. For example, the colours, type of fabric (silk, linen, cotton, rayon, etc.) and design on cloth have a different appeal to Singapore's different ethnic groups.

Second, Singapore's predominant Chinese population gives it a critical pivot of the 'bamboo network' in Southeast Asia. With Chinese families in the region making up 70 per cent of private businesses (Weidenbaum and Hughes 1996: 8), Singapore remains an important 'sink' for Chinese 'trust' funds and depositors. Chinese in neighbouring countries also come to Singapore for relaxation, security and comfort. The Singapore Chinese connection has been globalised through the extension of clan association link-ups with similar associations around the world (Yeung and Olds 2000). Singapore's varied clans have created good *guanxi* (interpersonal relationships) at a regional and global level and in turn Singapore's economy thrives.

Realising global retailing

Singapore has been viewed as a 'shoppers' paradise' from the 1960s to the mid-1980s. But now, most overseas visitors and tourists I meet say that Singapore is an expensive place to shop. This is not surprising as retailers say that operating costs have increased tremendously; 70 per cent of cost is in rentals and labour. Singapore's Orchard Road, for example, had the eleventh highest rentals in the world in 2001: US$184.60 per sq ft (*The Straits Times*, 16 November 2001: 14). Yet, when I travel overseas to Peking, Shanghai, Hong Kong, Taiwan, South Korea and Japan, I think we are still competitive in price for many goods.

Given the pro-globalisation policy of the government, the authorities have not left the retail sector alone. Singapore retail sector is a mix of local enterprise capitalising on new fads and activities and large foreign department chain stores, fast food outlets and branded products and services, all vying for a slice of the local tourist consumer market.

In an attempt to ensure that the Singaporean retail sector is world class, the PSB, together with the Singapore Retailers Association (SRA) and the Singapore Tourism Board (STB), have embarked on a major study as part of the Retail 21 initiative to benchmark Singapore's retail sector to see how 'world class' it is (*The Straits Times*, 18 September 2001: H4). As part of the Retail 21 ten-year master plan, the relevant bodies have been set several tasks to achieve. These are to:

- enhance retail efficiency;
- encourage retailers to be more innovative;
- improve customer satisfaction; and
- help shopkeepers upgrade and franchise or leave the business (*The Straits Times*, 8 March 2001: H1).

Essentially, Singapore needs to address three broad issues.

First, there is a need to enhance professionalism in the retail industry, if retailing is to be world class and have a global outreach. Specifically, many retail staff lack product knowledge and hence are unable to advise customers. Despite the consultancy and training programmes for small shopkeepers, only 3,000 shops have taken up these upgrading programmes out of a pool of 15,000 shops and 15,000 hawker stalls. One needs to remember that a satisfied customer is a repeat customer. Unfortunately, many Singaporean *small retailers* are increasingly being seen by locals and tourists alike, as 'rip off' dealers, 'hit and run' merchants who want to make a killing in sales without sustaining a long-term clientele. Unless steps are taken to address this issue, Singapore might end up with the same negative image that Hong Kong and Thailand have *vis-à-vis* Japanese and European tourists. These tourist places are increasingly being seen in a 'negative' light because people who feel 'cheated' are not going to recommend their relatives or friends these tourist destinations.

Second, Singapore's retailers need to develop, enhance and maintain Singapore's shopping experiences so that customers will experience a sense of excitement, enjoyment and satisfaction in Singapore shopping. While the excitement of 'bargaining' is an exotic experience for many tourists from developed countries, it can be a very sour experience if the price paid finally is still too high for a poor quality product. To make shopping an exciting and global experience, the STB and SRA have successfully inaugurated the two 'events' in retailing. The first is the big 'mega sale' for one month. The mega sale is statewide and demands that all retail outlets have a sale. This mega sale has been so successful that now Malaysia and Thailand are using the same concept to attract tourists. Second, is the increasing promotion of joint retail fairs in Orchard Road. In April 1999, Orchard Road was involved in a month-long fair with the Paris Champs Elysees retailers to feature French goods and in March 2002, Orchard Road and Ginza Tokyo promoted Japanese goods.

Third, the government is trying to increase the productivity of the retail sector. Currently, wholesale workers add S$70,000 to the economy but retail workers only add S$50,000. Even within the service sector, the retail worker value-added contribution is low. In 1998, the retail worker (shops/stores) added S$26,500 compared to the hotel/restaurant workers' S$31,700, and the social, personal and community services S$55,800 (*The Straits Times*, 8 March 2001: H1).

Reflections

Globalisation is nothing new to the world economy. There have been in world history great periods of international trade and commerce. What is different is the speed and scale of global forces affecting individuals, families and societies. Globalisation is a 'neutral' process, a reality we all need to accept and embrace. We can use the 'methods' and 'processes' of globalisation either positively or negatively. The choice lies with governments, political leaders, bureaucrats, businessmen and individual workers. But, like all processes of change, embracing the winds of globalisation will require radical changes in mindsets that will be a painful process with uncomfortable adjustments.

References

Appiah, Kwame Anthony and Gates, Henry Louis (1997) *The Dictionary of Global Cultures*, New York: Alfred A Knopf.

Bellett, John (1969) 'Singapore's central area retail pattern in transition', *Journal of Tropical Geography*, XXVIII (June): 1–16.

Bocock, Robert (1993) *Consumption*, London and New York: Routledge.

Burgess, Jacquelin and Gold, John R. (eds) (1985) *Geography and the Media: Popular Culture*, London: Croom Helm.

Chua Beng Huat (2001) 'Pop culture in China', *Singapore Journal of Tropical Geography*, 22(2): 113–21.

De Koninck, H. (1970) *Asian Art and Craft Retail Outlets in Singapore*, Unpublished Master's thesis, Department of Geography, National University of Singapore.

De Koninck, R. (1992) *Singapore: An Atlas of the Revolution of Territory*, Montpellier: Reclus.

Far East Economic Review (2000) 'Ready to Shop', September 7: 74.

Geertz, Clifford (1963) *Peddlers and Princes*, Chicago: University of Chicago Press.

Giddens, Anthony (1990) *The Consequences of Modernity*, Cambridge: Polity Press.

Huntington, Samuel (1996) *The clash of Civilization and the Remaking of World Order*, New York: Simon and Schuster.

Jessop, Bob (1999) 'Reflections on globalisation and its (il)logic (S)'. In: Kris Olds, Peter Dicken, Philip F. Kelly, Lily Kong and Henry Wai-Chung, Yeung (eds) *Globalisation and the Asia-Pacific*, London: Routledge, pp. 19–38.

Lau, K. J. (2000) *New Age Capitalism*, Philadelphia: University of Pennsylvania Press.

Lee, Kuan Yew (2000) *From Third World to First World – The Singapore Story: 1965–2000* Singapore: Singapore Press Holdings – Times Editions.

MacCannell, Dean (1999) *The Tourist*, Berkeley: University of California Press.

Marcuse, Herbert (1968) *One Dimension Man*, London: Sphere.

Nye, Joseph S. (2001) 'Globalization's democratic deficit', *Foreign Affairs*, 80(4): 2–6.

Ohmae, Keniche (1990) *Borderless World*, New York: Harper Perennial.

Storey, J. (1996) *Cultural Studies and the Study of Popular Culture*, Athens, Georgia: University of Georgia Press.

Swerdlow, Joel L. (1999) 'Global culture', *National Geographic*, 196(2): 2–11.

The Straits Times, Singapore, several issues.

Weidenbaum, M. and Hughes, S. (1996) *The Bamboo Network*, New York: The Free Press.

Yeung, Henry Wai-Chung and Olds, Kris (2000) *Globalisation of Chinese Business Firms*, London: MacMillan Press Ltd.

Yeung, Henry Wai-Chung (1991/1992) *The Orchardscape: Singaporean Cognition*, Unpublished Honours Thesis, Department of Geography, National University of Singapore.

Yeung, Yue-Man (1973) *National Development Policy and Urban Transformation in Singapore*, The University of Chicago, Department of Geography Research Paper No. 149.

7 Internationalization of retailing in China

Shuguang Wang

Introduction

During the last two decades, the world has become increasingly interconnected and interdependent. The homogenizing force which has brought the world together is globalization (Burbach *et al*. 1997), as the centre of gravity of firms is shifting away from domestic markets towards international markets (Elango 1999). In the 1980s, globalization of the world economy took place mainly in manufacturing. Since the early 1990s, the globalization of consumer services, of which retailing is a part, has intensified (Daniels and Lever 1996; Busillo 1998), meaning that 'the amount and variety of forms of international retail operations have increased' (Dawson 1994: 167).

The general process of internationalization of retailing is illustrated in Figure 7.1. This model is based on three theories: the *Eclectic Theory* that focuses on ownership advantages (both asset-based and transaction-based) and location advantages (Dunning 1988; Pellegrini 1991), the *Stages Theory* that emphasizes the concept of business distances, both geographical and cultural (Dupuis and Prime 1996) and the *Risk Theory* that focuses on risk-taking behaviours of multinational retailers (Eroglu 1992).

In the most fundamental sense, international operation of retailers is motivated by either or both of the following factors (also known as 'drivers'): saturation of domestic market and a strategic need to explore new markets and the desire to secure first-mover advantages (Yip 1992; Alexander 1993; Akehurst and Alexander 1995; Simpson and Thorpe 1999). Elango (1999) concludes that low domestic growth rates, strong import competition and high global market growth rates motivate the industry to seek international expansion; but only those firms that have adequate resources in administration and R&D and have achieved high operational efficiency, are likely to succeed in expanding into foreign markets. Indeed, the most successful international retailers are those based in USA, Western Europe and Japan, where domestic market growth rates are low, the retailers have the most resources, and import competition is strong due to interpenetration of international retailers.

Selecting a target market is the next step. Initially, they choose markets that have the least physical and psychic distances to minimize cost and degree of

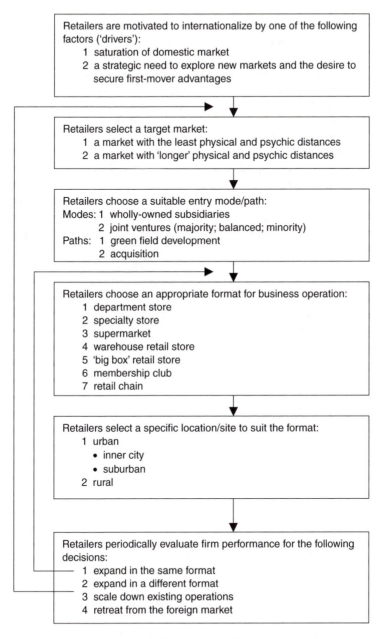

Figure 7.1 The process of internationalization of retailing.

uncertainty about sourcing and operation (Whitehead 1992). An example is the American retailers' use of Canada as a convenient experimental ground. As a firm gains more experience, it enters markets with greater physical or psychic distances (Erramilli 1991; Vida and Fairhurst 1998) but also great potential profitability. Recently, major international retailers have increasingly turned their attentions to the 'emerging markets' in Asia and Latin America (Wrigley 2000), which offer the attractions of potential rapid economic development and rising levels of affluence and consumer spending, combined with extremely low levels of penetration of Western forms of retailing and associated distribution systems.

Following the selection of a target market, the international retailers consider a suitable entry mode and path. Entry mode is defined as forms of capital participation in international enterprises (Sun 1999). Firms seeking entry into a foreign market usually take one of the following two modes: wholly owned subsidiaries and joint ventures. Each mode has relative advantages. In the former, foreign firms can impose their own operating methods with little friction, but they may also face higher risks (Sternquist 1998). In the latter, local partners can be relied upon for their expertise in exploring domestic markets, managing local labours and organizing local supplies of merchandise and intermediate products (Anderson 1993). Joint ventures can be broken into several sub-modes based on the percentage ownership of the equity: majority, balanced and minority (Sun 1999). Both wholly owned and joint ventures can be realized through two possible paths: green field development or acquisition of local firms (Vida and Fairhurst 1998). But which path to take depends on variations in the economic, cultural and regulatory environments of specific national markets. Usually, a firm chooses the most suitable entry mode and path to either minimize transaction cost or best overcome barriers. Their choice may also be constrained by regulations of the host country.

Format, which is characterized with a particular combination of store size, location, product mix, merchandise display and packaging, and customer service, is a micro-factor at the organization level, designed as the means by which corporate strategy is executed. It can be a department store, supermarket, warehouse store, 'big box' discount store, membership club or retail chain. As a general rule, for a format to be successful, it must serve a market better than competing formats. A firm may also need to modify a standard format in a foreign market, as many expansion failures result from an attempt to force standardized formats into a variable or unsuitable commercial environment (Simmons *et al.* 1998a).

A particular format must be supported by the right combination of a location and site in order to be successful. While some are well suited in both the inner city and the suburb (e.g. department stores and supermarkets), others require a suburban location (such as warehouse retail stores and 'big box' discount stores). Which location to take depends not only on the format itself but also on the settlement patterns of the local market and the corresponding transportation system.

As a necessary component of the internationalization process, foreign retailers periodically evaluate their firms' performance in the local (often culturally different) market and in view of competition from both local retailers and other international retailers. Depending on the review results, a firm may choose one of the following decisions:

- expand in the same format;
- expand in a different format;
- scale down its operation in the foreign market; and
- withdraw from the foreign market completely.

The case study is an important form of research for understanding the internationalization of retailing. As Dawson (1994: 268) correctly points out, 'any move towards multi-store operation has to acknowledge that culture varies through space'. In other words, the game is the same, but the rules can be different (Woodward 1996). While a literature review reveals many case studies, most of them have been conducted for Western countries, which also are members of the WTO. Few have studied non-WTO countries, where international retailers may face unconventional as well as conventional regulatory barriers, and they cannot dispute for these barriers within the framework of WTO rules. Accordingly, aggressive international retailers may take unconventional entry modes/paths to penetrate these markets.

China had been a non-WTO country until recently,[1] but because of its size, it became a dream market that major international retailers have wanted to penetrate. Before 1992, the retail sector in China had little direct influence from foreign retailers because the Chinese government prohibited their operations in China. In July 1992, China began to experiment with opening up its retail sector to foreign investment. Despite strict government restrictions, thousands of foreign-invested retailers now exist widely across the country. This raises a critical research question: how did so many foreign retailers investors bypass government regulatory barriers and gain entry into the highly protected market?

This chapter examines China's open-door policies and investigates the major foreign retailers that have gained entry into China in various ways. Revealing the experiences of China as a major non-WTO country should contribute to further understanding of the internationalization of retailing.

The regulatory environment and policy changes

China did not open its retail sector to foreign investment until 1992. This was more than ten years after the economic reform began and after its manufacturing and agricultural sectors were opened to foreign investment. Since 1992, China made three major policy moves towards opening up its retail sector.

The first move

In July 1992, China designated that six cities as well as the five Special Economic Zones (SEZ) could be opened to direct, overseas investment for experiment. The six cities were Beijing, Shanghai, Tianjin, Guangzhou, Dalian and Qingdao, while the five SEZs are Shenzhen, Zhuhai, Shantou, Xiamen and Hainan; all located in the Eastern Coastal Region. Overseas retailers were differentiated into two categories: retailers from foreign countries and those known as overseas Chinese-invested enterprises that were based in Hong Kong, Taiwan and Macao. The latter are treated as foreign retailers by the Chinese government, so they are included in this investigation. From the beginning, the Chinese government has been cautious, moving along with a deliberate sequence: from single-store operations to retail chains, and from joint ventures to whole foreign ownership. This is evidenced by a series of restrictions that the Chinese government imposed on overseas retailers in 1992 to control the experiment process (Editorial Board of Science and Technology Think Tank 1997):

- Each of the eleven designated cities or SEZs is permitted to establish one or two overseas-invested retail enterprises (four are approved for Shanghai because it contains the Pudong Development Zone). Other cities are not permitted to have overseas-invested retail enterprises (a geographical restriction).
- Overseas retailers must operate in joint ventures with Chinese partners; whole foreign ownership was prohibited. In joint ventures, foreign investors' shares must be less than 50 per cent (forcing minority equity participation for foreign investors).
- Application of Sino-foreign joint ventures should be submitted to respective municipal governments, but the authority of approval rests in the hands of the state government. Only state-approved joint ventures are entitled to preferential tax rates (strict state control over approval).
- Operation of foreign-invested enterprises is strictly limited to merchandise retailing; wholesaling is prohibited (a restriction on format).
- Overseas-invested retailers are also given the autonomy of importing and exporting certain types of merchandise for retailing, but total import must not exceed 30 per cent of their annual sales, and they are not allowed to act as import/export proxies of other retailers (a restriction on imports).

With the designation of the 11 cities and SEZs for experiment, 15 joint ventures were approved by the state government to establish in China (see Table 7.1).

The second move

While the initial opening up was a good first step, it had only limited success. All the fifteen overseas retailers were from East and Southeast Asia, which have relatively short physical and psychic distances from China. Local governments were not content with the strict state control, and domestic industry leaders complained that the selection and approval of the first fifteen overseas retailers simply wasted the government quotas, because what China really needs are the large international retailers from North America and Western Europe.

In October 1995, the state government took the second major step towards opening up the retail sector. This time, it authorized Beijing to experiment with

Table 7.1 The first eighteen Sino-overseas joint ventures approved by the State Council between 1992 and 1997

Enterprise	Host city	Foreign partner	Chinese partner
1992			
Beijing Lufthansa (Yansha Friendship) Shopping City Ltd	Beijing	Singapore New City Group Ltd	Beijing Friendship Commercial Services Corp.
Xin Dong'an Commerce Ltd	Beijing	Hong Kong Sun Hung Kai Properties Group	Beijing Dong'an Group
Dalian International Commerce and Trade Ltd	Dalian	Nichii of Japan	Dalian Commerce Ltd
Guangzhou Hualian-Broadway Ltd	Guangzhou	Hong Kong Broadway Ltd	Guangdong Corporation of Sugar, Tobacco and Liquor
Guangzhou Tianhe Plaza	Guangzhou	Hong Kong Zhengda International	Guangzhou Jiajing Commerce and Trade Co.
Qingdao No.1-Parkson Department Store Ltd	Qingdao	Malaysian Parkson Group	Qingdao No. 1 Department Store
Qingdao Jusco Ltd	Qingdao	Jusco of Japan	Qingdao Municipal Logistics Corp.
Shantou Gold & Silver Island Trading Ltd	Shantou	Hong Kong Zhengda International	Shantou China Travel Group
Shanghai No.1-Yohan Ltd	Shanghai	Yohan International of Japan	Shanghai No. 1 Department Store
Shanghai Run-Hua Ltd	Shanghai	Hong Kong Huarun	Shanghai Hualian Department Store
Shanghai Orient Plaza Ltd	Shanghai	Hong Kong, Shanghai Industrial Investment Ltd	Shanghai Commercial Development Corporation
Shanghai Jusco Ltd	Shanghai	Jusco of Japan	Shanghai Shenhua Ltd and 4 others
Shenzhen Wal Mart-Yichu	Shenzhen	US Wal-Mart	Shenzhen International Trust Investment Co.
Tianjin Huaxin Plaza Ltd	Tianjin	Hong Kong Shun Tak Group	Tianjin Hualian Commercial Building
Tianjin Chia Tai International	Tianjin	Chia Tai Group of Thailand	Tianjin Leader Group
1995–1997			
Huatang Commerce Ltd Co.	Beijing	Ito-Yokado of Japan	China Sugar-Liquor Corp.
CTA -SHV Makro Ltd Co.	Beijing	SHV Markro of the Netherlands and Taiwan Fengqun Investment Ltd Co.	China Native Products Import/Export Corp.
Weilai Central Department Store	Wuhan	Taiwan Fengqun Investment Ltd Co.	Wuhan Central Department Store Group

Source: Beijing Intelligence Tapping and Management Consulting Ltd, 1997: 8; China Association of Commercial Chains, 2000: 733.

expanding joint ventures from single-store operations to retail chains; it also allowed the expansion of foreign involvement from retailing to wholesale, and from general consumer goods to groceries. As a measure of precaution, the state government still insisted that partnership with Chinese retailers is necessary, and Chinese partners must have a larger share of ownership.

Two international retailers were subsequently approved to form chains. These were Japan's Ito-Yokado and the Netherlands' Makro. The former is linked to the China Sugar-Liquor Corp., while the latter was linked to China Native Products Import/Export Corp. Both Chinese partners were affiliated with government ministries: Interior Trade and Foreign Trade, respectively. In addition to Ito-Yokado and Makro, the state government approved the entry of a Taiwanese enterprise, Weilai Central Department Store in Wuhan of Hubei Province (Sternquist 1998). This increased the total number of state-approved joint ventures from 15 to18 (see Table 7.1).

The third move

In June 1999, the state government of China made its third move with the following new policies (State Economic and Trade Commission and Ministry of Foreign Trade 1999):

- In addition to the previously designated cities and SEZs, the experiment is expanded to include all provincial capitals and the cities that are independent of their provinces in economic planning (a geographic expansion).
- Joint Sino-foreign retail enterprises are allowed to engage in wholesaling as well as retailing (an expansion in business scope).
- New criteria are set forth for the selection of foreign retailers and Chinese partners. Future overseas entrants must be large, experienced retailers with a good reputation and performance record (i.e. with minimum business capital of US$200 million and having achieved minimum annual sales of US$2 billion); they should have well-established international distribution networks and be able to help export made-in-China products. Chinese partners must also be large retailers with minimum capital of 50 million *yuan* (US$6.2 million) and having achieved minimum annual sales of 300 million *yuan* (US$37.5 million) (more stringent in choosing new overseas entrants and domestic partners).
- Favourable treatments are given to the joint ventures that are willing to set up business operations in the western region of China (see Table 7.2).
- Wholly foreign-owned enterprises are still prohibited, but majority-foreign ownership is allowed in joint-retail chains that have potential to purchase large quantities of made-in-China products and export these products to other countries (an expansion on foreign ownership).
- Foreign retailers cannot charge more than 0.3 per cent of the annual sales of a joint venture for technology transfer or for using their registered trade marks (a restriction on foreign-franchised retail establishments).
- Hong Kong-, Taiwan- and Macao-invested joint ventures continue to be treated as foreign-invested enterprises; the above policies apply to them as well.

Table 7.2 Differential treatments to Sino-foreign joint retail ventures in China

Region of operation[a]	Minimum capital required for business registration (million yuan)		Maximum contract life to be granted (year)
Eastern Coastal and Central Regions	Retail: Wholesale:	50 (US$6.25 million) 80 (US$10 million)	30
Western Regions	Retail: Wholesale:	30 (US$3.75 million) 60 (US$7.5 million)	40

Source: State Economic and Trade Commission and Ministry of Foreign Trade 1999.

Note
a See Table 7.3 for provinces in each region.

The above new policies are still too recent to have any recorded effects, but their significance is threefold. First, China reiterates that the state government has the ultimate control over the approval of the entry of foreign retailers. It is not likely that local governments will approve as many foreign retailers as they did in the 1990s. Secondly, China raised the entry threshold and wants to select only the large international retailers as future entrants. This makes the entry of smaller retailers (including those of the overseas Chinese) difficult. The intention is to trade China's lucrative consumer market for capital, information technology, merchandising techniques and managerial expertise. Thirdly, China wants to ensure that only the large domestic retailers that have adequate resources and experience should become partners. This will raise the level of participation by the Chinese retailers in business decision making, so that their role is not reduced to a liaison between the joint ventures and the Chinese government.

Overseas retailers in China

Despite the fact that the state government approved only 18 overseas retailers between 1992 and 1997, the number of such enterprises increased rapidly. Some government sources say there are now over 300 international retailers in China; but according to the *1997 China Statistical Yearbook*, a total of 1,697 foreign-invested and 1,088 overseas Chinese-invested retail establishments existed in China in 1996 (Table 7.3). They spread widely in 26 of the 30 provinces. No published list of overseas retailers is available. Table 7.4, which is compiled from scattered sources, lists the major international retailers and their locations.

While most of overseas retailers did not have state approval, they are not underground businesses. They were all approved by local governments. So, negotiating a joint venture through a local government became the most common entry path. Local governments are not content with the strict state restrictions. The cities that are not designated for experiment argue: why should only the selected cities and the SEZs be allowed to have foreign retailers and investment, which contributes further to regional disparity? The designated cities also question: why are only one to two joint ventures allowed while so many international retailers want to come

Table 7.3 Geographical distribution of overseas-invested retail enterprises, 1996

Region	Province	Foreign		Overseas Chinese		Total overseas	
		No.	(%)	No.	(%)	No.	(%)
Eastern	Beijing	563	(33.2)	64	(5.9)	627	(22.5)
Coastal	Fujian	81	(4.8)	107	(9.8)	188	(6.8)
	Guangdong	162	(9.5)	318	(29.2)	480	(17.2)
	Guangxi	23	(1.4)	7	(0.6)	30	(1.1)
	Hainan	10	(0.6)	31	(2.8)	41	(1.5)
	Hebei	2	(0.1)	28	(2.6)	30	(1.1)
	Jiangsu	27	(1.6)	35	(3.2)	62	(2.2)
	Liaoning	33	(1.9)	16	(1.5)	49	(1.8)
	Shandong	18	(1.1)	40	(3.7)	58	(2.1)
	Shanghai	629	(37.1)	289	(26.6)	918	(32.9)
	Tianjin	7	(0.4)	6	(0.6)	13	(0.5)
	Zhejiang	19	(1.1)	4	(0.4)	23	(0.8)
	Sub total	1,574	(92.8)	945	(86.9)	2,519	(90.4)
Central	Anhui	28	(1.6)	11	(1.0)	39	(1.4)
	Heilongjiang	7	(0.4)	8	(0.7)	15	(0.5)
	Henan	1	(0.1)	28	(2.6)	29	(1.0)
	Hubei	12	(0.7)	11	(1.0)	23	(0.8)
	Hunan	8	(0.5)	5	(0.5)	13	(0.5)
	Inner Mongolia	5	(0.3)	9	(0.8)	14	(0.5)
	Jiangxi	5	(0.3)	10	(0.9)	15	(0.5)
	Jilin	11	(0.6)	19	(1.7)	30	(1.1)
	Shanxi	15	(0.9)	4	(0.4)	19	(0.7)
	Sub total	92	(5.4)	105	(9.6)	197	(7.1)
Western	Gansu	0	(0.0)	1	(0.1)	1	(<0.1)
	Guizhou	0	(0.0)	2	(0.2)	2	(<0.1)
	Ningxia	0	(0.0)	0	(0.0)	0	(0.0)
	Qinghai	0	(0.0)	0	(0.0)	0	(0.0)
	Shaanxi	0	(0.0)	0	(0.0)	0	(0.0)
	Sichuan	14	(0.8)	26	(2.4)	40	(1.4)
	Tibet	0	(0.0)	0	(0.0)	0	(0.0)
	Xinjiang	13	(0.8)	4	(0.4)	17	(0.6)
	Yunnan	4	(0.2)	5	(0.5)	9	(0.3)
	Sub total	31	(1.8)	38	(3.5)	69	(2.5)
Total		1,697	(100.0)	1,088	(100.0)	2,785	(100.0)

Source: State Statistics Bureau 1997.

Note

a Chongqing did not become a municipality directly under the central government with provincial status until March 1997.

to invest? Consequently, local governments took the liberty of approving their own joint ventures, with the hope that China would soon join the WTO, when the state government would be obliged to approve all of those that are already in operation.

Table 7.4 Major foreign retailers in China, 2002

Foreign retailer	Home country	Format	City of operation and number of stores
Wal-Mart (Including Sam's Club)	USA	Discount department store/membership club	Dalian (2); Dongguan (1); Fuzhou (1); Guangzhou (1); Kunming (2); Shantou (1); Shekou (1); Shenyang (1); Shenzhen (4)
Carrefour	France	Hypermarket	Beijing (4); Chengdu (1) Chongqing (2); Dalian (1); Dongguang (1); Hangzhou (1); Harbin (1); Nanjing (1); Ningbo (1); Qingdao (2); Shanghai (6); Shenyang (1); Shenzhen (2); Suzhou (1); Tianjin (2); Wuhan (1); Wuxi (1); Zhuhai (1)
Metro	Germany	Warehouse retail store/ membership club	Fuzhou (1); Hangzhou (1); Nanjing (1); Ningbo (1); Qingdao (1); Shanghai (4); Wuxi (1)
Parkson	Malaysia	Department store	Beijing (2); Changchun (1); Changzhou (1); Chengdu (1); Chongqing (1); Dalian (1); Hohhot (1); Jinan (1); Qingdao (2); Shanghai (2); Shijiazhuang (1); Xi'an (1); Wuhan (1); Wuxi (1)
Makro	The Netherlands	Warehouse retail store/ membership club	Beijing (2); Guangzhou (1)
Ikea	Sweden	Big box store	Beijing (1); Shanghai (1)
Price smart	USA	Warehouse retail store/ membership club	Beijing (3); Qingdai (1)
B&Q	UK	Big box store	Shanghai (1)
Ito-Yokado	Japan	Department store/ supermarket	Beijing (1); Chengdu (1)
Jusco	Japan	Department store	Guangzhou (1); Qingdao (2); Shanghai (1)
Daiei	Japan	Supermarket	Tianjin (6); Dalian (1)
Seiyu	Japan	Department store	Beijing (1); Shanghai (1)
Isetan	Japan	Department store	Shanghai (2); Tianjin (1)
Sogo	Japan	Department store	Beijing (1)
Mycal-Nichii	Japan	Department store	Dalian (1)
Lawson	Japan	Convenience store	Shanghai (90)
Seibu	Japan	Department store	Shenzhen (1)
Lotus	Thailand	Hypermarket	Shanghai (4)

Sources: Chen 1999; Xu 1999; websites of respective retailers; site visits and personal interview of the managers of foreign and domestic retailers by the author.

Foreign retailers with no state approval are not eligible for state-instituted preferential treatments, but tax reform made it possible for local governments to offer their own incentives to attract foreign retailers. Before tax reform, all corporate tax went into the state government's coffer. Under the current system, corporate tax is split between the state and local governments, and the latter often waive their share of the corporate tax for foreign retailers. In addition, such local taxes as municipal development tax and education tax are often also waived, at least for the first few years of business operation.

Local governments went so far that in 1997 the state government had to issue an urgent circular to reiterate that local governments have no authority to approve joint ventures in retailing (*People's Daily*, 11 August 1997). In 1998, the State Planning Commission, Ministry of Foreign Trade, Ministry of Interior Trade and State Bureau of Industry and Commerce joined forces to scrutinize 277 joint retail ventures that did not have state approval. After this examination, only 41 were ordered to close; 42 were given state approval; and 194 were told to reorganize (without closing) and await future approval (Beijing Government 1999). This was interpreted as a signal of loosening state control in the Chinese retail economy. It shows that the state government quietly allowed most of them to exist. The Ministry of Interior Trade even sponsored a high-level forum in Shanghai in 1998 to discuss what could be learned from the locally approved German Metro's operation in Shanghai (Liu, X. J. 1999). In 2001, under the pressure of domestic retailers and other foreign retailers, the State Economic and Trade Commission (which oversees foreign retailers operating in China) admonished Carrefour for flouting the rules of the state government in setting up and expanding businesses in China, and suspended its further expansion for six months (*China Economic Review* March 2001c). Subsequently, Carrefour negotiated and signed an agreement with the State Economic and Trade Commission, which not only allows all existing Carrefour stores to remain open but also allows Carrefour to resume opening of new stores (*China Economic Review* 2001c, 2002).

During a personal interview, the general manager of a foreign-invested store[2] disclosed three principles that his management has followed in dealing with the various levels of government in China: (1) trust the local government that approved the joint venture and keep the local government informed of the foreign retailer's needs and difficulties, with no reservation and no exaggeration; (2) be understanding of the local government's position and situation; if the local government has to temporarily retract from its own offer of incentives due to changes in the larger political environment (such as the above-mentioned state circular and scrutiny of locally approved joint ventures), the foreign retailer would not lodge complaints; (3) whenever facing news media, save no words to praise the state government for its open-door policies and preferential treatment to foreign retailers; never openly criticize or embarrass the state government.

In addition to seeking local government approval for forming joint ventures, other entry paths have been reported or observed. In 1995, the Chinese government made the following commitments to the newly established WTO as part of its negotiation efforts for a membership (Xiao and Qiu 1999):

- foreign-invested manufacturers are allowed to sell a portion of their production in China;
- foreign retail chains are allowed to select Chinese retailers as their franchised outlets;
- foreign companies are permitted to participate in managing Chinese-owned retail establishments in China.

Some joint ventures in manufacturing took the advantage of China's preferential policies that allow them to sell part of their production in China without paying tariff. They either opened factory outlets or established franchised specialty stores to sell their products – typically apparels. Examples of this practice are firms such as Pierre Cardin (French), Giordano (Hong Kong) Crocodile (Hong Kong) and Play Boy (American). Some Chinese retailers contracted their day-to-day management to foreign retailers, thus effectively becoming cooperatives. This practice was adopted by Beijing's Scitech that at one time was managed by Japan's Yohan International (Han 1998). Other emerging enterprises became franchisees of various foreign retailers. This approach was adopted by Beijing's Lafayette (French) and Sogo (Japan) department stores (Wang 1999). There are also some foreign investors who applied to invest in real estate development such as office towers and hotels; when the buildings are completed, they would use part of them for retail. The Malaysian Parkson has done this in a number of cities.

In China, all foreign-invested retail establishments are joint ventures. This is dictated by state regulations, but it may also be an entry mode that foreign retailers preferred. When a foreign retailer attempts to enter a culturally different market with substantial psychic distances, local partners can be helpful in exploring the domestic market, managing local labour and organizing local supplies. Despite forced minority equity participation, in almost all cases, foreign investors insist on the control over business management. They can agree to have a Chinese national to be the chair of the board of directors, but the general manager (or CEO) must be appointed by them, usually someone from their home countries.

There are also some foreign retailers who obtained ownership control after a joint venture went into business. This was done through supplementing investment. Since the Chinese partners often do not have access to additional funds, the foreign retailers would provide all the new investment, thus becoming controlling shareholders. It is reported that of the eighteen state-endorsed joint ventures that were approved between 1992 and 1997, more than half have foreign retailers as larger shareholders (Liu, X. Y. 1999).

Foreign retailers in China do business in a variety of retail formats. Those from Asian countries mostly adopted the department store format. The Japanese Yohan, Jusco, Sogo, Isetan and Seiyu, and the Malaysian Parkson are good examples. There is also a major difference between the Japanese retailers and the Malaysian

Parkson. The former tend to focus on retailing, whereas the latter combines retailing with real estate development. In both Beijing and Qingdao, Parkson invested heavily to develop office towers with only part of the buildings used for retailing. Those from Hong Kong mostly take the format of franchised specialty stores, which requires low investment and involves low risks. Examples are Giordano, Crocodile and Goldlion.

The European and North American retailers came later than the Asian retailers, but they all adopted the so-called new formats of hypermarket (Carrefour), Cash & Carry warehouse retail store (Metro, Makro, Ikea), discount department store (Wal-Mart) and membership clubs (Sam's Club, Pricesmart, Metro and Makro). The new formats use a number of measures to reduce operation cost. While large in store size, their interior finish is plain and simple with minimum decoration. They also adopt the open-shelf form of service so that the number of workers and the total labour cost are reduced. Metro, Sam's Club and Makro are all operated as membership clubs. Those who purchase a membership are mostly committed customers with certain levels of purchasing power. This allows the membership clubs to focus on one group of customers with the most business potential. Promotion fliers are sent only to the members, and costly mass advertisement on TV and in newspapers is avoided. The membership system also allows the foreign retailers to monitor sales and changes in consumption patterns. This gives them a competitive edge over the domestic retailers. Metro, Makro, Sam's Club and Price Smart, all in warehouse format, not only deal with end users, but also target small retailers as well as institutions, which usually make bulk purchases. Most importantly, this format allows them to bypass government restrictions that prohibit foreign retailers from engaging in wholesale business in China, thus becoming a disguised form of wholesaling under the name of retailing.

The Wal-Mart discount department store and the Carrefour hypermarket are not membership clubs, but they have their distinctive way of promoting business. Wal-Mart offers 'everyday low prices', so no expensive forms of advertisement is needed. Carrefour offers discounts on a rotation basis: a few different items a time, intending to attract the loyal customers for frequent visits.

While most of the above international firms are retail chains in their home countries, they have yet been able to form nation-wide chains in China. The fact that they have different business partners in different Chinese cities has made it difficult for them to form any nation-wide chain.

Foreign-invested retail enterprises heavily concentrate in the Eastern Coastal Region, where the large and wealthy markets are located (Table 7.3). In the Eastern Coastal Region, they heavily concentrate in the two largest cities of Shanghai and Beijing. By 1996, these two cities accounted for 70 per cent of all foreign-invested retail enterprises in China. The overseas Chinese-invested enterprises have somewhat different geographical patterns, with the heaviest concentration in Guangdong Province (29.2 per cent), followed by Shanghai (26.6 per cent) and Fujian (9.8 per cent). The high concentrations in Guangdong and Fujian can be explained by the fact that these provinces were the birthplace of many overseas Chinese investors and are in close proximity to Hong Kong, Taiwan and Macao, where the parent companies are located. It is not clear why Beijing has been much less favoured by overseas Chinese retail investors than Shanghai. What is also interesting is that few large international retailers chose Beijing as their landing field. For example, Wal-Mart and Carrefour landed in Shenzhen; Metro, Ikea and B&Q started in Shanghai, Makro in Guangzhou, and Parkson in Qingdao. One explanation is that because their entry in China was not approved by the state government (except for Wal-Mart), they avoided having their first operations established in Beijing, which is under close watch of the state government.

Within urban centres, location strategies of foreign retailers have been changing. Early entrants of the new format retailers tend to locate in urban fringe close to highways. Examples are the American Wal-Mart and Sam's Club in Shenzhen, the German Metro in Shanghai, and the Dutch Makro in Beijing. This is a typical location principle in Western countries. In China, however, peripheral locations have not been able to attract the crowds of shoppers that are needed to support the businesses, mainly because car ownership is still low even in large urban centres. In Beijing, private auto ownership is only 3 vehicles per 100 people (Beijing Statistics Bureau 1998), compared with 46 in Toronto and 51 in Dallas-Fort Worth (Simmons *et al.* 1998b). Recently, foreign retailers have opened new stores within residential areas and on major bus routes. The most obvious are the French Carrefour stores in Beijing, Shanghai and Qingdao. Some foreign retailers even provide free buses from affluent suburban residential areas to their stores.

Impact on local retailers and Chinese responses to foreign competition

Internationalization of retailing has mixed impacts on the host country. On the positive side, Chinese consumers have benefited from wider selection of goods, lower prices and better services. Foreign retailers have also brought capital, new operation concepts and merchandising technology. Nowadays, almost all the new retail formats that have been developed in the Western economies can be seen in China. They are operated not only by foreign retailers but also by Chinese retailers. On the negative side, foreign retailers have introduced competition, which poses threats to the existence of some local retailers.

Foreign retailers have not made significant impacts on China's retail sector as a whole. They account for less than 1 per cent of the total number of stores and less than 3 per cent of the total retail sales in the country (Huang 2000). However, in large urban centres, such as Beijing, Shanghai, Guangzhou and Shenzhen, domestic retailers have felt the pinch. The latest census of commercial activity in Beijing shows that foreign-invested retail establishments are much larger than other retail enterprises (Beijing Statistics Bureau 1999). For instance, the foreign-invested retailers account for only 0.4 per cent of the total retail enterprises in Beijing; yet, they employ 2.4 per cent of the total retail workers in the city (excluding the self-employed vendors), with an average of 179 workers per enterprise; this is three times as large as the state-owned establishments. The foreign-invested are also the largest in store size with an average of 5,252 m^2 per store; this is also about three times as large as the state-owned retail enterprises. Scale economy plus high efficiency makes the foreign-invested much more competitive than domestic retailers. In 2000, Carrefour sold US$1 billion of merchandise in China, becoming the third largest retailer in the country (*World News Connection*, 24 February 2001).

Lower price is another reason that Chinese consumers are attracted to the foreign retailers. Wal-Mart brought with it the all-familiar slogan of 'every day low prices' to Shenzhen; and the Dutch Makro pledged lowest prices in the City of Guangzhou. Domestic retailers have accused them of unfair competition in offering prices below production costs. As reported in China Commerce Daily (quoted in Hong 1998), only six months after Carrefour opened its store in Shenzhen's Nanshan District, one Chinese department store within Carrefour's trade area had to close due to heavy losses, and several others were struggling to survive. The victims all blamed the highly price-competitive Carrefour for their failure. Also in Nashan District, on 18 December 1997, a Chinese retailer opened a supermarket right within the trade area of Carrefour to take on the French retailer. It mobilized considerable resources (including the use of local news media and fliers) to publicize the grand opening, hoping to attract a big crowd. To their greatest surprise, the general manager of Carrefour with a group of Carrefour employees appeared outside the Chinese supermarket on its opening day, distributing Carrefour fliers. The grand opening did attract a big crowd, but many shoppers, after touring the new supermarket, left for Carrefour because Carrefour was offering lower prices on almost everything on that day (Wang 2000).

In another case, a Taiwanese investor opened a 4,000 m² warehouse-format retail store in the City of Chengdu in Sichuan Province in November 1997. This store, named Good & Plenty, offered prices lower than those at state-owned local stores. This prompted several state-owned department stores to join forces in order to fight back. They discussed the possibility of imposing minimum prices in the city, and threatened to boycott local suppliers if they would continue to supply merchandise to Good & Plenty. In response, the Chengdu Bureau of Industry and Commerce investigated the Taiwanese retailer for possible improper pricing practice, but could not find sufficient evidence that Good & Plenty's prices were below production cost (Hong 1998).

Foreign retailers argue that they are able to offer low prices because of their low production costs and more efficient distribution systems (Cai 1997; Yi 1997). They are able to negotiate with suppliers for low wholesale prices when they buy in large quantities and pay in cash. They also turned to Sino-foreign joint manufacturers for merchandise to replace expensive imports (*People's Daily*, 29 August 1999). It is reported that Wal-Mart purchases 80–85 per cent of its merchandise from producers and suppliers in China with cash. Carrefour sources 95 per cent of its products from China (*Eurofood*, 13 February 2001). Most Chinese retailers do not have the same resources and usually rely on using credit for their purchase. Producers and suppliers are generally unwilling to offer the same low prices to the Chinese retailers due to their experiences of notorious debt problems. Foreign retailers are also willing to accept lower profit margins than the

Chinese retailers. For instance, Makro sets its profit margin at 9–12 per cent, lower than the 15–30 per cent range expected by most Chinese retailers (Fei 1998). Carrefour's operating profit target for 2002 is set at 4.3–4.4 per cent (SIAM Future Development Co. Ltd 2002). Undoubtedly, foreign retailers in China expect a profit, but their business plans are long term, and their strategy is to steadily expand market shares by building their reputation and popularizing their brands (which they consider as an intangible asset), even though this may require low profit margins in early stages of operation. Foreign retailers also make great efforts to increase operating efficiency and reduce labour costs. According to a report by Fei (1998), Makro's operation in Beijing has a workforce of 420 employees. Of this total, 350 are store-based and only 70 work at the head office. Its large store of 17,000 m^2 in Guangzhou carries 25,000 stock keeping units (SKU's), but only 600 employees support its various operations. In contrast, a Chinese enterprise of the same scale typically employs 1,500–2,000 workers. Smaller staff brings substantial savings on wages, even though average wage is much higher in the foreign-invested enterprises.

Another power that the large international retailers possess is their ability to 'help' Chinese manufactures export their products. They also use this power to negotiate for lower prices with Chinese manufacturers and suppliers. Wal-Mart, Carrefour, the Japanese Jusco, the Malaysian Parkson and the Swedish Ikea all purchase made-in-China products in large quantities, not only for their stores in China but also for their stores at home and in other countries. It is reported that Carrefour purchases US$200 million worth of goods each year from China to sell in its 5,000 stores in other countries (*La Tribune*, 2 September 2001).

During a personal interview in Beijing, a manager of a domestic retailer disclosed that many of the workers in Beijing's Carrefour store are not Carrefour employees. They are workers sent and paid by Chinese producers, who are eager to have their products sold through Carrefour's international distribution network and therefore are willing to send their own workers to the Carrefour stores to promote their products. Similar practice has been observed in other foreign-invested retail stores in China, such as the British B&Q in Shanghai – a big box store specializing in hardware and home furnishing materials.

To cope with the increasing foreign competitions, a variety of responses have been proposed or made either by domestic industry leaders or by the Chinese government. Domestic retailers appeal to governments, both state and local, to eliminate any preferential policies that have given foreign retailers a competitive edge (Li and Ni 1997). They strongly feel that the existing government policies have actually contributed to unfair competition: while foreign retailers have more resources, they pay less tax; they are therefore able to offer lower prices to make themselves more competitive. Elimination of preferential treatments will create a level field for fair competition between domestic and foreign retailers.

Some analysts have advised that the state government implement policies to control the timing and location for entry of foreign retailers. Such policies should reduce or spread the impacts of foreign retail competition over time and space, and give local Chinese retailers greater time to respond to the impacts.

At the same time, large domestic retailers (especially those in the same city) have taken actions to consolidate among themselves or to merge the willing small businesses to form retail chains. This has received strong support from the Chinese government, which decided to emphasize the development of indigenous retail chains as a means to modernize China's retail industry and thereby responding to foreign competition (Li 1997a,b; Gu 1998). In June 1995, the then Ministry of Interior Trade (MIT) issued the *Blueprint for Development of Retail Chains in China*. This document gave new impetus to the establishment of retail chains in a number of provinces. By January 1996, a permanent government agency – the Office of Commercial Chains Administration – was created under the auspice of MIT. In March 1997, MIT issued *The National Standards for Operation and Management of Commercial Chains* in an attempt to streamline this new form of retail organization in China (Ministry of Interior Trade 1997). To supplement the *National Standards for Operation and Management of Commercial Chains*, MIT in November 1997 issued the *Operation Guidelines for Commercial Franchising*. The state government has also begun to provide special assistance to the large, high-performing chains. It selected sixty chains as recipients of the State Technology Improvement Foundation Grants, and gave nineteen of them permission to import and export their own merchandise – the same privilege that is granted to foreign retailers. To follow suit, the China Bank of Industry and Commerce provided 6 billion *yuan* in loans to support the growth of major Chinese chains (Office of Commercial Chains Administration 1997). In consideration of China's particular situation, the state government now encourages franchising as a means to fast track the development of domestic chains. Both Lianhua (United China) and Hualian (China United), the two largest retail chains in China, have recently resorted to this form of growth by providing management to franchised stores and supplying merchandise to them through the chains' distribution networks. In other reports, two of Beijing's largest retailers – Wangfujing Co. Ltd and Dong'an Group – have merged to form the capital's first 'super-retailing' group: Beijing Wangfujing-Dong'an Group Co. Ltd, in order to fend off foreign competition (*China Economic Review* 2000c; Fang 2001); four publicly-traded department store groups in Wuhan have also planned to merge for the same purpose (*China Economic Review* 2000a); in Hunan Province, Changsha Friendship Group Co. Ltd and Changsha Apollo Commercial City merged into Hunan Friendship Apollo Co. Ltd (Fang 2001). Trans-regional merger has also begun to occur. Supermarket operator Shanghai Hualian and Beijing Xidan have merged some of their existing operations to form a new joint venture named Beijing Xidan-Hualian Supermarket, being 77 per cent owned by Hualian, 19 per cent owned by Xidan and 4 per cent belonging to another Beijing retailer – Chaoshifa (*Eurofood*, 13 February 2001).

In the mean time, the government continues to push for the transformation of state-owned companies into joint-stock enterprises. This approach is seen as the most effective means of raising business capital and reducing the barriers associated with trans-regional and trans-sectoral retail chain expansion.

Industry leaders have also recognized the importance of shifting away from emphasis on department stores as the main retail format to development of new format stores, such as hypermarket that combines the functions of a discount department store and a supermarket. Warehouse retailing, which has the advantage of combining retailing with wholesaling, is another format that some domestic retailers are pursuing. As retailing enters the low-profit era in China, wholesaling will become a new battleground between domestic and foreign retailers.

Conclusion

Now that China has become a full member of the WTO, the Chinese government may soon legalize most of the joint ventures that had been approved by the local governments, and the presence of foreign retailers in the country is to increase further. Carrefour closed all its operations in Hong Kong in 2000 and has since accelerated opening of new stores in Mainland China (*Singtao Daily*, 30 August 2000). In October 2000, the CEO of America's Wal-Mart, Lee Scott, paid a business visit to China, making contact with China's high-ranking officials as well as local officials. Shortly afterward, Wal-Mart reversed its low-profile growth pattern in China and announced opening of eight new stores in the very near future (Fang 2001): 5 in Beijing, 1 in Shanghai, 1 in Tianjin and 1 in Jinan (*People's Daily*, 19 November 2001; Chinaonline, 15 November 2001; SIAM Future Development Co. Ltd, 2001; *People's Daily*, 9 October 2001). Wal-Mart also plans to set up its Asia-Pacific headquarters and a global purchasing centre in Shenzhen (*People's Daily*, 6 October 2000; *World Journal*, 2 November 2001). Metro and Parkson announced similar plans to open more stores at new locations (Fang 2001). Clearly, after a decade of learning the Chinese business environment and the way of overcoming political and cultural barriers, the foreign retailers have accumulated enough experiences and are poised to launch new waves of expansion in China.

The department store as a retail format has become obsolete not only in China but in other countries as well. As China further opens its retail market, the losers will be the domestic retailers and the Asian retailers who still do business in this traditional format. For example, the Japanese Yohan International already withdrew from its operations in Shanghai; another Japanese retailer, Jusco, had to close a store in Shanghai due to business losses (*China Economic Review* 2000b). As one of the first state-approved foreign retail chains, Ito-Yokado still has only one store in Beijing. The winners will be European and American retailers, who possess the most resources and advanced IT technologies, and do business in new retail formats. Once the regulatory barriers are pulled down, they may easily expand by taking the path of acquisition, just like what Wal-Mart did in Canada. The surplus retail spaces resulting from department store closures in many large cities will make this possible. Those willing to set up operations in the Western region may also be winners in a long run by taking first-mover advantages. If they can quickly occupy a large urban market with multiple stores, they will effectively pre-empt subsequent entrants.

Notes

1 China began to negotiate with GATT (the predecessor of WTO) in 1986 for restoring its membership (which China relinquished after 1949). After fifteen years of hard negotiations, China finally cleared all hurdles and became a full member of the WTO in November of 2001.
2 The store cannot be named here, to respect the store manager's request for confidentiality.

References

Akehurst, G. and Alexander, N. (1995) 'Developing a framework for the study of the internationalisation of retailing', *The Service Industries Journal*, 15 (4): 204–10.
Alexander, N. (1993) 'Internationalisation: interpreting the motives', *International Issues in Retailing, ESRC Seminars: Research Themes in Retailing*, Manchester Business School/Manchester School of Management, 15 March.
Anderson, O. (1993) 'On the internationalisation process of firms: a critical analysis', *Journal of International Business Studies*, 2nd Quarter: 209–31.
Beijing Government (1999) *A Preliminary Analysis of the Current Situation of Foreign-Invested Commercial Enterprises in Beijing* (*Beijing Waizi Shangye Qiye Fazhan Xianzhuang Jianxi*).
Beijing Intelligence Tapping and Management Consulting Ltd (1997) 'A report on opening-up of China's retail sector' (Zhongguo lingshouye duiwai kaifang fazhan baogao), *Science and Technology Think Tank* (*Keji Zhinang*), 11: 7–12.
Beijing Statistics Bureau (1998) *1997 Beijing Statistical Yearbook*, Beijing.
Beijing Statistics Bureau (1999) *Census of Commercial Activity in Beijing* (*Beijing Shi Shehui Shangye Pucha Ziliao Huibian)*, Beijing: China Commerce Publishing House (Zhongguo Shangye Chubanshe).
Burbach, R., Nunez, O. and Kagarlitsky, B. (1997) *Globalization and Its Discontents: The Rise of Postmodern Socialism*. New York: Pluto Press.
Busillo, T. (1998) 'The world is a stage for retail', *Home Textile Today*, 19 (22): 31–3.
Cai, Z. (1997)' The rise of Wal-Mart in China' (Yijun tuqi Wo-er-ma.), *Science and Technology Think Tank* (*Keji Zhinang*), 11: 13–15.
Chen, L. (1999) 'Investment and operation strategies of Japanese retailers in China' (Riben lingshou shangye de zhongguo touzi zhanluo ji jingying zhanluo), *Commerce Enterprise Management* (*Shangye Qiye Guanli*), 9: 57–9.
China Association of Commercial Chains (2000) *China Chain Store Almanac*. Beijing: China Commerce Publishing House.
China Economic Review (2000a) 'Chinese stores unite to fight', *China Economic Review*, August.
China Economic Review (2000b) 'Mixed fortunes for foreign groups', *China Economic Review*, August.
China Economic Review (2000c) 'Beijing stores announce merger', *China Economic Review*, October.
China Economic Review (2001a) 'Carrefour to open 10 more stores', *China Economic Review*, February.
China Economic Review (2001b) 'Foreign retailers plan expansion', *China Economic Review*, March.
China Economic Review (2001c) 'Carrefour faces possible restructuring', *China Economic Review*, September.
China Economic Review (2002) 'Carrefour to resume expansion', *China Economic Review*, January.

Chinaonline (2001) 'Wal-Mart awaits approval of first Shanghai store', *Chinaonline* 15 November http://english.sina.com/news/trade/2001/1115/trade.html

Daniels, P. W. and Lever, W. F. (eds) (1996) *The Global Economy in Transition*. Essex, England: Addison Wesley Longman Limited.

Dawson, J. A. (1994) 'Internationalization of retailing operations', *Journal of Marketing Management*, 10: 267–82.

Dunning, J. H. (1988) *International Production and the Multinational Enterprise*. London: Allen and Unwin.

Dupuis, M. and Prime, N. (1996) 'Business distance and global retailing: a model for analysis of key success/failure factors', *International Journal of Retail & Distribution Management*, 24 (11): 30–8.

Editorial Board of Science and Technology Think Tank (1997) 'An overview of regulations on foreign investment in retailing in China' (Waishang touzi lingshou shangye de youguang guiding), *Science and Technology Think Tank* (*Keji Zhinang*), 11: 4–6.

Elango, B. (1999) 'An empirical examination of the influence of industry and firm drives on the rate of internationalization by firms', *Journal of International Management*, 4: 201–21.

Eroglu, S. (1992) 'The internationalisation process of franchise systems: a conceptual model', *International Marking Review*, 9 (5): 11–39.

Erramilli, M. K. (1991) 'The experience factor in foreign market entry behaviour of service firms', *Journal of International Business Studies*, 3 (22): 479–501.

Eurofood (2001) 'Chinese firms act together to combat presence of foreign giants', *Eurofood*, 13 February: 8.

Fang, N. (2001) 'Foreign retailers speed up advance into Chinese market', *Beijing Review*. http://www.bjreview.com.cn/2001/NationalIssues/China200114b.htm

Fei, L. (1998) 'An investigation of Shenzhen's Wal-Mart and Guangzhou's Makro for their operations', (Wangpai yu duice: guanyu Shenzhen Wo-er-ma he Guangzhou Wan-ke-long jingying qingkuang de diaocha) *China Business and Trade* (*Zhongguo Shangmao*), 9: 44–7.

Gu, G. (1998) 'The "white book" on retail chain development in China' (Zhongguo lian-suo fazhan baipishu), *Science and Technology Think Tank* (*Keji Zhinang*), 3: 4–11.

Han, J. (1998) 'The story of Scitech' (Saite de chengzhang guiji), *Science and Technology Think Tank* (*Keji Zhinang*), 2: 29–31.

Hong, S. (1998) 'Who are slashing prices to increase sales?' (Jiujing shui zai dijia Jjngxiao?), *Science and Technology Think Tank* (*Keji Zhinang*), 6: 7–10.

Huang, H. (2000) 'The opening up of China's retail chain sector to international competi-tion' (Zhongguo liansuoye de duiwai kaifang), *China Chain Store Almanac 1990–2000* (*Zhongguo Liansuo Jingying Nianjian 1990–2000*). Beijing: China Commerce Publishing House (Zhongguo Shangye Chubanshe).

La Tribune (2001) 'Peking raps Carrefour on the knuckles', *La Tribune*, 2 September.

Li, L. (1997a) 'Must raise the level and standards of chain operation and management' (Qieshi tigao liansuo jingying guimohua he guifanhua shuiping), *Science and Technology Think Tank* (*Keji Zhinang*), 8: 4.

Li, L. (1997b) 'Speech at the national forum on development of commercial chains'. In: *Almanac of China's Domestic Trade 1997*, pp. I-1–I-5. Beijing: Ministry of Interior Trade.

Li, Z. and Ni, X. (1997) 'The Chinese retail market is feeling the impacts of 'foreign' stores' ('Yang' dian zhuangji zhongguo lingshouye shichang), *Outlook Weekly News* (*Liaowang Xinwen ZhouKan*), 25: 26–7.

Liu, X. J. (1999) 'Operation and management at Metro' (Mai De Long de jingying yu guanli), *Commerce Economy Research* (*Shangye Jingji Yanjiu*), 6: 33–6.

Liu, X. Y. (1999) 'GATT and the opening up of China's retail sector' (Fuwu maoyi zong xieding yu woguo lingshouye de duiwai kaifang), *Issues of International Trade* (*Guoji Maoyi Wenti*), 10: 51–5.

Ministry of Interior Trade (1997) 'National standards for operation and management of commercial chains' (Liansuodian jingying guangli guifan yijian), *Science and Technology Think Tank* (*Keji Zhinang*), 9: 4.

Office of Commercial Chains Administration, MIT (1997) 'A report on retail chain development in China' (Zhongguo lianso jingying fazhan baogao), *Science and Technology Think Tank* (*Keji Zhinang*), 8: 5–13.

Pellegrini, L. (1991) 'The internationalisation of retailing, 1992 Europe', *Journal of Marketing Channels*, 1(2): 3–27.

People's Daily (1997) 'Local governments are prohibited from approving foreign invested retail enterprises' (Jinzhi difang shenpi waiguo touzi shangye qiye) *People's Daily* (overseas edition), 11 August: 2.

People's Daily (1999) 'Overseas retailers attempt to increase sales by carrying more medium- and low-priced merchandise' (Zhongguo lingshouye waiqi tiaozheng celue, zengjia zhong di dang shangpin shiying shichang), *People's Daily*, 29 August: 2.

People's Daily (2000) 'Wal-Mart to set up Asia-Pacific headquarters in China', *People's Daily* (English edition) 6 October http://english.peopledaily.com.cn/200010/06/ eng20001006_51930.htm

People's Daily (2000) 'Wal-Mart to open new chain store in China', *People's Daily* (English edition) 15 November http://english.peopledaily.com.cn/200011/15/ eng20001115_55191.htm

People's Daily (2001) 'US chain store opens branch in SW China', *People's Daily* (English edition) 10 May http://english.peopledaily.com.cn/200105/10/eng20010510_69589.htm

People's Daily (2001) 'US chain store to open branch in Northeast China', *People's Daily* (English edition) 14 September http://english.peopledaily.com.cn/200109/14/ eng20010914_80237.htm

People's Daily (2001) 'Retail multinationals expand China operations', *People's Daily* (English edition) 9 October http://english.peopledaily.com.cn/200110/09/ eng20011009_81856.htm

People's Daily (2001) 'Wal-Mart to open five branches in Beijing', *People's Daily* (English edition) 19 November http://english.peopledaily.com.cn/200111/19/ eng20011119_84874.htm

SIAM Future Development Co. Ltd. (2001) 'Wal-Mart prepares site for 1st store in northern China', http://www.siamfuture.com/thainews

SIAM Future Development Co. Ltd. (2002) 'Carrefour/China: China store openings to start in 2003', http://www.siamfuture.com/thainews

Simmons, J., Jones, K. and Yeats, M. (1998a) 'The need for international comparisons of commercial structure and change', *Progress in Planning*, 50 (4): 207–16.

Simmons, J., Jones, K. Kamikihara, S. and Yeates, M. (1998b) 'International comparisons of commercial structure and public policy implications', *Progress in Planning*, 50 (4): 291–313.

Simpson, E. and Thorpe, D. I. (1999) 'A special store's perspective on retail internationalisation: a case study', *Journal of Retailing and Consumer Services*, 6(1): 45–53.

Singtao Daily (2000) 'Carrefour closes all operations in Hong Kong' (Jialefu quanxian jieye gaobie Xianggang), *Singtao Daily*, 30 August.

State Economic and Trade Commission and Ministry of Foreign Trade (1999) 'Interim stipulations about foreign-invested commercial enterprises' (Waishang touzi shangye qiye Shidian banfa), *Essays on Commerce Economy* (*Shangye Jingji Wenhui*), 5: 38–40.

State Statistics Bureau (1997) *China Statistics Yearbook.* Beijing: China Statistical Publishing House.

Sternquist, B. (1998) *International Retailing.* New York: Fairchild Publications.

Sun, H. (1999) 'Entry modes of multinational corporations into China's market: a socio-economic analysis', *International Journal of Social Economics*, 26(5): 642–59.

Vida, I. and Fairhurst, A. (1998) 'International expansion of retail firms: a theoretical approach for future investigations', *Journal of Retailing and Consumer Services*, 5 (3):143–51.

Wang, P. (1999) 'Zhuangsheng-Sogo Department Store' (Zhuangsheng-Chongguang Baihuo), *Commerce Economy Research* (*Shangye Jingji Yanjiu*), 3: (inside of back cover).

Wang, X. H. (2000) 'Ren-Ren Lo battling Carrefour' (Renrenlo dou fa Jialefu) (Printed from *China Journal* website; original source unknown).

Whitehead, M. B. (1992) 'Internationalisation of retailing: developing new perspectives', *European Journal of Marketing*, 26(8/9): 74–9.

Woodward, W. C. (1996) 'In global retailing, the game's the same, but the rules can be different', *Chain Store Age*, December: 9B–13B.

World News Connection (2001) 'French firm Carrefour denies ordered to shut down stores in China', *World News Connection*, 24 February.

World Journal (2001) 'Wal-Mart to move its global purchasing center to Shenzhen, China' (Wo-er-ma quanqiu caigou zhongxin mingnian qian Shenzhen), *World Journal*, 2 November: B16.

Wrigley, N. (2000) 'The globalisation of retail capital: themes for economic geography'. In: G. Clark, M. Gertler and M. Feldman (eds), *Handbook of Economic Geography*. London: Oxford University.

Xiao, Z. and Qiu, F. (1999) 'The circulation sector is opened further to meet new waves of foreign investment' (Liutongye kaimen ying dachao), *Essays on Commerce Economy (Shangye Jingji Wenhui)*, 5: 43–45.

Xu, Y. M. (1999) 'How do Japanese retailers play the China card?' (Riben lingshouye de zhongguo pai), *International Economic Cooperation* (*Guoji Jingji Hezuo*), 2: 29–32.

Yi, H. (1997) 'Makro: a golden egg-laying chicken' (Wan-ke-long: yizhi hui sheng qian de ji), *Science and Technology Think Tank* (*Keji Zhinang*), 12: 7–8.

Yip, G. S. (1992) *Total Global Strategy: Managing for Worldwide Competitive Advantage.* Englewood Cliffs, NJ: Prentice Hall.

8 International transfer of retail know-how through foreign direct investment from Europe to China

Amelia Yuen Shan Au-Yeung

Introduction

The extent and impact of retail internationalisation has become increasingly prominent in the last fifteen years. Internationalisation has appeared to be inevitable for those Fast Moving Consumer Goods (FMCG) retailers who desire to maintain a strong and competitive position in the marketplace. Owing to the opportunities offered in transitional economies in recent years, several Western FMCG retailers with their 'superior' retail expertise have ambitiously expanded their operation domains into these largely untapped markets. Modern Western retailing has evolved over a long period of time in Europe and North America, whereas structured retail development in transitional economies, such as China[1] and Central Europe, only began about a decade ago. Therefore, there is a gap in the level of retail development between the developed countries and the countries in transition. This provides retailers from developed countries with an opportunity to exploit the under-developed retail industry in transitional economies. Due to the differences in economic, social, cultural, technological and political conditions between the developed and the developing countries, retailers are confronted with many complications when they transfer their retail expertise from their developed domestic countries to the developing host countries. This is because their retail expertise is rooted in a specific set of underlying social, economic and political conditions and level of infrastructure development.

This chapter discusses what the transfer of retail know-how from a developed country to an emerging economy actually entails and examines the complications that European FMCG retailers encountered in their process of transfer. Particular attention is focused on the transfer of four aspects of retail know-how: retail formats, supply chain relationship management practice, supply chain information technology and human resource management policy. The first section presents an analytical framework of international flows of retail know-how. The next section investigates the retail environment in China. The third section analyses how these differences affect the transfer of retail know-how regarding the four aspects mentioned earlier. Problems encountered and the corresponding adjustments to their retail know-how by European retailers are also examined in this section. Drawing on these problems and adjustments, the final part of this section suggests

Table 8.1 Details of respondents interviewed

Location in China	Company	Position of respondents
Guangzhou	1	President, South China Region
Shanghai	2	Chief Operating Officer, Region Asia, Chief Executive Officer, Chief Purchasing Officer, food, Chief Purchasing Officer, non-food
Beijing	3	General Manager, China
Beijing	4	General Manager, Manager, Food commercial division

a conceptualisation of the kind of know-how on which adaptation should be made during the transfer process. The fourth section evaluates the impact of the transfer of European retail know-how on the local Chinese retail industry. The chapter concludes with some managerial implications for retail practitioners and suggestions for future research in the field of international retailing.

The geographical scope of the present study is confined to the three regions with the highest average disposable income in China, namely Beijing, Shanghai and Guangdong (mainly Shenzhen and Guangzhou).[2] Methodologically, this study adopts the case study approach that stresses 'the rigorous and fair presentation of empirical data' (Yin 1994: 2) and allows 'an investigation to retain the holistic and meaningful characteristics of real-life events' (Yin 1994: 3). Case studies with four leading European food retailers were conducted. Primary data were obtained from in-depth, semi-structured interviews and author's observation during store visits. Secondary data from newspaper, retail magazines, retailers' annual reports and journals were also used. The details of respondents of interviews are in Table 8.1. Due to confidentiality, all the names of the companies and respondents being interviewed in this chapter are pseudonyms.

Analytical framework: international flow of know-how

The concept of retail know-how

The term 'retail know-how' has not been well defined in the literature. Kacker (1988) defines it broadly as the business concepts, operating policies and techniques employed in a retail business in a given environmental setting. He further suggests that the term includes two elements: the managerial element, which embraces concepts, policies and systems; and the technical elements, which are the techniques employed in areas such as site selection and store layout. Drawing on Bucklin (1972), Betancourt and Gautschi (1990), Ghosh (1990), Goldman (1981), Hollander (1970), Kacker (1985, 1988), Mason and Mayer (1987) and Messinger and Narasimhan (1997), Goldman (2001), on the other hand, advocates that 'know-how' is one element of 'format' and 'offering' is the other element. 'Know-how' is the internal part of a retail format that determines a retailer's operational strength and strategic direction whereas 'offering' comprises the external elements that are related to the delivery of the functional, social, psychological, aesthetic and entertainment benefits that attract customers to stores. These conceptualisations of retail know-how are vague and inconsistent. Building from the existing literature, a more comprehensive concept of 'retail know-how' is presented in this chapter. Retail know-how identifies the main elements that define a retailer's strategy, which in turn determines the retailer's competitive position in a market. 'Retail know-how' can be used interchangeably with 'retail expertise'. The author identifies three components of retail know-how: retail technology, retail culture and retail format. The first two components are the internal characteristics of a retail organisation, with retail culture being the embedded characteristics and retail technology the explicit characteristics; while the third component is the visible characteristics of the outlets of the retailer (Figure 8.1).

Retail technology. Retail technology,[3] according to Goldman (2001), contains the systems, methods, procedures and techniques that a retail firm employs; and determines the firm's operational strength and strategic direction. Therefore, the author suggests that it comprises four areas. First, there is information technology, which a retailer uses to manage the flow of information, physical materials and finance throughout the whole supply chain. Second, there is supply chain relationship management, which is about selecting and negotiating with suppliers, and establishing and maintaining relationships with them. Site selection and store development is the third area. The fourth area is cash flow management, which is mainly about retail financial formula for different formats.

Retail culture. Goldman (2001) claims that retail culture consists of concepts, norms, rules, practices and experiences. It determines a retailer's ability to evaluate situations, identify trends and opportunities, and deal with problems.

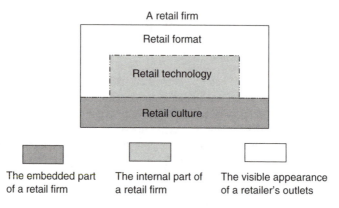

Figure 8.1 Three components of retail know-how.

A retailer must have a learning-oriented culture in order to be competent in these tasks. Organisational learning, which is defined as the capacity or process within an organisation used to maintain or improve performance through experience (Nevis *et al*. 1995), provides an approach for continuous adjustment of organisational issues and knowledge utilisation in a turbulent competitive climate (Kiernan 1993 and Stata 1994 in Morgan *et al*. 1998). Retailing is an industry directly interacting with consumers. With rapid development of technology and intensifying competition, together with rapid changes in consumers' taste, retailers could not sustain their favourable positions in the market without a continuous fine-tuning of the organisation and its processes. In other words, retailers could not survive in a turbulent competitive environment without a learning orientation.

The capacity to learn is termed organisational capability. Grant (1996a in Morgan *et al*. 1998) considers the concept of organisational capability within the boundaries of a knowledge-based view of the firm. He advocates that analysis of the organisation as an integrator of knowledge is an appropriate frame of reference for researchers to diagnose organisational capability. He further interprets it as a consequence of complicated assimilation of knowledge, where productive activity is a function of the firm's capacity to harness and integrate knowledge attributed to multiple individuals and groups. It is important to emphasise that organisational capability depends on the firm's mechanisms and processes of knowledge integration, not simply the extent of knowledge that individuals and groups possess *per se*.

Owing to the highly dynamic nature of the market environment, effective organisations are always loosely coupled in order to maximise the buffer effect between them and their environments. Organisational capability can act as such a buffer in the following four aspects (Morgan *et al*. 1998). First, learning activities are always designed and organised according to the predicted future circumstances with the aim of minimising the incidence and potential impact of serious environmental disturbances. Second, since learning organisations usually enjoy good relationships with suppliers, customers and related constituencies, an attitude of mutual accommodation is evidenced when anticipated problems arise. Third, flexibility within the learning organisation means that rapid company responses are possible in order to exploit and respond to emerging opportunities or threats. Finally, information usually flows efficiently within learning organisations and this leads to significant reduction of transaction costs and economies of information.

Retail format. Retail format is the third component of retail know-how. It is the physical elements of a retail outlet that are visible to consumers, such as assortment, store atmosphere, services inside the store, physical location and price. Simultaneously, each retail format comes with a specific cash flow and Return on Investment (ROI) management philosophy.

According to the above conceptualisation of 'retail know-how', the concepts of self-service and discounting within specialty retailing is an example of retail know-how and this retail know-how is manifested in the format of a category killer, such as ToysRUs. The concept of one-stop shopping, department-based store design, and a merchandise mix of soft and hard items is another example of retail know-how, which is transformed into the format of a department store.

The vehicle of flow

'Flow' is the movement of retail know-how from one enterprise to another within the same regions or between different regions (Kacker 1988). There are two different kinds of flow. A flow that is unplanned or incidental is called diffusion. Diffusion may take place during overseas business trips and in professional meetings or seminars. A flow that is planned and purposive is called a transfer. The vehicles of transfer include foreign direct investment, management contracts, franchising and supplies of equipment and support services. This chapter is concerned with foreign direct investment in retailing and therefore only retail transfer will be discussed.

The flow process: preconditions, problems and consequences

'No technology or innovation evolves in a vacuum' (Kacker 1988: 44). Retail technology or concepts are created to respond to human needs. Human needs, in turn, are shaped by a given social, cultural and economic environment. The development of retail technology, on the other hand, is constrained by dimensions such as information technology and political regulation. Retail know-how thus evolves in response to different contexts. Retailing know-how that is developed in an environment with a certain family size distribution, store patronage patterns, levels of retail industry growth, urbanisation and presence of supportive infrastructure may not be effective in an environment with different business conditions. In other words, the environmental dimensions of a host country affect the effectiveness of retail know-how transfer. Field investigation and analysis of secondary data reveal that the process of transfer of retail know-how may experience serious problems in the absence of certain preconditions or basic infrastructure (Kacker 1988). Consequently, a retailer may need to adjust the original retail know-how that they intend to transfer in order to adapt to the host environment.

Apart from the environmental dimensions, Goldman (2001) believes that the global position of a retailer also affects the adjustment of their retail know-how in the host country. When deciding how much adjustment to undertake during the process of retail know-how transfer, a retailer must consider the following four factors. The first factor is scale economies and standardisation that global sourcing of products and equipment, standardisation of operations, elimination of duplication and the global use of specialised skills can derive. The second factor is experience and learning that can be generated by operating in diverse environments. The third factor is global flexibility that enables retailers to move resources, expertise, innovative concepts and methods across countries. The last factor is specialisation that a retailer can enjoy by serving global segments.

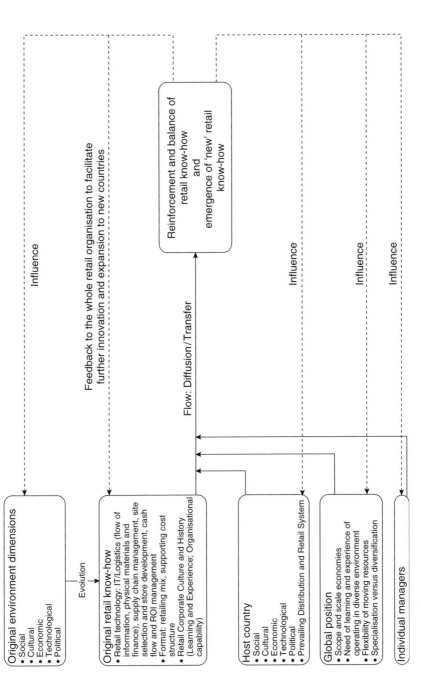

Original environment dimensions
• Social
• Cultural
• Economic
• Technological
• Political

Evolution

Original retail know-how
• Retail technology: IT/Logistics (flow of information, physical materials and finance), supply chain management, site selection and store development, cash flow and ROI management
• Format: retailing mix, supporting cost structure
• Retail Corporate Culture and History (Learning and Experience; Organisational capability)

Host country
• Social
• Cultural
• Economic
• Technological
• Political
• Prevailing Distribution and Retail System

Global position
• Scope and scale economies
• Need of learning and experience of operating in diverse environment
• Flexibility of moving resources
• Specialisation versus diversification

Individual managers

Influence

Feedback to the whole retail organisation to facilitate further innovation and expansion to new countries

Reinforcement and balance of retail know-how and emergence of 'new' retail know-how

Flow: Diffusion/Transfer

Influence

Influence

Influence

Figure 8.2 Analytical framework of international flow of retail know-how.

The environment of the host country and the retailer's overall strategy at the international level determine the extent of adaptation that a retailer undertakes in the host country. As a retailer continues to fine-tune their retail know-how in response to the environmental factors in the host country, 'new' retail know-how emerges. Following the tenets of organisational learning, this know-how should then feed back to headquarters in the home country to enhance the capabilities of the retailer as a whole and another flow cycle of 'new' retail know-how begins. Figure 8.2 presents an analytical framework of the international flow of retail know-how.

Retail environment in China: a market in transition

Economic reform in China has been underway for more than two decades. The aim of the economic reform is to transform the command economy into a new hybrid system: a socialist market economy with Chinese characteristics. This is said to be different from a fully fledged market economy. China can be considered to be a case of a semi-reformed planned transition economy. For example, collective farms still remain but the household-responsibility system emerging within them offers incentives similar to those of private farming. Responsibility capitalism is emerging in the field of service sector and small industry but domestic industry is still dominated by large state-owned enterprises that show most of the standard features of a command economy (Knell and Yang 1992 and Lardy 1991 in Lavigne 1995). The boom in the Chinese economy reflects the factors of genuine liberalisation and decentralisation in agriculture:

- the emergence of a new private sector;
- the opening up of the economy through current account convertibility of the currency; and
- the position of the country in the early stages of take-off.

Following this line, China is an economy that embraces both pure capitalism and aspects of standard socialism (Lavigne 1995). This is what the Chinese government calls a 'socialist market economy with Chinese characteristics'.

Retailing in China is also gradually moving towards modernisation and has remarkable prospects. Any study of retailing development in China during the last fifteen years will reveal a dramatic change. Nevertheless, the development of modern retailing is still affected by the legacy of the command economy.

Prior to economic reform, China, like other communist countries, was a shortage economy. Production and distribution of commodities were planned and monitored by the central planning bureau, the Ministry of Commerce and Ministry of Materials. Most of the marketing and distribution channels at that time were state-owned. Wholesaling and retailing existed merely for administrative purposes. In contrast with a market-led economy emphasising allocative and technical efficiency, a centrally planned, command economy treats equity as its primary concern. Production preference was given to those goods considered essential or basic to the health and well-being of the majority of the population. Luxury goods were supposed to be produced using extra capacity after the basic needs of the populace have been fully met. The aim of the distribution system was to ensure that goods were allocated according to need and were available to all who needed them. Consequently, there was very limited investment in product development and innovation. Product ranges were typically limited and life cycles were much longer than in a market economy. Products were engineered to cope with capricious supplies of capital and material inputs. There was hardly any incentive to design products to meet the needs of consumers. Systematic market research was almost unknown and was virtually precluded by the organisation of industry. The concept of customer service hardly existed (Mun 1988). As a result, today much of management in China suffers from a lack of a thorough understanding of market trends and changes, and the principles of pricing. They also have difficulties in organising a sales force and modern distribution channels that are fully customer oriented (Wortzel and Wortzel 1987).

There is also a lack of adequate supporting infrastructure for the development of modern retailing. For example, road and transportation infrastructure is not well developed, a consistent supply of electricity is not guaranteed and a well developed legal and regulatory system has yet to be seen.

Although profound changes in distribution structure, consumption behaviour and the environment for foreign-invested enterprises in retailing have been brought about by economic reforms, all the above problems still present challenges for the transfer of foreign retailers' know-how into China.

Transfer of retail know-how through foreign direct investment

Magnitude of transfer

As reported in China Daily, by the end of 2001, there were a total of 356 foreign retailers in China, with a total annual turnover of more than RMB52.6 billion (US$6.4 billion), which accounted for 4 per cent of China's total retail sales volume in that year (compared to 2.5 per cent for the year of 2000). Moreover, their purchasing volume in China in 2001 totalled RMB249 billion (US$30 billion), which equalled 12 per cent of the national volume of commodity exports. All these foreign-invested retailers made up 1 per cent of China's total foreign capital inflow by the end of 2001. In Shanghai alone, there were close to 100 foreign-Sino retail joint ventures and they accounted for 8 per cent of the turnover of the whole city. Furthermore, Shanghai had retail revenue of US$300 million through trade with multinational chain stores in 2000. In Beijing, the retail sales of foreign retailers during the first two months of 2001 equalled RMB1.07 billion (US$128.9 million), which contributed 4 per cent of the city's total retail sales of RMB26.89 billion (US$3.24 billion).

Out of the 356 foreign retailers, 29 enterprises entered China with state approval. Most of them originating from Asia and a few from Europe and North America.

Among them, Wal-Mart has successfully opened seven supercentres and one 'Sam's Club', with a total investment close to RMB905 million (US$113 million). Carrefour has opened 27 chain stores in 15 Chinese cities. Metro has opened 15 Cash and Carry outlets. Furthermore, Metro has successfully signed an official investment agreement to set up the Metro Warehouse Management Company, which is the first wholly foreign-owned wholesaler in western China. Further expansion of these retailers in terms of number of outlets and into different cities is expected. No officially published list of foreign retailers that have entered China is available to the public from the Chinese government. Based on the author's research, the major active foreign retailers in China are listed in Table 8.2.

Table 8.2 Foreign retailers active in China

Foreign retailer	Country of origin	Year of first entry	Retail format(s)
Auchan	France	2000	Hypermarket
Carrefour	France	1996	Hypermarket
Continent (Promodès)[a]	France	1999	Hypermarket
CRC	Hong Kong	1992	Supermarket
Daiei	Japan		Convenience Store
IGA (PRD)[b]	Hong Kong	1997	Supercentre
Ito-Yokado	Japan	1992[c]	GMS[d]
Jusco	Japan	1995	Department store with supermarket
EK Chor Distribution Company (CP Group)	Thailand	1997	Supercentre (Lotus)
Makro	The Netherlands	1992[e]	Cash and Carry
Metro	Germany	1996	Cash and Carry
Park'n Shop	Hong Kong	1988	Supermarket/Superstores
Royal Ahold[f]	The Netherlands	1996	Supermarket
Seiyu	Japan	1995	Department store with supermarket
Wal-Mart	USA	1996	Supercentre and Warehouse Club
Dairy Farm[g]	Hong Kong	1992	Supermarket/Convenience Store

Notes

a Promodès merged with Carrefour in August 1999.

b PRD stands for Pearl River Distribution. It is a company from Hong Kong and they bought the franchise of IGA, which is from USA, and operates in China.

c Ito-Yokado obtained a business licence in 1992 but opened its first retail outlet in China in 1996.

d GMS stands for General Merchandise Store. It is, basically, similar to a department store with a supermarket at the lowest level.

e Makro is one of the first two foreign retailers that obtained licences from the Chinese Central Government to set up chain stores. It obtained the licence in 1992.

f When the author was conducting her fieldwork in Shanghai in the summer of 1999, Ahold was undergoing restructuring. When the author attempted to contact them again in winter 1999/Spring 2000, it was found that they had closed their operations in China. Commentators suspected that this is due to the company's poor financial performance in China.

g Dairy Farm started managing supermarkets in Beijing inside 2 hotels in 1989. Its investment in China started with convenience store 7-Eleven in 1992 and then supermarket Wellcome in 1994. However, they withdrew its supermarket operation from China in 2000/2001 and decided to focus on its convenience store operation.

Process of transfer: problems and adjustments

Supply chain management. Based on the four case studies, there were four major problems with supply chain management in China. Each of these problems was identified by the four European retailers interviewed. These four problems were

- different distribution structure in China,
- difficulty in getting high quality products,
- late delivery due to both transportation infrastructure and suppliers' ability to deliver, and
- lack of a computerised stock control system on the supply side in China.

In China, foreign retailers have to go through the wholesale market and various agencies for fresh food. They cannot obtain fruit and vegetables directly from farmers. Nor can they deal directly with slaughter houses for meat. The wholesale market is the only legal means of distribution of fresh food to retailers. For many other products, retailers also have to go through agencies instead of dealing directly with manufacturers. According to the Chief Non-Food Purchasing Officer of Company 2, this is

> because of the existing distribution network system in China. When a manu-
> facturer tries to sell product in China, they cannot do it themselves because
> there are no national chains established yet. So, what they do is that in each
> city, they appoint dealers. Their dealers then have the authority to sell their
> products in that area. In the supply chain between manufacturers and retail-
> ers, there are many tiers. You will have a regional distributor, and then a lower
> level and then another lower level of distributors. This system of distribution
> has been running for the last twenty years. Before that there was the state-
> owned distribution system, which was also similar. You went to the provin-
> cial distribution network, then into the district and then the city level
> distribution network. Although the state-owned distribution system no longer
> exists, each vendor has their own distribution network. The dealers in
> Shanghai do not have the right to sell in say Nanjing because Nanjing is the
> territory of another dealer. The right to sell is exclusive. Therefore, when the
> foreign retailers come in, we still need to deal with these local networks
> although we are in the process of reducing the number of layers that we have
> to go through.

On the other hand, foreign retailers also claimed that controlling the quality of the products supplied was an important issue. They had to maintain very tight control on the quality of products at the receiving department where products were first delivered by the suppliers. This is especially the case for fresh food because the concept of a cold chain was not common among suppliers in China. There was no cooling system and technology in some slaughter houses and not all delivery trucks had freezers or refrigerators. Moreover, products sometimes did not arrive in the packaging specified by the retailers. Consequently, retailers had to check the quality and packaging of products, and the delivery temperature in the case of fresh food, very strictly when they arrived. Any item that did not match their quality and packaging requirements would be rejected. The Chief Operating Officer of Company 2 also mentioned that they needed to spend time and be patient in explaining to suppliers their requirements and educate them about the importance of quality. The Chief Food Purchasing Officer of the same company also claimed that many suppliers in China normally do not understand the importance of issues such as combined truck loads, pricing, quality and packaging.

The transportation infrastructure and system in China is another area that foreign retailers pay attention to, although late delivery is not too severe. According to the Chief Operating Officer of Company 2, transportation infrastructure is poor. The highway system is not well established although it is improving. Moreover, commercial transport, especially in Beijing, is limited to certain hours. Big trucks are not allowed on ring roads outside specified hours. Furthermore, the transportation industry in China is largely controlled by the army, according to the President of Company 1. All these factors make transportation of products from suppliers to retailers difficult. Consequently, retailers had to adjust their stock level very carefully, especially during festival periods. In addition, retailers may need to 'work around things' in China. Because of the distribution and transportation infrastructure, the president of Company 1 reported that he sometimes found transporting products with up to five tricycles was more economical and efficient than using trucks. He claimed that this did not make sense to him when he first worked in China but he was convinced at a later stage. Late delivery was also caused by lack of product on the manufacturers or suppliers side.

Another major issue with supply chain management is the poor quality of information technology (IT) utilised by local distributors. Local suppliers do not have the knowledge or the financial resources to invest in IT. Therefore, Electronic Data Interchange (EDI) could not be implemented by foreign retailers. According to the General Manager of Company 4, some of their suppliers did not even have fax machines. Multinational suppliers in China have the knowledge and financial resources to implement EDI but did not appear to be enthusiastic about investing in it, because the overall scale and number of retailers who have the capacity to do so in China is not significant enough to justify such investment.

Although the level of IT is low, many local suppliers are catching up. Many of them are implementing barcode systems on their products so that retailers can make use of EPOS system to better manage their retail performance.

Retail format. A strong correlation between internationalisation of a given form of retail activity and its success in the country of origin has been found (Tordjman and Dionisio 1991). Particular European countries appear to have acquired a distinctive competence in a particular form of retail distribution and that the types of operation that are exported are mainly market leaders in their country of origin. For example, French hypermarkets (such as Carrefour), German discount stores (such as Aldi), and Dutch and German cash-and-carries (such as Metro) are dominant concepts in their country of origin that have reproduced abroad the key factors in their success. Different types of retailing possess different competitive advantages. That of hypermarkets lies in their low costs and high productivity; that of discount stores lies in their reduction in cost through reduction in assortment and service; that of cash-and-carry on cost reduction through bulk purchasing and reduction in service.

All four European retailers in the author's sample claimed that adjustment on format was only made to assortments when they transferred their retail formats to China. They believed that their retail format was one source of competitive advantages and therefore the same rules and concepts relating to format are observed regardless of where they operate. Nevertheless, it was pointed out that assortment is different in different markets in order to fit market needs. For example, the CEO of Company 2 said that they only sold living fish from aquariums in China because Chinese people put much emphasis on freshness of food.

Human resources policy. Training for local staff was recognised to be very important by foreign retailers because there is no reservoir of experienced retail human resources available due to the legacy of the command economy. Training was provided both in-house and by headquarters or other overseas operations. All of the four European retailers stated that they sent local managerial staff abroad to learn about the retail system and appropriate management skills. The retailers interviewed claimed that their local staff were open minded, capable and willing to learn. Furthermore, they all believed that human resources are the most important factor underlying successful retailing. The President of Company 1 stated

> To me, human resources is probably the most crucial issue ... because when our company expands, we can find the site, put up the building relatively easily but we need competent people to run it.

The Chief Non-Food Purchasing Officer of Company 2 also pointed out that

> Basically, we (ourselves and our competitors) sell similar merchandise and the price is already down to the bone. There is no meat left. The thing that makes differences between our competitors and us is human resources. What type of people you have, how your people react to market changes and how they serve customers are very important. I believe that building up a team and make everyone in the team strong should be given the first priority.

The opinion of these two respondents implies that there is a tacit component of retail know-how that can only be developed and utilised when there is a reservoir of competent human resources. Without this tacit component, all fast moving consumer goods retailers will become almost homogeneous because the ultimate factor that differentiates one retailer from another is human resources. Therefore, food retailers should endeavour to develop their individual members in terms of responsiveness to consumer demands and market changes.

In order to develop human resources in the host country, experienced members of the organisation are needed. Consequently, expatriates are brought in. Apart from giving training to local staff, another important function of expatriates is to transfer the 'culture', 'style' or the 'personality' of the retail organisation into the foreign subsidiary. As mentioned before, this is the embedded underlying foundation from which unique retail technology and formats are developed. Therefore, ensuring an adequate transfer and preservation of its culture when foreign direct investment is undertaken is crucial to a retail firm.

At the commencement of a foreign subsidiary, there is usually a large proportion of expatriates at the management level. However, as expatriates are expensive and local people are usually more capable of understanding and being sensitive to local conditions, the proportion of local staff at the management level will gradually increase in time. All retailers interviewed disclosed that this was the case for them. Nevertheless, Company 1 and Company 2 specifically claimed that they would maintain the number of expatriates in the Chinese subsidiary reported at the time of interview, which was about 1 per cent of the whole workforce in the company at the time for both companies. The Chief Operating Officer of Company 2 emphasised

> We are not decreasing the number of expatriates here any more because we need to have some expatriates here to make sure that every store is run under the same 'store culture' and our core concept and style is maintained.

He and the General Manager of the same company further commented that their job is more about empowering local staff than running bureaucratic rules. Therefore, they pointed out that besides possessing adequate knowledge of and experience in the retail industry, expatriates should be open minded about different cultures, believe in trust and team building and seek to develop the staff members of the company. His view was that

> Expatriates should be open-minded, modest, willing to listen to people, learning oriented, and very importantly, able to work with people but not rule people.

In other words, the more important duty of expatriates is to develop a local team of people who possess the ability to understand local market conditions, swiftly respond to market changes and capitalise on unexpected opportunities and yet perpetuate the culture and style of the retailer.

Organisations ultimately learn via their individual employees improving their own mental models. By making these individual mental models explicit, new shared mental models are developed (Kim 1993). When a foreign food retailer launches its operation in a transitional economy, such as China, some standard procedures being adopted in the domestic country might not be appropriate in the host country. One example could be the selection of the food merchandise range and the size of packaging, because the eating habits of the Chinese are different from elsewhere. Adaptation is necessary and therefore, a branch in China would want to serve the link between the shared mental model of the headquarters and its actions in order to seize an opportunity. The implication of the link between organisational learning and individual learning is that emphasis should be placed on developing individual expertise at local levels and ways have to be found to make mental models of individuals explicit and transfer them into the organisational memory. This can be done by both formal and informal sharing of experience and knowledge between members in different overseas operations and headquarters. The Chief Operating Officer of Company 2 stressed the importance of this point

> I am a member of the board in our headquarters. Board members of operations from all over the world talk about their experience together regularly.

The General Manger of Company 4 explicitly pointed out that

> I have been working in many subsidiaries of our corporation in different countries and my past experience always helped when I had to develop a new operation in a new country.

When the experience gained and the knowledge developed from operations in one market is brought back to the headquarters and shared among operations across the world, the retail know-how of the whole corporation is enhanced and further international expansion of the company is facilitated. The General Manager of Company 2 claimed that

> Our corporation have specialists in almost all areas in retailing, such as purchasing and new store construction. They are responsible for all international projects. These specialists have very close contact with operations all over the world. They continuously accumulate experience in different countries, both developed and developing. Consequently, they continuously develop new retail expertise. As a result, they give very strong support to subsidiaries anywhere in the world. This support is crucial to the international expansion of our company.

Therefore, food retailers should appreciate the significance of developing a structure that can ensure effective assimilation of knowledge developed from its operations in different markets and creation of further retail expertise that can strengthen the corporation's capability for its international operations and expansions.

Implications: perpetuation versus adaptation

The discussion above illustrates that each of the two components of retail know-how, retail technology and retail format, further consists of a conceptual and an executive part. For example, in the reference to delivering products with tricycles, timely delivery of products is an important step towards avoiding stock-out in an outlet. Effective use of transportation for product delivery is crucial to keeping cost low. These are conceptual know-how that gives rise to competitive advantages over one's competitors. Some interviewees termed them 'core know-how'. Conceptual know-how is almost generic and hence should be transferred directly with hardly any modification.

Given the transportation infrastructure and other related conditions in China, which differs from that in Europe, using big trucks to transport products, which is perceived as the most sensible method in Europe, becomes inefficient and relatively more costly sometimes in the country. In such cases, adjustment to this method of transportation should be made. As the example indicates, transporting products with up to five tricycles was found to be more economic and efficient than using trucks in some cases. In other words, this is a better way to operationalise or, using some interviewees' terms, 'execute' the conceptual know-how mentioned in the last paragraph under some circumstances. Consequently, tricycle transporting instead of the normal practice of truck transporting becomes an executive know-how under certain circumstances in China. Executive know-how is dependent on the operational environment and therefore adaptation may be needed on such know-how during the transfer process. As discussed earlier, the experience of a foreign subsidiary in developing 'new' know-how should be

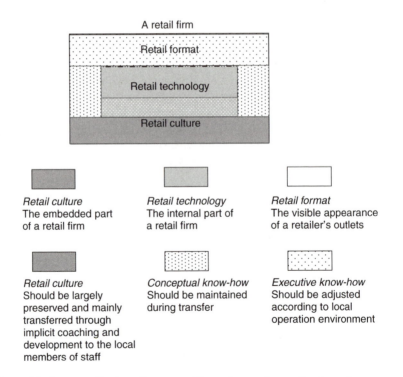

Figure 8.3 Conceptualisation of conceptual know-how and executive know-how.

shared among the entire organisation through an effective structure to enhance a learning-oriented culture, which in turn is conducive to further innovation in retail know-how to suit the ever-changing market.

During the transfer, the content and extent of adaptation of executive know-how depends on the experience, sensitivity, risk-averseness and innovativeness of the team of staff involved in the host country. As mentioned before, corporate culture gives rise to a unique personality of a retailer and retailers believe that this is what differentiates them from their competitors at a deeper level. Therefore, a firm should transfer their corporate culture effectively to the team in the foreign subsidiary so that the team's knowledge, sensitivity, risk-averseness and innovativeness align with those of the whole retail organisation (see Figure 8.3). It is because in this case, the content and extent of adaptation that a foreign subsidiary makes during the process of transfer will reflect the corporate culture and hence the personality of the firm will be preserved regardless of the adaptation made. The transfer of corporate culture, again, as pointed out earlier, is largely done through implicit coaching and development of local human resources by appropriate expatriates.

Impact of transfer on local Chinese retail industry

Before 1992, the distribution and retail sector in China was under-developed. In order to compensate for the lack of capital, technology and management techniques, the Chinese government partially opened the market to foreign retailers in 1992, in order to facilitate modernisation of distribution and retailing. There is no doubt that the transfer of retail know-how from Europe to China will benefit China in terms of its modernisation process in the long run. Nevertheless, in the short run, small local retailers suffer as a result of lack of competitiveness.

Although foreign retailers are still in the process of learning about the Chinese market and searching for the optimal way to serve the market, and that most retailers interviewed did not make any net profit at the time of interview, they have had some significant market effect on the retail industry in China. According to the 1999 Market Statistical Yearbook of China (China National Bureau of Statistics 1999), Metro Cash and Carry ranks the fourth among all chain store enterprises with a capital of RMB50 million (US$6.02 million) or above in China in 1998 in terms of annual sales. With only four outlets at the time, their annual sales in that year reached more than RMB2 billion (US$0.24 billion). In fact, three retailers interviewed believed that they were occupying good market positions in the cities in which they operated. The Chief Operating Officer of Company 2 claimed that they had a market share of about 16.5 per cent in the FMCG retailing sector in Shanghai at the time of interview. The General Manger of Company 4 believed that they were occupying either a first or second position in the retail sector in Beijing in terms of market share, while Company 1 were occupying third or fourth position in Guangzhou.

Due to their high volume of sales and favourable market positions, foreign food retailers have already started to induce changes in the retail industry in China.

One impact is that they have changed consumers' expectation regarding services, pricing and quality. They introduced a new experience of food shopping to Chinese consumers. Consumers are made aware that they could now purchase goods of high quality at a low price. Consequently, all the players in the field are compelled to improve the quality of products and services they offer and reduce their prices. As described by a practitioner in a non-European foreign retail firm in China.

> Players like Makro and Carrefour are influencing the market. They deal with suppliers everyday and the quantity they are talking about is big. They make a lot of joint promotions with the suppliers. Therefore, they always sell products at a discounted price. Their behaviour has become one of the factors to be considered in pricing decisions in the market. For example, if Carrefour today sells this product at 3 Rmb, it's not long before everybody else follows, because otherwise they are going to lose. Consumers are sensitive to these things. They believe that if Carrefour can sell it at such a low price while the product quality is maintained at a good level, all the other retailers should be able to, and should, do so as well.

However, the majority of local retailers do not have the financial and knowledge capacity to invest in and employ the 'Western' retail know-how and hence lose out in the competition. This has led to the development of animosity of some local retailers towards their foreign counterparts. Political opposition is one means through which they channel their animosity. For example, the Chief Non-Food Purchasing Officer of Company 2 reported that some small local retailers tried to create negative propaganda or complained to local government.

The proliferation of foreign retailers in China is highly likely to accelerate in terms of speed and importance as China's entry into the WTO promises gradual abolition of all restrictions on FDI in the retail sector within five years. This situation is conducive to a possible domination of foreign retailers in the retail and distribution sector. Some commentators believe that the Chinese government does not want such domination to happen and hence they further believe that the recent domestic retail restructuring processes in Beijing and Shanghai are backed by the government to guard against such domination (China World Trade Corporation 2000). The most notable domestic retail merger and acquisition was the one between Hualian and Xidan in 2001,[4] which aimed to create a large nation-wide retail organisation that would hopefully be competitive against foreign retailers in the country.

Foreign retailers' entry into China has induced strategic thinking and re-engineering among the major local retail organisations. As local retailers gather further momentum to catch up with modernisation and improvement in efficiency, an interesting interplay between local and foreign retailers is expected. This, together with the complicated interactions between different stakeholders related to the retail industry, such as governmental policy makers and consumers, will undoubtedly lead to the emergence of a new retail landscape in China.

Conclusions

This chapter discusses some of the major problems faced by foreign retailers during their transfer of retail know-how into China, and the root causes of these problems. Adjustments that foreign retailers have made are investigated. The implication is that retail know-how is continuously modified in response to the environmental factors that affect retail operations. Maintaining the conceptual retail know-how in the process of transfer is important but adjusting certain executive know-how such as assortments in stores to adapt to local situation and needs is also crucial. The author identifies the most important issue behind success as the development of competent human resources and the development of a learning orientation in the whole retail organisation. Development of expertise in internationalisation must be routinely included as part of retail human resource training and development. In order to achieve this, there needs to be a channel in international retail firms through which experience and knowledge that are developed are systematically built, stored, shared, utilised and continuously updated so that retail know-how can evolve appropriately and efficiently to suit the ever-changing retail environment.

Furthermore, this study demonstrates that cross-border transfer of retail know-how to a developing country has a very deep, wide and strong underlying impact on the host country's industrial structure in both the retail and other related sectors. The transfer process also carries profound repercussions on the cultural and social aspects of the host country. For instance, the process has been radically transforming consumers' expectation and lifestyle in China. In other words, cross-border transfer of retail know-how is not only a process of transferring know-how that is related to the retailing industry but also a process of transferring culture and lifestyle to a certain extent, especially when the recipient country is a developing country.

Notes

1 China in this chapter does not include Hong Kong Special Administrative Region and Macau.

2 According to the Chinese National Statistics Bureau 1999, the average disposable income in the urban area in Beijing, Shanghai and Guangdong in 1998 was RMB8471.98, RMB8773.10 and RMB8839.68, respectively. They are the highest among all the cities in China. The average disposable income in China as a whole in the same year was RMB5425.05.

3 The term 'retail technology' in this chapter does not only mean 'information technology'. This term is used to mean 'ways of doing things in various aspects of retailing'.

4 Hualian is one of the China's largest supermarket chains whereas Xidan is one of the most important department stores in Northern China. In order to remain competitive under the attack of the large international retailers, Hualian saw the urgent need of forming a joint-investment subsidiary with a renowned partner and concentrating on its supermarket business in the short run. The Xidan–Hualian alliance was forged on 3 February 2001. With the formation of this alliance, the group started a new phase of development and moved into Beijing soon afterwards. It also plans to open 6,000 outlets throughout China within five years with the aim of developing itself into a nation-wide retailing trust in the long run.

References

Betancourt, R. and Gautschi, D. (1990) 'Demand complementarities, household production, and retail assortments', *Marketing Science*, 9 (Spring): 146–61.

Bucklin, L. P. (1972) *Competition and Evolution in the Distribution Trades*. Englewood Cliffs, N.J.: Prentice Hall.

China National Bureau of Statistics (1999) *Market Statistical Yearbook of China 1999*, Beijing: China Statistics Press.

China World Trade Corporation (2000) *Chain Store must Prepare for WTO*. Online available from URL: http://www.chinawtc.com/chinaindustries3.shtml (accessed 20 April 2001).

Davies, K. (1993) 'The lure of one billion new customers: foreign investment in the retail sector of the People's Republic of China', *Working Paper 9301: Institute for Retail Studies, University of Stirling*.

Ghosh, A. (1990) *Retail Management*. Orlando, FL: The Dryden Press.

Goldman, A. (1981) 'Transfer of a retailing technology into the less developed countries: the supermarket case', *Journal of Retailing*, 57 (Summer): 5–29.

Goldman, A. (2001) 'The transfer of retail formats into developing economies: the example of China', *Journal of Retailing*, 77(2): 221–42.

Hollander, S. (1970) *Multinational Retailing*. East Lansing, MI: Michigan State University Press.

Kacker, M. (1985) *Transatlantic Trends in Retailing: Take-overs and Know How*. London: Quorum.

Kacker, M. (1988) 'International flow of retailing know-how: bridging the technology gap in distribution', *Journal of Retailing*, 64(1): 41–67.

Kim, D. H. (1993) 'The link between individual and organisational learning', *Sloan Management Review*, 35 (Fall): 37–50.

Lavigne, M. (1995) *The Economics of Transition: From Socialist Economy to Market Economy*. London: Macmillan.

Mason, J. B. and Mayer, M. L. (1987) *Modern Retailing: Theory and Practice*. 4th edn, Plano, Texas: Business Publications, Inc.

Messinger, P. R. and Narasimhan, C. (1997) 'A model of retail formats based on consumers' economising on shopping time', *Marketing Science*. 16(1): 1–23.

Morgan, R. E., Katsikeas, S. S. and Appiah-Adu, K. (1998). 'Market orientation and organisational learning capabilities', *Journal of Marketing Management*, 14(4): 353–81.

Mun, K. C. (1988) 'Chinese retailing in a changing environment'. In: Kaynak, E. (ed.) *Transactional Retailing*, pp. 211–26. Berlin: Walter de Gruyter & Co.

Nevis, E. C., DiBella, A. J. and Gould, J. M. (1995) 'Understanding organisations as learning systems', *Sloan Management Review*, 36 (Winter): 73–85.

The Asian Wall Street Journal (issues published between June 1991 and November 1997).

The China–Britain Trade Review (issues published between July 1993 and February 1998).

The Economist (issues published between January 1991 and September 1997).

Tordjman, A. and Dionisio, J. (1991) 'Internationalisation strategies of retail business', *Commission of the European Communities, DG XXIII, Series Studies*. Commerce and Distribution. 15.

Wortzel, H. V. and Wortzel, L. H. (1987) 'The emergence of free market retailing in the People's Republic of China: Promises and consequences', *California Management Review*, 29(3): 59–76.

Yin, R. K. (1994) *Case Study Research: Design and Methods*. London: Sage Publications.

9 The reform of the distribution system in China

Opening the system to the outside world

Han Jinglun

Introduction

China is the most populous developing country in the world with a population of 1.3 billion people. This makes up one quarter of all the world's consumers. For many years, before the 1980s, this large market offered few opportunities for international marketers. The reasons for this were:

- China operated a rigid command economy. From 1949 to 1978, the economy developed slowly, and China participated in little trade with the outside world. No foreign investment was allowed or invited in this period.
- Consumer incomes increased only slowly during this period, and Chinese consumer markets remained poor.

Under such circumstances the Chinese government was concerned with ways to reform its closed and rigidly planned economy, develop China's consumer market and raise the purchasing power of the consumers. Deng Xiaoping is credited with beginning this reform process in the late 1970s, turning China into what it terms a Socialist Market Economy. This was the beginning of the dramatic development of the Chinese consumer market after 1978. Since then, China's economy and its distribution system have changed and developed rapidly. According to Chinese Statistics, GDP in 1978 was RMB¥358.8 billion. By 1992, this had increased to RMB¥2,043.6 billion, a jump of 670 per cent. By 2000, again GDP continued to increase to more than RMB¥8,900 billion, a 400 per cent improvement on 1992.

In 1992, total retail sales were put at RMB¥1,099.4 billion, and was growing quickly, increasing 16.7 per cent over the previous year. The Statistics Bureau of the People's Republic of China (PRC) stated that retail sales growth was 20 per cent in 1994. During the period from 1995 to 2000, the annual average increase was 10 per cent. By 2000, retail sales were estimated at RMB¥3,047.3 billion.

In preparation for entry into the World Trade Organization (WTO) in 2001, the Chinese government relaxed and removed many of the tariff and non-tariff barriers to trade for numerous consumer and industrial products. Furthermore, it also promises to undertake a wide range of changes and reforms in its import regime, phasing out many internal trade regulations, import controls, quotas, licensing requirements and other restrictions, including those affecting service sectors such as finance, insurance, banking, telecommunications, transportation, the stock market and so on. The purchasing power of Chinese consumers has risen year after year and living standards are improving accordingly.

It is not surprising to find that China has become a market of considerable interest to overseas companies and particularly those from industrial nations. Many have undertaken considerable investment in China including a number of major retail companies. Many companies are currently in the process of examining and evaluating the structure and characteristics of the distribution system in China. The distribution system within such a geographically large and culturally diverse market makes market entry particularly challenging.

A historical review of the old distribution system in China

China's distribution system before the 1978 Reform

From 1949 to 1978, China operated a planned economy. In accordance with this philosophy, China structured its central distribution system and marketing channels into three levels. Within this structure, products were distributed from the manufacturers to the retailers and then to the consumers through three levels of wholesalers, specifically provincial, municipal and district level wholesalers (see Figure 9.1).

Characteristics of the pre-Reform system

The characteristics of this system were as follows. All types of products were produced by the state-owned agents (enterprises) at different levels. At the same

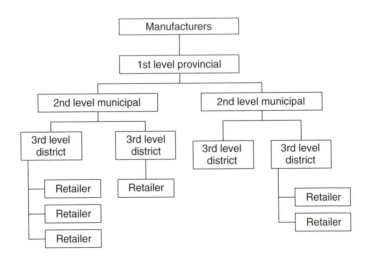

Figure 9.1 Traditional pre-Reform distribution channels in China.

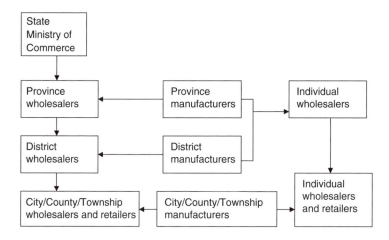

Figure 9.2 The dual distribution system.

time, the majority of product types were distributed by state-owned wholesalers from the state level down to the lowest administration level.

The distribution structure of this system consisted of two types of organizations (see Figure 9.2). In the first type were planning and administrative organizations. They included State Ministry of Commerce, Provincial (municipal) Commercial Bureaus, the District Commercial Offices and the City or County (township) Commercial Offices. All these organizations were responsible for providing information for the formulation of the state economic plan and also responsible for coordinating all business activities among organizations.

The second type was the operational organization. These operational organizations were the wholesale stations within the ministerial system. They included four grades of so-called wholesales stations, called Grade 1, 2, 3 and 4. These four grades of wholesale stations were responsible for, first, implementing the mandatory economic plan and, second, dispatching products at different levels of administration from the state level down to the township level.

The nature of ownership for pre-Reform distribution organizations

In general, there were three types of distribution network in China before 1978, namely state owned, collective and private owned. It was the state-owned distribution networks that monopolized the distribution system and commercial channels before 1978. Collective-owned distribution networks were small and less important. Private-owned distribution networks were negligible, and largely abandoned during the Cultural Revolution. The distribution system and commercial channels before the Reform were rigid. Their efficiency was low.

The disadvantages of the planned distribution system

Until 1978, the pre-Reform distribution system within the planned economy was based on three levels of wholesalers (Figure 9.3). Products from manufacturers were transported to first-level wholesalers in the large cities like Beijing, Shanghai and Tianjin for intra-provincial sale. They were then distributed to second-level wholesalers in municipal districts. Retailers in cities were at the end of the distribution channels. Product was distributed according to 'need and equal availability' to provide for the 'health and well-being' of the population. This channel for delivering products through two or three wholesale units is shown in Figure 9.3 by arrows that represent economic links and the route of products from producers to retailers.

Under the centrally planned economy, all trade was organized by the Ministry of Commerce although different consumer goods had different administrative channels. For example, packaged food products came under the Corporation for Tobacco, Sugar and Wines. The retail level followed the administrative division of distribution so that packaged food products and staple food such as oil

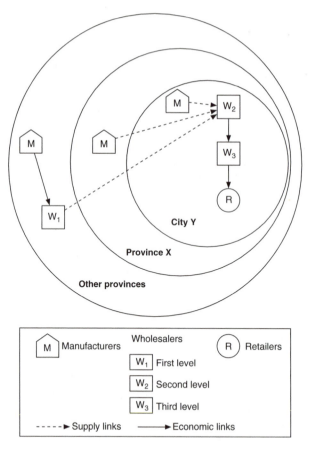

Figure 9.3 Distribution channels in the centrally planned economy before 1978.

and rice were sold in different retail outlets. In such cases, the planned nature of production and distribution was centred upon a specific physical and administrative base. Naturally, none of the actors within the system were required to compete for survival.

Under these circumstances, the disadvantages of this distribution system are clear.

- This system was highly rigid. First, the scope of business was determined according to the centralized economic plan. Secondly, marketing channels were operated within a narrow and specific territory. Thirdly, all distribution activities were monopolized by state-owned commercial units. Although there were still some collective-owned distribution channels, these do not play a major role in delivering products to market.
- The efficiency of the system was low throughout. The consumer market was served via central planning or, in other words, a top-down approach. The allocation of production and distribution quotas was decided in accordance with the central government's priorities. Market forces were restrained and suppressed, and there was no competition allowed among producers, wholesalers and retailers in the system.

The reform of China's distribution system

China's economic reforms began in 1978 and have now continued for almost twenty-five years. These economic reforms have changed the lives of Chinese consumers, not least through the development of a new form of distribution system in the country.

The four stages of reform of the distribution system

In the command economy before 1978, both the wholesale and retail sectors in China were under the control of the Ministry of Commerce and the Ministry of Materials and Equipment. Those Ministries planned and monitored the operation of the distribution system and distribution channels. Wholesaling and retailing were essentially administrative matters and concerned with the physical process of delivering products to consumers. Beginning in 1978, and continuing to the present, measures have been taken to reform the rigidity of the distribution system. This reform has gone through four major stages as described in the following sections.

Stage one (1978–1985)

During this stage, the initial reforms were made which were required to establish enterprise autonomy within a non-planned economic system. First, efforts were made to establish a new commodity circulation system, within which state-owned commerce operated as the leading player. At the same time, collective organizations were encouraged to develop within certain limits. Individuals, or in other words private businesses, were allowed to engage in activities in the distribution system for the first time. Moreover, efforts were also made to establish a new city-based wholesale system consisting of multiple channels, but with fewer intermediate links. This system was established to provide a comprehensive network to deliver goods smoothly between different provinces, cities, districts, counties and towns.

Secondly, according to the '10 Regulations' promulgated by the State Council in May 1984, the Chinese government decided to delegate more rights to the various enterprises. These included financial control, planning and operations, fixing and regulating prices for some goods, personnel autonomies and rights to individual workers and staff. By doing so, enterprises could now sell their own products and also products in excess of state targets. And at the same time, they could explore new markets and had the freedom to select their customers and middlemen.

Stage two (1986–1988)

During this stage, a production contract system was introduced between government and enterprises and much more was done to change distribution channels from a vertical linkage system to a horizontal one. In the end, a dual distribution system was set up. Under the new system, manufacturers could sell their products to the state as stipulated in the production contract. In addition, they were also allowed to sell their products directly to state-owned and collective-owned wholesalers or retailers, or even to private retailers in the free market in certain places. This dual distribution system offered horizontal connections to different enterprises which helped to promote and distribute products to the markets in different levels. It was also good for removing and eliminating bureaucratic and geographical barriers in China's distribution channels.

Stage three (1989–1991)

Much progress was made in the reform of distribution in China until 1989. However, problems such as inflation, corruption and economic and political privileges continued to create barriers to free and fair trade. The Chinese government decided to take further measures to attempt to solve some of these problems. For example, government organizations at all levels were required to relinquish control of some prices for different goods and to enlarge the role of supply and demand in setting prices. In addition, more steps were taken to create a competitive distribution environment by reducing intermediate links in distribution channels, establishing more markets and introducing various forms of regional economic cooperation. As a result, China was able to reduce the inflationary pressure on some prices and provide the basis for the most recent stage of reform.

Stage four (1992 to present)

The most recent stage of reform was announced at the Third Plenary Session of the 14th Central Committee of CPC during Deng Xiaoping's inspection tour of southern China. Maintaining its goal of establishing the so-called Socialist Market Economy, China announced a significant opening of its markets to the outside world. Further reform of the distribution system was a key part of this latest policy, and consisted of the following measures.

First, a new ministry was established called the Ministry of Domestic Trade. This was created through the merger of the former Ministry of Commerce and the Ministry of Materials and Equipment. The formation of this new ministry allowed a more unified policy leadership, simplified commercial organization, strengthened regulations for the distribution system, the basis for further on-going reforms and changes.

Secondly, the structure of distribution channels was re-organized into two levels: national level and local level. Several large-scale wholesale centres were established and a greater diversity of economic elements was allowed, providing the opportunity for more privately and semi-privately owned commercial enterprises. The retail sector was, for the first time, opened to foreign investors. Joint ventures between Chinese and overseas companies were permitted to sell their products within the domestic market.

Thirdly, and related to this last point, the right to undertake import and export business was extended. More enterprises and research institutions were allowed to trade directly with overseas organizations, whereas earlier, the right to handle imports and exports was confined to strictly limited companies as designated by the State.

After these measures were taken, China's commercial system and its distribution channels became more flexible. State-owned commercial enterprises were given more autonomy in terms of their business scope, pricing, staffing and the distribution of profits or responsibility for losses. Their wholesale power over distribution activities was declining gradually while that for collective and private commercial enterprises was increasing steadily. Collective and private commercial enterprises, wholesalers and retailers became more motivated and began to play a more important role in the distribution system. In addition, several international enterprises soon entered the Chinese market and currently are taking an active part in China's distribution system and channels. At this stage, different commercial entities with different kinds of ownership have begun to compete nearly on the same footing in the same market.

The present situation of distribution channels in China

Great changes have taken place in China's distribution system and its commercial channels during a period of over twenty years of reform. The old rigid centralized distribution system is being replaced by a structured, flexible, more efficient and diversified distribution system with multiple types of ownership. This new system is tailored to the principles of a socialist market mechanism.

It goes without saying that any changes in a country's economic structure and its commercial system will bring opportunities and challenges for distribution activities. China's market has been changing from formerly being a 'sellers' market' to becoming a 'buyers' (customers') market'. Compared with the old distribution system in China, the new one shows some specific characteristics and continued improvement.

Multiple forms of enterprise ownership exist in the distribution system

In the ownership of enterprises, there are multiple forms of industrial, agricultural and commercial enterprises, namely state-owned, collective, private and foreign-funded enterprises. Private commercial enterprises are encouraged to develop while foreign-funded commercial enterprises are allowed to operate with some freedom within the distribution system. All these enterprises are now competing on a nearly equal basis in the market.

Different players in distribution sectors

In different distribution sectors, channel design and management activities have been dramatically re-shaped with the emergence of many new channels and channel members of different types. The dealership system has been introduced in major cities, such as Guangzhou, Shanghai, Beijing, Tianjin and in provincial capital cities. In urban areas, many industrial manufacturers such as garment makers and household appliance producers rely on these middlemen to distribute their products to retailers and consumers. In the coastal cities there are a lot of jobbers from inland provinces who take an active part in distributing products to the retailers and consumers in the more remote and less-developed provinces and regions.

Retailers have more power in marketing channels

Channel power is no longer in the hands of state-owned wholesalers although the state-owned distribution system and channels still function under more flexible and efficient rules. With the shift of channel power from suppliers to retailers, there are many powerful retailers emerging in Chinese marketing channels. These have the freedom to purchase products from different manufacturers or wholesalers, and to sell products to customers in different places. Therefore, with more outlets, they have more power to challenge state-owned manufacturers and wholesalers, to make good use of their ability to control the selling space and to get favourable buying terms.

The role of private channel members is increasing

In China's distribution system at present, there is already a large number of private enterprises involved in all aspects of distribution from manufacturer to retailer. They control their own channels and scope of business activities with more effective and efficient ways. This is a factor to which more attention must be given.

Table 9.1 Number of supermarkets in Asia-
        Pacific countries

Country	Number of supermarkets
China	51,470
Japan	20,830
Australia	5,400
Korea	2,460
Taiwan	1,380
New Zealand	1,200
Hong Kong	690
Philippines	630
Indonesia	530
Thailand	450
Malaysia	360
Singapore	160
Asia-Pacific excluding China	34,090

Overseas joint venture enterprises function in China's distribution channels

At present, there have been some joint venture department stores, retailers and supermarket outlets. Overseas operators offer high technology, good quality merchandise, capital, qualified personnel and advanced management, and more experience in distribution sectors. Through these abilities these members provide opportunities and, at the same time, challenges for the domestic distribution system.

China's distribution system already offers well organized, structured, highly efficient and smooth network and infrastructure, with multiple organizational types and different kinds of wholesalers and retailers with different markets. Retail formats include shopping centres, large department stores, grocery and chain stores. The current market makes it convenient for international manufacturers to sell their products to Chinese end-users. Each of the above-mentioned channel members has been developing quickly compared with other countries in Asia (see Table 9.1). There are 50 per cent more supermarkets in China's cities and towns than in eleven other Asia-Pacific countries combined.

Any one of the various existing operators and networks in China can be used as an effective and reliable channel for international manufacturers to distribute their products, either through direct or indirect channels (see Figure 9.4).

The opening of China's distribution system to the outside world

China's policy to open more to the outside world has been a motivating force in reforming China's distribution system and channels. Introducing foreign capital

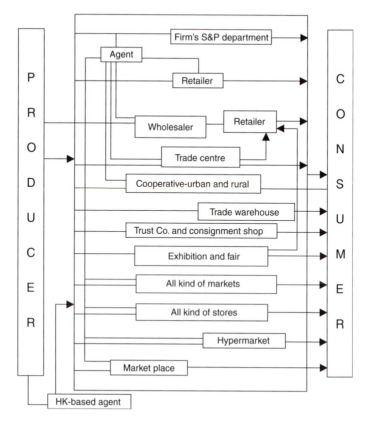

Figure 9.4 Distribution channels in China for consumer products.

in the distribution system has played an important role in the innovation of business types and operations.

The process and achievements of opening China's commercial sectors

It is said that the first international commercial enterprise to enter China was the Yaohan Department Store, a Japanese company, which signed a Cooperative Agreement of Intention with Shanghai First Department Store in 1991. This is regarded as the prelude for China's commercial sector to initiate an introduction of foreign capital into the distribution system.

Strictly speaking, a formal opening to the international investors was only initiated in 1992. In July of 1992, the State Council of the PRC made 'the Written Instructions Concerning Issues of Utilizing Foreign Capital in Commercial Retailing Sectors'. The above 'Written Instructions' stated that investing in the retailing sector was allowed only in the six big cities of Beijing, Shanghai, Guangzhou, Tianjin, Dalian and Chingdao, and in five large Special Economic Zones of Shenzhen, Zhuhai, Xiamen, Shantou and Sanxia (Three Gorges).

According to this Written Instruction, one or two trial retail enterprises could only be established through joint venture or cooperative venture. In such an agreement, the Chinese side must hold 51 per cent or more of the total shares of the investment. In addition, these retail enterprises were not allowed to operate wholesale businesses. The amount of commodities imported from abroad was restricted to a maximum of no more than 30 per cent of total sales. At that time, foreign investors were required to obtain a business license from the Ministry of Foreign Economy and Trade after they had first applied to the Ministry of Planning which was then further approved by the Ministry of Economy and Commerce.

In June 1999, China promulgated the regulations of 'the Trial Methods for Foreign Investors to Invest in Commercial Enterprises'. In accordance with these regulations, the opening areas for retail businesses are extended from the original six large cities and five large special economic zones to all provincial capitals, capitals of autonomous regions, cities under direct supervision of the Central Government and planned, separated-list cities. At the same time, foreign investors were permitted to operate wholesale business for their own imported products.

Encouraged by these new regulations, a large number of foreign investors have come to China to invest in wholesale and retail businesses as shown in Table 9.2. By the end of 2000, the number of Sino-foreign retail joint ventures formally approved at State level had reached 28. In addition, there were another 277 Sino-foreign retail joint ventures approved by local authorities. The total value of investment was estimated at US$2.0 billion (Ministry of Domestic Trade 2001). According to estimates from the Ministry of Domestic Trade three years after

Table 9.2 Major international retail enterprises entering China

Company	Country	Entry	First store	Number of stores (2000)
Yaohan	Japan	1991	1991, Shenzhen	Merged with China's Friendship Group
Seven-Eleven	Japan	1992	1992, Shanghai	26
Carrefour	France	1993	1995, Beijing	26
Daiei	Japan	1994	1995, Tianjin	14
Metro	Germany	1995	1996, Shanghai	8
Jusco	Japan	1995	1995, Guangzhou	4
Makro	The Netherlands	1996	1996, Guangzhou	4
Wal-Mart	USA	1996	Shenzhen	8
Auchan	France	1997	1998, Shanghai	1
Ahold	The Netherlands	1997	1997, Shanghai	50
Ito-Yokado	Japan	1997	1998, Beijing	1
IKEA	Sweden	1998	1998, Shanghai	2

Source: Research Institute of Circulating Economy (1999).

China was admitted to enter WTO, restrictions relating to international commercial enterprises in terms of operating area, number, ratio of shares and forms of operation will be abolished completely. As a result, international commercial enterprises have a bright future in China.

One example is Carrefour, currently the second largest retailer in the world. It entered China in 1995, and by 2000 operated 27 stores in Beijing, Shanghai, Tianjin and other large cities. Five stores were added in 2000, and Carrefour had plans to open at least another eight stores in 2001. The business volume for Carrefour in China is estimated at RMB¥8.0 billion for 2000 (Nanfang Daily 2001) Carrefour is already the third largest retail business in China.

International commercial enterprises entering China

It can be concluded that all successful international commercial enterprises entering China have pursued a strategy of adapting to global markets. On the other hand, it is equally clear that these same companies have had to implement a policy of localization in China. Some of the most important problems and solutions facing overseas retailers in China are summarized in the following sections.

Selecting the appropriate format

When international commercial investors first came to China, department stores were the primary choice as cooperative partners. More recently, international retailers have focused their attention on new and less well established formats, particularly supermarkets, general merchandise stores, hypermarkets, membership wholesale clubs and other forms of chain store operations. Anecdotal evidence suggests that these newer formats account for two-thirds of total overseas retail company sales volume. Department stores, however, have declined.

Advanced managerial techniques

International retailers and other commercial enterprises have significant advantages as compared to domestic competitors. These advantages exist in operational management, market positioning and customer targeting, merchandising, customer information systems, material and product flows, and customer relationship management systems. International commercial enterprises also pay more attention in combining these competitive advantages with specific features of the local market.

One example of this is the Dutch cash and carry wholesaler Makro. The company is said to be highly successful in China (Zhai 2001), but initially experienced problems with slow payment systems operated by Chinese manufacturers and suppliers. Because the Makro cash and carry system guarantees immediate payment once Makro takes title to merchandise, local Chinese manufacturers and suppliers have been happy to work with Makro.

Long-term commitment to the market

Blessed with abundant capital funding and skilled management, the majority of international commercial enterprises entering China are currently implementing a long-term strategy approach to China. This reflects confidence in the political and business future of China as a whole, as well as recognition of the great opportunities within such a large consumer market.

Many international companies have employed an aggressive pricing strategy, and this has proved highly successful. Carrefour, for example, opened its first superstore in Beijing in 1995. The store proved very popular for three months, with long waiting times to enter the store and at cash registers. The majority of merchandise on offer at Carrefour was manufactured in China, but prices were lower than local domestic competitors. While Carrefour initially makes less profit through this approach, in the long run, it wins more customers and aims for profitability.

As China prepared for entry into the WTO, the commercial environment and distribution system became much more attractive to international commercial enterprises, and many are already operating and well established in the Chinese market. I believe that all international commercial wholesale and retail enterprises should continue to actively invest in China and continue the pace of expansion within the market.

Conclusion

Great changes have taken place in China's distribution system and distribution channels since the beginning of the 1978 Reform. Over time, the distribution system has adapted and changed, and continues to improve. The organizational structure and functions of state-owned wholesale and retail enterprises in China's distribution system were rigidly enforced before 1978. These same enterprises which were recently part of the planned economy system are now becoming more flexible, efficient and customer-oriented. International investors in commercial business will rely on these enterprises in order to achieve a rapid entry into China's distribution system because state-owned wholesalers and retailers are more reliable.

Collective and private wholesale and retail enterprises are also playing a more important role. These enterprises will make an increasing contribution to the reconstruction and establishment of a customer-oriented distribution system in China. International investors can also take advantage of these non-state enterprises, although their influence in the market is more limited.

China gained membership of the WTO in 2000. Membership will bring opportunities for China's enterprises in commercial and distribution fields. Undoubtedly, one of the biggest challenges facing domestic enterprises will be competition with international companies. In the long term, this is a challenge they should meet without difficulty. Through competition, domestic enterprises in commerce and distribution will learn how to combat overseas entry, but there will be enough opportunity for both domestic and international firms within the market. So far, total sales volume for all the overseas funded retailers account for only

10 per cent of the market (Anon 2001). It will take time for international retailers to accumulate larger market shares, and, despite some predictable domestic opposition, domestic companies probably have little to fear in the long run. Even if international firms do come to account for 20 or 30 per cent of the market, it is only a matter of time before domestic firms come to the fore.

For international investors in China's distribution system, immediate and rapid investment is the obvious and preferable strategy. Without strong growth early on, international companies will increasingly find it difficult to compete with domestic competitors.

References

Anon (2001) 'Makro case study', http://7158.com.cn/qhsz1.htm

China Statistical Publishing House (1999) *China Statistical Yearbook (1999)*. Beijing: China Statistical Office.

Davies, Howard (1995) *China Business: Context & Issue*. Hong Kong: Longman Asia.

Gronroos, Christian (1999) 'Internationalization strategies for services', *Journal of Service Marketing*, 13(4/5): 290–7.

Han, Jinglun (1987) 'On the changes and future development trend of China's market', presented at the 16th EMAC Annual Conference, Toronto, Canada, June.

Han, Jinglun (1990) 'On China's investment environment', *Journal of China's New Information*, 3(7/9): 8–12.

Han, Jinglun and Mayer, Charles (1990) 'Performances of the joint ventures: 6 cases from Tianjin'. In: C. Engholm (ed.) *The Development of China's Industry*, JAI Press, 1(B), pp. 263–75.

Han, Jinglun (1994a) *The Magnificent Spectacle of the Global Trade Warfare: A War of Century without Bloodshed*. Tianjin: Tianjin Social Science Research Institute.

Han, Jinglun (1994b) 'China's economic reform and opening to the outside world', Working paper, Nankai University.

Han, Jinglun (1994c) *Service Marketing: The New Battlefield for Enterprise Competition*. Tianjin: Tianjin People's Publishing.

Han, Jinglun (1998) *The Most Current International Business*. Tianjin: Tianjin University Press.

Han, Jinglun (2000a) *International Trade Theory and Practice*. Tianjin: Nankai University Press.

Han, Jinglun (2000b) *The Road to Prosperity for the Maple Leaf Nation: Canadian Trade and Investment Strategies*. Guiyang: Guizhou People's Publishing House.

Ho, David and Leigh, N. (1994) 'A retail revolution', *China Business Review*, 21(1): 22–8.

Li, Zunyang (2001) 'On the development trend of China's retailing business', *China Chain Store Almanac 1990–2000*, China Commerce Publishing House, pp. 173–80.

Ministry of Domestic Trade (2001) http://finance.sina.com.cn/b/20010815/95692.html

Nanfang Daily (2001) 'Carrefour sales', *Nanfang Daily*, March 2.

Polsa, Pia (1998) *The Distribution of Consumer Goods in the People's Republic of China: An Empirical Study of Packaged Food Products*, Swedish School of Economic and Business Administration, Finland.

Zhai Bian (2001) 'The marketing position of Macro', *China Business and Trade*, 2.

10 The role of government in creating competitive advantage in the globalized economy

The case of Shanghai, China

Wen Hong and Roger C. K. Chan

Introduction

Among the big cities in China, Shanghai is always a topical research area because of its glorious history, its strategic location and the leading role it plays in China. Shanghai's prime strength centers on its location. Situated at the connection node of the Yangtze River and China's coastline, the city provides a gateway to a market of some 400 million people (Zhao and Zhang 1998) and, concurrently, an outlet for their produce to the Asia-Pacific region and beyond. Its development history can be traced back to 1842 when it became a treaty port and was opened to the outside world. Through providing the window between central China and the outside world, Shanghai developed rapidly from a small village into one of the world metropoli. By the 1930s, Shanghai was the premier center of trade, transport and industrial venture, and also a financial center or banker both internationally and domestically.

The fate of Shanghai changed dramatically after the liberation of China by the Chinese Communist Party. It paid a heavy price under the central command economy, the "Close-Door" policy, and the ideology of transforming it from a "consuming" city into a "productive" one. Shanghai had to accommodate to a narrower focus centered on heavy industry, and lost its leading position in the world hierarchy.

China's economic reform and opening to the outside world ushered in a new era for Shanghai and China. Since 1979, the central government has introduced reform policies to liberalize gradually the highly command economic system, increase the role of the market in the circulation of goods, services, capital and labor force, and reopen China to the outside world. China's economy is rapidly integrating with the world economy since then. Foreign Direct Investment (FDI), in the form of joint ventures, cooperative projects and wholly foreign-owned enterprises has increased rapidly. By the end of 1995, China became the second largest destination for FDI in the entire world after the USA (Wu 2000a). Its total export value in 1997 reached more than US$200 billion, which made it the eighth largest exporting country (Chai 2000).

As China is playing an increasingly important role in the world economic system, Shanghai is brought into a new development stage. In 1990, as the key of the overall reform strategy, the central government decided to open Pudong, the eastern part of Shanghai, and declared that "...we should open more cities along the Yangtze River, while concentrating on developing and opening the Pudong Area of Shanghai. We want to make Shanghai one of the international economic, financial and trade centers as soon as possible and to bring about a new leap in economic development in the Yangtze Delta and the whole Yangtze Basin." (Chai 2000). Shanghai has witnessed great development since then, which is the focus of the economic reform and development of the whole country throughout 1990s. Its GDP in 1999 is more than five times of that in 1990, with a yearly average growth rate of about 20 percent. In the coming decade, according to its development proposal, Shanghai will catch up with other international metropolitan cities in Southeast and East Asia, like Hong Kong and Singapore.

Re-examining Shanghai's development process in the 1990s, it can be found that the most marked characteristics shaping its urban transformation are the interplay between the forces of government and market, and the interplay between local and global forces. First, China's economic transition from a centrally planned economy to a market-oriented one undoubtedly underlies all of the processes effecting urban change in Chinese cities today. Market forces are becoming an indispensable part in decision-making and shaping Shanghai's economic and spatial transformation. On the other hand, the liberalization of state control makes the local government more self-determinant, contrasting with the pre-reform situation when they were the passive agents of central government (Wang 1988). Local government plays a leading role in Shanghai's economic transformation. The continuous reform and economic liberalization raise the fundamental question of what would be a proper role of government and market, and how should they interact with each other to revitalizing Shanghai's economy?

Second, through revitalizing its role as a node connecting the Yangtze River Basin and the outside world, Shanghai is taking new function and new responsibility in the urban system in both local and international terms. Internationally, the impact of Transnational Corporations (TNCs) and FDI on Shanghai's economy has been becoming more and more significant. From 1990 to 1999, the accumulated FDI in Shanghai reached US$410.4 billion (Statistical Yearbook of Shanghai 2000). The contribution to industrial output of foreign or Sino-foreign joined enterprises rose from 15.5 percent in 1993 to 47.2 percent in 1998 (Tang and Luan 2000). The global forces, however, should be seen as a triggering factor rather than a determinant of urban change in Shanghai (Wu 2000a). Shanghai has a tight economic connection with the Yangtze Region and the whole nation. Its industrialization process before the 1990s mainly relied on domestic markets. Such a local connection continues to influence its development from 1990 onwards. Eng (1997) argued that Shanghai is different from the cities in the Pearl River Delta where external influences are dominant. Instead, both global and local forces are imperatives for urban change in Shanghai. With China's entry into WTO, which will integrate it with the global economy to an unprecedented degree, Shanghai as a leading city will no doubt become the "bridgehead" for TNCs to set up their operations in China, with a view to exploring its huge market.

The interplay and even conflict between the global and local forces may even become more complicated. Then, what would be the proper strategy for Shanghai to participate in the new International Division of Labor? What can government do to create and sustain its competitive advantage in the international competition?

While considering the answers to these questions, this chapter begins with an explanation of why some nations can achieve a higher niche in the urban hierarchy formed in the international competition. It then examines what government can do and how it interacts with the market in the process of upgrading a nation's position in the hierarchy. This discussion is then applied to Shanghai. The chapter concludes with some policy suggestions and planning implications about appropriate role of government in creating competitive advantage in the globalized economy.

The global context

Globalization

The most significant development in the world economy during the past few decades has been the increasing globalization of economic activities (Dicken 1998). Major cities in the world are being integrated into a global network through the flow of commodities, information, capital and people. The specificity of any particular territory as a unit of production and consumption is thereby being undermined as the world economy becomes increasingly interconnected and interdependent (Borja and Castells 1997).

At the heart of globalization are the technological innovation and the change of international trade pattern. First, the last century has witnessed an undeniable technological revolution mainly based on information technologies. While facilitating the flow of resources, technology becomes the vital element deciding a country's competitive advantage and then its position in the New International Division of Labor (Castells 1989; Porter 1990; Dicken 1998; Mascitelli 1999).

Second, the lowering of national barriers through international trade agreements, the formation of trading blocs and interregional alliances, and the deregulating of markets within and between nations, are other driving forces that further increase the competition between cities for providing goods and services for the world market (Brotchie *et al.* 1995). TNCs become the main players in the globalization process, locating their production activity outside their home base to tap into cheaper land, labor force and market place. FDI has thus become a fashionable and often-quoted concept for the purpose of reflecting the extent of integrating with the global economy of a particular state (Chan 2000).

These two groups of driving forces push the processes of economic integration and intensified international competition, by which the relative importance of cities in the global hierarchy is changing. Cities, that can achieve and sustain competitive advantage in the international competition, are reinforced as new global or regional centers, or ascend in the urban hierarchy, overtaking others in the course of transition.

The New International Division of Labor

What the globalization of competition implies is the emergence of a New International Division of Labor which reflects a change in the geographical pattern of specialization at the global scale (Dicken 1998), and also reflects a shift in global hierarchy (Evans 1995).

Storper and Salais (1997) observes that there are three tiers existing in the International Division of Labor. Core areas are those where high technology and knowledge, high value-added are generated and mastered. Routine Production Regions are those with a concentration of branch plant, subsidiaries and assembly lines of TNCs. Excluded Regions are those that do not enroll in the international production circuits in an important way. While a core area is a creator of market and technology and maintains sustainable economic development, a routine production site can only enjoy limited and uncertain developmental possibility in limited industrial sectors, and expects the possibility of being substituted by another production site. Excluded regions, of course, will be excluded from global economic development circles and remain at the lowest level in global hierarchy. The economic activities of every modern nation are unavoidably articulated into this hierarchy; their places in production for the global market have significant implications for its economic development and the welfare of its citizens (Evans 1995).

National competitive advantage

Further research into the International Division of Labor will raise such questions: what decides a nation's place in the International Division of Labor? Why can some nations gain a higher niche in the hierarchy?

The classical explanation is Ricardian's theory of comparative advantage: all countries will be better off if each concentrates on what it does best. Production activities compatible with its natural resource and factor endowments are most rewarding for each country, and they are the sectors in which its comparative advantages lie. As a consequence, a nation's comparative advantage based on its given nature factor endowments decides inherently its niche in the International Division of Labor. As manufactures and services become increasingly "tradable," this theory cannot explain why the value-added process happens in certain location. Evans (1995) argued that this theory makes sense only in a world where international trade consists of unprocessed raw materials.

The following version, of Hechscher and Ohlin, bases the comparative advantage of a nation on so-called "factors of production" such as land, labor, natural resources and capital. However, as more and more industries have become knowledge-intensive, and the globalization process has made access to the factors of production increasingly less important in the value-added process, so factor comparative advantage cannot explain sufficiently why certain nations become the home base of international headquarters while others are the base of assembly lines.

More recent versions, notably the ideas of national "competitive advantage" (Porter 1990) and "constructed comparative advantage" (Evans 1995) give a sound explanation. Porter (1990) substitutes the concept of comparative advantage with competitive advantage. He argues that the competitive advantage of a nation is based upon the advantages of its firms in particular industry. Firms, not nations, are on the front line of international competition. To achieve competitive success, firms from the nation must possess a competitive advantage in the form of either lower costs or differentiated products that command premium prices. To sustain advantage, firms must achieve more sophisticated competitive advantage over time, through providing higher-quality products and services or producing more efficiently. On the other hand, the home nation is the base on which the essential competitive advantages of the enterprise are created and sustained. Differences in national economic structures, values, cultures, institutions and histories etc. contribute profoundly to the competitive success of its firms. The characteristics of a nation, that allow its firms to create and sustain competitive advantage in particular fields, are the competitive advantage of nations.

Porter pointed out further that there is a three-tier hierarchy of sources of national competitive advantage in terms of sustainability, in which innovation-driven advantage is at the highest level, investment-driven advantage is at the second level and basic-factor-driven advantage is at the lowest level. Upgrading in an economy is the movement from basic-factor-driven level towards more sophisticated sources of competitive advantage.

Explaining the International Division of Labor

Porter's concept of competitive advantage offers us a convincing way to explain what decides a nation's position in the International Division of Labor. At the initial stage, a nation draws its advantage solely from basic factors of production, whether they are natural resources, or an abundant and inexpensive semi-skilled labor force. Indigenous firms in such an economy compete on the basis of price in industries that require little technology and knowledge. More advanced product design and technologies are obtained from other countries. Foreign firms provide most of the access to foreign markets. Nations at such a stage are only routine production sites or even are excluded from the International Division of Labor. With access to abundant factor endowments becoming less important than the technologies and skills, their economy is fundamentally vulnerable to changes in markets, technology and the loss of factor advantage to other countries. "Today's low labor cost country is rapidly displaced by tomorrow's" (Porter 1990).

Nations may upgrade their economy into the investment-driven stage, in which their national competitive advantages are based on their ability to invest or attract foreign investment. Through local and foreign investment, they construct modern infrastructure and acquire complex technology, which will allow these nations to compete in more sophisticated industries. Their economies thus become less vulnerable to the external environment and more sustainable. However, since their technology and skill capability are mainly acquired from foreign suppliers, who generate and master the high value-added process and command a large part of the investment, investment-driven economies remain fragile (Porter 1990; Storper

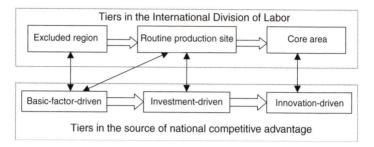

Figure 10.1 The relationship between the sources of a nation's competitive advantage and
its position in the International Division of Labor.

and Salais 1997), and can only serve as routine production sites in the
International Division of Labor.

In contrast, an innovation-driven economy pushes ahead the skill and technology level in product, marketing and other aspects of competition. Such capacity
to innovate upgrades the industries in which the nation's firms can successfully
compete, and thus allows firms to locate less sophisticated routine production
activities into other nations to tap into cheaper natural resources and labor forces.
Nations at such a stage of economic development then serve as headquarters,
which influence and even command the global economy, and thus achieve a niche
in a core area in the International Division of Labor. As more and more industries
have become knowledge-intensive in the post-Second World War period, the
innovation-driven characteristic of a nation gives its firms the power to circumvent
scarce factors through new products and processes, and then sustain long-term
economic prosperity (Porter 1990).

The above discussion manifests the causative relationship between the sources
of national competitive advantage and its position in the International Division of
Labor (Figure 10.1). To gain a higher position in the International Division of
Labor, a nation must upgrade its competitive advantage to a high-order one.
Stimulating innovation becomes a necessary strategy for achieving a niche in the
core area.

The role of government in creating competitive advantage

While this section focuses on the role of government in creating competitive
advantage, understanding the role of firms in international competition and the
government–firm relationship are key issues in establishing the appropriate role
of government.

Firms and business environment

Business firms provide the organizational context for most business activities. As
discussed before, it is firms, not nations, who compete in international markets.

As a result, it was assumed that a society's fortunes were tied up with the success of business firms; the competitive advantage of firms determines the status of a nation's economy and its ability to progress in international competition.

On the other hand, firms should not be conceptualized as economic machines responding to an external market and cost conditions in a "borderless" world. They are inescapably embedded in the external environment, which comprises a wide range of influences: economic, demographic, social, political, legal, technological, etc (Buchholz 1992; Hayter 1997; Worthington and Britton 1998; Yeung 1998). Such an external environment is referred to as the "business environment" within which a business firm's long-term planning and daily operation are facilitated and constrained.

A review of business management literature indicates the importance of the business environment for a firm from perspectives of both business strategy and organization theory (e.g. Globerman 1986; Pounder 1991; Buchholz 1992; Worthington and Britton 1998). Buchholz (1992) argued that "...all skills at internal managing – financing, manufacturing, marketing, research and development and the like – all these put together will not influence a firms destiny as much as what happens in political, social, and economic arenas." From the perspective of business strategy, scholars emphasize the importance of the business environment to a firm's long-term planning and decision-making. Globerman (1986) stressed that "a critical aspect of evolving an overall international business strategy ... is an ongoing assessment of the firm's environment." From the perspective of organization theory, however, scholars stress the need for overall organizational adaptation to the environment as the determination of a business firm's daily operation. Business organizations must interact with, and adapt to their environment in order to survive. Kast and Rosenweig (1985) argued that "the business organization is an open system that exchanges information, energy and materials with its environment. In this view business organizations are dependent for their survival on an exchange of goods and services with the environment" (cited in Pounder 1991: 1).

Geographers and urban planners illustrate the importance of the external environment for business organizations in terms of "spatial attractiveness," "locational advantage," "place embeddedness," or similar concepts (e.g. Storper 1992; Markusen 1996; Schneider and Kim 1996; Storper and Salais 1997; Yeung 1999). Although advancement in technology has greatly facilitated the flow of information, capital, commodity and people throughout global space, the uneven geography of productivity in the International Division of Labor and the increasing trade specialization manifest the importance of location. Storper (1992) observed that technology and knowledge-intensive outputs of the world economy continue to be produced in relatively few core places, while routine production activities spread globally. Such a process of "territorialization" of high technology and knowledge-level activities and "de-territorialization" of routine production activities give rise to a "globalized-localized system of production" (Storper 1998).

The underlying reason for the "territorialization" and "place-embeddedness" of high technology and knowledge-level activities is that particular economic structures, values, cultures, histories, institutions of certain area, provide the basis for innovation (Porter 1990; Blakely 1995; Evans 1995; Storper and Salais 1997; Dicken 1998). Dicken (1998) argues that the most important functions of location are its role as a container of distinctive business practices and its role as a regulator of economic activities within its territorial basis. As all economic activities are embedded in certain territorial basis, the locational distinctiveness means that "ways of doing things" tend to vary across national boundaries. Porter (1990) also emphasizes in his theory of national competitive advantage the locational differences that determine the extent to which an area is economically competitive. Porter states, "Competitive advantage is created and sustained through a highly localized process, ... the home nation is the source of the skills and technology that underpin competitive advantage."

Apart from the fundamental importance of the business environment for firms, a point that needs to be emphasized is that although firms are often able to exercise some degree of control over their internal activities and process, it is often very difficult, if not impossible, for them to control the external environment in which they operate (Worthington and Britton 1998). Thereby, it is vital that firms, especially small- and medium-sized enterprises (SMEs), have the right conditions to survive and flourish to achieve the competitive advantage of certain economic sector in a nation.

Government–firm relationship: business environment as an interface

While the business environment of a firm is related to every aspect of our society, the most important environmental influences come from government (Buchholz 1992).

The need for government involvement in the day-to-day working of the economy is generally accepted (Worthington and Britton 1998). Economists have traditionally pointed to the problem of "market failure" as the reason for governmental intervention in the economy. Government intervention can be portrayed as the attempt by government to deal with the problems inherent in the operation of the free market. Scholars of global political economy examine the role of government through studying the relationship between economy and government involvement, and argue that economies are always embedded in the state as well as market (Evans 1995; Yeung 2000). Such an opinion rejects a conceptual separation between the economy and state. It insists, however, that the economy is necessarily a combination of markets and government action. The role of government is to intervene in market operation to "beat structural imbalance" inherent within capital accumulation (Yeung 2000). As Evans remarked (1995) that "... withdraw and involvement are not the alternative. State involvement is a given."

The critical question, therefore, is not whether a role for government should exist, but what the role should be and where the boundaries should be drawn between private and public action. Neo-liberalist countries, for example USA and UK, tend to prefer limited state influence directed toward improving the operation of the free market. In contrast, direct intervention is the key instrument deployed by the developmental states in Asia to regulate their domestic economy (Yeung 2000). Either way, the actions of the state in the economy are the most important

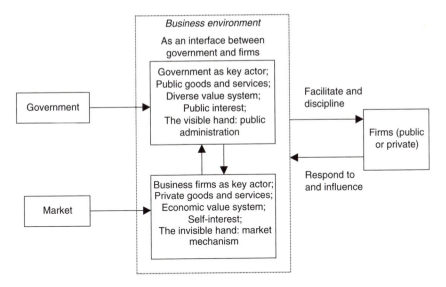

Figure 10.2 The relationship between governments and firms in a market-based economy: business environment as an interface.

influence at both the macro and micro level and shape fundamentally the business environment in which enterprises function. Government can be even seen as the biggest enterprise at national or local level (Worthington and Britton 1998). As a result, we would argue that government is the most important influential actor of the business environment. In effect, the business environment serves as an interface in the process of government–firm interaction (Figure 10.2). The role of government in achieving national competitive advantage can be thus defined as providing an appropriate business environment in which business activities especially higher-level activities and innovation are facilitated and promoted.

The role of government in creating competitive advantage: a dynamic perspective

Generally, government may exert an influence on the business environment directly or indirectly. Government may act as a controller and producer in a direct way. As a controller, government sets up and enforces rules aimed at providing restriction and also stimulation. As a producer, government may take direct responsibility for delivering certain types of goods, such as public goods which private capital cannot provide successfully. Indirectly, however, government acts as a guide and assistant, and responds to the market in a different way. Instead of replacing private producers, government assists in the emergence of new entrepreneurial groups or in guiding existing indigenous firms into new production activities, and helps local entrepreneurs to tackle global challenge.

But which way will be more appropriate for government involvement to achieve favorable business environment – a direct way, an indirect way, or both?

Maybe a dynamic perspective should be applied in answering this question. First, the presence of diversified social, economic, institutional, cultural backgrounds indicate that governments should respond distinctively to facilitate the operation of firms in international competition. Second, even within the same national territory, the economic development is a dynamic process in which the economy will go through several qualitatively different stages. Government's involvement should change accordingly to achieve higher-order competitive advantage. The point here is that the proper role of government in a certain development stage reflects the sources of its competitive advantage.

At a lower development stage, a nation draws its competitive advantage mostly from basic factors of production or investment. Foreign firms provide the technology and the access to global market. There is little indigenous private strength. Then, government should be the leading force in education and training, research and development, infrastructure construction, information provision and capital allocation. Some direct intervention, such as subsidy, technological assistance and tariff protection would be needed to promote and stimulate the development of entrepreneurs. The role of governments in the industrialization process in the "Newly Industrialized Countries" (NICs) serve as good cases, in which governments act as "bureaucratic entrepreneurs" and facilitate directly the economic upgrading.

Government's appropriate role will be markedly different in a higher development stage. The appropriate philosophy of intervention and types of intervention changes (Porter 1990). Allocation of capital, protection, licensing controls, export subsidy and other forms of direct intervention may lose relevance or effectiveness in innovation-based competition. As the economy broadens and deepens, government cannot hope to keep track of every existing and new industry and all the linkages among them. Increasingly prosperous international firms are also less amenable to guidance. Instead, the private sector must be the source of the impetus and skills to innovate, and guide its own developmental directions. Government's efforts are best spent in indirect ways such as stimulating the creation of advanced factors, encouraging new business formation.

Although the role of government is embedded, it is not static. Maybe such a dynamic perspective can explain why neo-liberalism countries are mainly the most developed countries in the world, since indirect involvement is a proper way for government to intervene given their development stage.

The role of government in creating competitive advantage in Shanghai

Shanghai's development in the 1990s

Shanghai has achieved great strides in its development since the launching of Pudong Project in 1990. The GDP in 1999 was 403.5 billion yuan, which is more than five times of that in 1990 when it was, 75.63 billion yuan. The highest growth rate of GDP reached 35.7 percent in 1993 and the average has been about 20 percent per year during the 1990s (Table 10.1).

Table 10.1 GDP and investment in Shanghai during the 1990s

Year		1990	1991	1992	1993	1994	1995	1996	1997	1998	1999
GDP	Amount (billion yuan)	75.6	89.4	111.4	151.2	197.2	246.3	290.2	336.0	368.8	403.5
	Growth rate (%)	8.6	18.2	24.7	35.7	30.5	24.9	17.9	15.8	9.8	9.4
Investment on fixed assets (IFA)	Amount (billion yuan)	22.7	25.8	35.7	65.4	11.2	160.2	195.2	197.8	196.5	185.7
	Growth rate (%)	5.7	13.7	38.4	83.0	71.8	42.6	21.9	1.3	−0.6	−5.5
	IFA/GDP (%)	30.0	28.9	32.1	43.3	57.0	65.0	67.3	58.9	53.3	46.0
Investment on infrastructure (II)	Amount (billion yuan)	4.72	6.14	8.4	16.8	23.8	27.4	37.9	41.3	53.1	50.1
	Growth rate (%)	30.1	30.0	37.5	98.9	41.9	14.9	38.3	9.0	28.7	−5.6
	II/GDP (%)	6.2	6.9	7.6	11.1	12.1	11.1	13.1	12.3	14.4	12.4
Investment on real estate (IRE)	Amount (billion yuan)	0.82	0.76	1.27	2.2	11.7	46.6	65.8	61.4	57.7	51.5
	Growth rate (%)	—	−7.3	67.1	73.2	433.6	297.1	41.1	−6.6	−6.0	−10.7
	IRE/GDP (%)	1.1	0.9	1.1	1.5	6.0	18.9	22.7	18.3	15.6	12.8

Source: Statistical Yearbook of Shanghai (2000).

Consideration of the recent development reveals that Shanghai has experienced substantial industrial restructuring. The contribution of tertiary industry to the whole urban economy rose from 31.9 percent in 1990 to 49.6 percent in 1999, while the secondary industry decreased from 63.8 to 48.4 percent and the primary sector from 4.3 to 2.0 percent (Table 10.2). Along with industrial restructuring, the urban spatial structure transformed significantly. Within the inner ring, the total area of buildings for the secondary industry dropped 11 percent while that of office, commercial building and housing increased by 120, 70 and 50 percent respectively (Tang and Luan 2000).

The impact of TNCs and FDI on Shanghai's economy is becoming increasingly prominent. Between 1990 and 1999, the accumulated FDI in Shanghai reached US$26.64 billion with the annual ratio of the FDI to GDP increasing every year (Table 10.3). The contribution to industrial output of foreign or Sino-foreign joined enterprises rose from 15.5 percent in 1993 to 50.6 percent in 1999 (Table 10.4). By 1997, there were 55 of the world's largest 100 industrial enterprises locating their regional headquarters or production branches in Shanghai. Besides, the number of foreign financial organizations in Shanghai increased from 79 in 1993 to 160 in 1998 (Tang and Luan 2000).

Alongside the economic development, investment in the built environment also grew significantly. This can be illustrated by the data on the investment in fixed assets, infrastructure and real estate (Table 10.1). Investment on infrastructure enjoyed a substantial rise from 4.7 billion yuan in 1990 to 50.1 billion yuan in 1999, with the proportion on transportation facilities, telecommunication facilities and utility facilities increasing greatly. The upgrading of infrastructure improved the investment environment. By the end of 1999, the improved infrastructure network enabled Pudong to become an integral part of Greater

Table 10.2 Sector structure of the Shanghai economy

Year	GDP		Primary sector		Secondary sector		Tertiary sector	
	Billion yuan	%	Billion yuan	%	Billion yuan	%	Billion yuan	%
1978	0.27	100	0.01	4.0	0.21	77.4	0.05	18.6
1990	75.6	100	3.3	4.3	48.3	63.8	24.1	31.9
1991	89.4	100	3.3	3.7	55.1	61.7	30.9	34.6
1992	111.4	100	3.4	3.1	67.7	60.8	40.3	36.1
1993	151.2	100	3.8	2.5	90.0	59.6	57.3	37.9
1994	197.2	100	4.9	2.5	114.3	57.8	78.0	39.6
1995	246.3	100	6.7	2.5	141.0	57.3	99.1	40.2
1996	290.2	100	7.2	2.5	158.3	54.5	124.8	43.0
1997	336.0	100	7.6	2.3	174.4	52.2	153.0	45.5
1998	368.8	100	7.9	2.1	184.7	50.1	176.3	47.8
1999	403.5	100	8.0	2.0	195.4	48.4	200.1	49.6

Source: Statistical Yearbook of Shanghai (2000).

Table 10.3 FDI in Shanghai during the 1990s

	1990	1991	1992	1993	1994	1995	1996	1997	1998	1999
FDI (billion US$)	0.18	0.18	1.26	2.32	3.23	3.25	4.72	4.81	3.64	3.05

Source: Statistical Yearbook of Shanghai (2000).

Table 10.4 Output from foreign-owned enterprises in Shanghai

Year	Industrial output (IO) (billion yuan)	Output of foreign-related enterprises (OFE)	
		Billion yuan	OFE/IO (%)
1993	299.0	46.3	15.5
1994	375.8	83.8	22.3
1995	395.7	115.9	29.3
1996	433.0	150.5	34.8
1997	544.8	211.9	38.9
1998	550.4	259.8	47.2
1999	566.6	286.8	50.6

Source: Statistical Yearbook of Shanghai (2000).

Shanghai. There are four bridges, a tunnel and a metro line linking both sides of the Huangpu River. This increase in accessibility and consequent reduction in commuting time further boosted Pudong.

Positioning Shanghai in the International Division of Labor

Although Shanghai is a latecomer to the international competition, the great changes in the role it plays in both the domestic and international hierarchy makes it one of the most discussed growth regions in China and also within the Pacific Rim. Shanghai in the last ten years has attracted vast international capital (Table 10.4), and most of it came from TNCs. Rose (1997) and Wu (2000a) observe that compared with the Pearl River Delta Region, inward investments in Shanghai are characterized by multinational origins, high levels of technology, and higher-order enterprises such as headquarters, representative offices, management or sales offices of firms which have manufacturing functions located in suburban Shanghai or neighboring provinces. These characteristics derive from several advantages that Shanghai enjoys compared with other big cities in China. Apart from the favorable geographic location, Shanghai has a superb hinterland and is a window to a vast consumer market compared to most cities of the world. The leaders of central government believe that Shanghai will be the key to China's take-off, so give Shanghai more political backup and more preferential policies than the other part of China. Shanghai has a relatively better-trained labor force, good infrastructure and a relative less corruption and bureaucracy, which make doing business here relatively easier.

However, in evaluating Shanghai's development in the light of the International Division of Labor, we will find that this city is by no means comparable with cities at the top of the global hierarchy for two fundamental reasons.

First, Shanghai's fast economic growth during the reform period was mainly induced by vast capital investment rather than through increasing added value and upgrading the technological level. The contribution rate of capital to local GDP growth in Shanghai was 65.6 percent (Chai 2000), with means that in its 20.4 percent annual local GDP growth rate in the last decade, 13.4 percent comes from the increase in investment. It shows that the source of Shanghai's competitive advantage is based on investment rather than innovation. Such a characteristic makes economic growth in Shanghai vulnerable to the availability of capital. Once facing the "bottleneck" of capital resources, the growth in the economy cannot be sustained. Meanwhile, since the provision of goods and services in Shanghai remain in low-to-medium-technology and low-value-added level, the utilization efficiency and rate of return on investment is relatively low. The waste and poor performance of capital will increase the possibility of a capital crisis, which makes the economy fragile.

Secondly, although Shanghai has become the largest FDI destination in East Asia, and has attracted some TNCs setting up their Regional Headquarters here, it still remains a concentration site of subsidiary enterprises and branch organizations other than the home base of TNC headquarters, R&D activities and of innovation. TNCs invest here to tap into preferential policies, cheap land and resources, abundant and skilled human resources, and to explore the vast market in Shanghai's hinterland. Its indigenous entrepreneurship is not strong enough to compete in the international market, which weakens greatly Shanghai's competitiveness. Taking the hi-tech business in Shanghai as an example, a questionnaire survey conducted by the author in June 2001 shows that 24.7 percent of responding hi-tech firms are regional headquarters, which have subsidiaries in other cities in China and 30 percent of the respondents are Sino-foreign jointed venture or wholly owned foreign. However, all these headquarters in Shanghai are totally China-based trans-province enterprises, and all the foreign investments are subsidiary branch plants. Neither regional headquarters of foreign-based TNCs nor China-based TNCs, that have an operation in a foreign market, are found among the respondents (Hong 2001). In contrast, a city in "core area" is always the home of TNCs and FDI, an incubator and transmission hub of new technology, and a cradle of new ideas and entrepreneurship. Economic growth in Shanghai is investment-driven. Shanghai still serves as a routine production site in the International Division of Labor.

Reviewing the role the Shanghai municipal government played in 1990s

Castells (1998) argued that it is the "bureaucratic entrepreneurs" that had led the emergence of new capitalism in China. This argument is seen in Shanghai's development in the 1990s. Although the market forces were apparently working and shaping this city's transformation since the 1978 reform, research finding have shown that state control was not weakened (e.g. Olds 1997; Han 2000; Yatsko 2000; Wu 2000b). Rather, reform created powerful local states that controlled enterprises and intervened in resource allocation (Han 2000; Wu 2000b). Heavy government intervention remained as the distinguishing characteristic in Shanghai's development process in the 1990s.

First, the industrial restructuring process is pushed ahead by local government efforts. The municipal government recognized that a strong tertiary sector is critical for Shanghai to become the economic center, and thus adopted a development principal, which puts the tertiary sector as priority. According to this principle, major efforts are devoted to the tertiary sector while actively adjusting and upgrading secondary industry and keeping the steady increase of primary industry (Zhao and Zhang 1998). The municipal government then formulated detailed plans, which emphasizes the growth of the commercial and financial sectors as well as the development of real estate, tourism and information services, to push ahead and guide the restructuring process. Industrial enterprises that were non-profitable ones, or pollution-sources, or low efficient land users and substandard houses, gave way to the profitable tertiary industry and higher standard apartment development. From 1990 to 1999, one-third of the 13,200 industrial enterprises was closed down; another one-third was moved out from the city proper. For the first time, the contribution of the tertiary industry to the whole urban economy in 1999 reached 50 percent. In such a process, more than 1 million people lost their job in the old industries, which would be impossible without the power of government.

To attract foreign investment, the Shanghai government tries to improve the investment environment. With the land-use system reform in China, administrative allocation was gradually replaced with land leasing. As the municipal government controls the land leasing, its role in urban development is thus enhanced. Government financed mega-infrastructure building and huge urban redevelopment projects with the revenue gained from land leasing. More than ten huge infrastructure projects were finished in 1990–1997, including a subway project, new airport project, deep-water port project, etc. In the same period, about 18 million square meters old housing were demolished, accompanied by 436,200 families, about 1 million people, moved out from the inner city where they used to live. The striking numbers illustrate the efficiency of Shanghai municipal government in urban construction.

Government also intervenes directly in the economic activities of business enterprises. For example, about half of hi-tech business in Shanghai are government-owned or half-government-owned (Hong 2001). Government is also involved in real estate development. There were instances of the government establishing official or quasi-official development enterprises as one of the actors in the market. For instance, when the development of Pudong was announced in 1990, the Pudong Development Corporation was set up by the government to take charge of land development in Pudong area. On the one hand, government acts as a developer, looking after its own economic profits as an economic entity, and competing with private sector in the market; on the other hand, government acts as a manager that guarantees public goods. Conflict of interest, both apparent and real, is inevitable. It is not unknown that government would sometimes compromise the public interest to ensure its own economic gains. The original detailed plan of Pudong District was changed several times for this reason. Meanwhile, since the government would have to bear the business loss of official corporations, the soft budget constraints tend to allow the corporations to act unreasonably and without regard to commercial reality and principles.

Through reviewing the role that the municipal government played in the 1990s, it can be seen that the Shanghai government achieves tangible objectives and improves the physical environment. In contrast, the Shanghai government has not done enough work in building a modern city's software system, including the free flowing of economic and business information, lowering the administrative burden on entrepreneurs, increasing the availability of venture capital, consultation and business support services, providing a well-regulated capital market, being consistent in policy, etc. This point can be illustrated further using the development of the business support service industry in Shanghai.

Traditionally, the role services play in the efficient functioning of economy has been neglected in China owing to the ideological perception of "production" as a material term and services as "unproductive." Shanghai had to transform from a "consuming" city into a "productive" one, and focused on heavy industries. Business support services were rarely provided by professionals. Industrial enterprises under the planned economic system were 'small but all-functional" ("*xiao er quan*") social units and depended primarily on themselves to providing business support services. Rarely possessing specialized knowledge and skills, such services were of low quality, with high transaction costs impeding the development of enterprises and reducing the efficiency of the whole economy.

The general attitude toward services changed, since the introduction of market-oriented reforms, as Shanghai proposes to be an "international economic, financial, and trade center." The contribution of the tertiary industry to the whole urban economy increases gradually, as we showed earlier. However, a significant gap still exists between Shanghai and global metropolises in terms of the share of services to total value added, and the quality of the services provided. The gap in business support services is larger than in services generally, and imposes a considerable negative influence on its business environment. Figure 10.3 is an advertisement for an American corporation, and demonstrates the poor quality of logistical systems in China.

Several important points account for the underdevelopment of business support services in Shanghai. First, due to its intangible and non-storable nature, the significance of business support services is not properly evaluated and fully understood. The government has been aware of the vital importance of technological level in economic upgrading. However, the major efforts are devoted into constructing hi-tech parks and attracting international hi-tech firms, while building up mature logistical network and support system is not gaining proper emphasis.

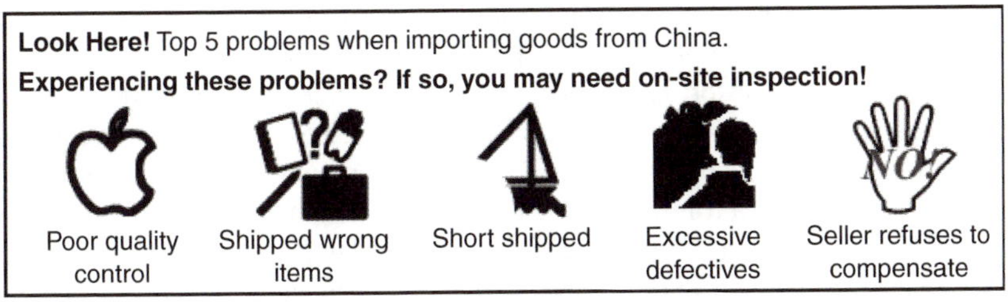

Look Here! Top 5 problems when importing goods from China.
Experiencing these problems? If so, you may need on-site inspection!

| Poor quality control | Shipped wrong items | Short shipped | Excessive defectives | Seller refuses to compensate |

Figure 10.3 An advertisement from an American on-site inspection corporation.

Source: http://www.chinainspect.com/

Secondly, the development of business support services (e.g. consulting, marketing, quality control, research and development, information-related services, etc.) depend on the availability of specialized knowledge and skills, that cannot be acquired overnight by the introduction of market-oriented reforms, but require a longer period of time and a more determined policy to build an efficient producer service sector (Stare 2001). Business support services were controlled by government previously and only recently have been opened to market provision. The majority of local business support services in Shanghai lack professional knowledge, skills and experiences, and thus fail to meet the growing requirements of firms.

Thirdly, the introduction of market-oriented reform into the business support services is slower and later than other economic sectors. For example, telecommunication in China is not yet exposed to market competition. With the absence of market competition and international rules and standards, China's telecommunication services charge very high prices, that are not proportional to local average personal income. The range and quality of services and their adaptation to customer needs also fail to meet the market requirements. Additionally the bank and insurance sectors in China are not fully exposed to international competition although there are some foreign banks and insurance companies established in China. Their monopolistic operation is one of the key reasons for their substandard services.

Taking into account the increasing role it plays, promotion of the development of business support services and other elements of the software system of a modern city would be an important strategy for Shanghai to improve its business environment. As international competition grows, it is vital to be aware that it is the entrepreneurial culture and appropriate business environment other than the roads and other physical infrastructure that make the Silicon Valley the cradle of the New Economy. The soft parts of the business environment are actually what Shanghai needs to realize its final objectives.

The changing role of Shanghai government

Shanghai has accumulated a decade's rapid development and transformation, and has upgraded its economy from a basic factor-driven stage into an investment-driven stage. China's entry into the WTO will be another opportunity for this city to revitalize its traditional role. Appropriate government response are vital for Shanghai to grasp the opportunity to upgrade its position.

Great government effort is the most marked characteristic in Shanghai's place-promotion process, which has successfully integrated Shanghai's economy into the global network, and upgraded Shanghai's economy into the investment-driven stage. However, such a role will not work to push Shanghai from the routine pro-duction site up to the core area in the International Division of Labor. This point has already been made manifest by Shanghai's deficiency in building up the entrepreneurial culture and the software system. As the planned economy changes toward a market-oriented one, a new administrative model that is compatible with market-oriented economic reform is of critical importance. The functions of local government should shift from direct intervention to the fostering of the market and guaranteeing its normal operation; from a producer and a controller to a referee and a manager who provide a favorable business environment in which indigenous entrepreneurship are facilitated and boosted. To this end, the urban management system would experience a de-regulation (diminishing the government direct control over market) and re-regulation process (regulating and promoting indigenous entrepreneurship with more market-oriented rules). That means the local government should:

- disassociate itself from micro-economic activities and be responsible for macro adjustment and social development;
- exercise indirect control over enterprises and their economic activities;
- build up a simplified, unified and efficient administrative structure; and
- set up an international acceptable standard of management.

From such a point of view, the WTO membership would be a good opportunity for China to accelerate its market-oriented reform. WTO is founded on the core principles of national treatment and non-discrimination, which require China to treat foreign firms the same as domestic firms. Complying with WTO rules and its trade agreement will undoubtedly catalyze the de-regulatory and re-regulatory process in China. However, WTO membership will bring rigorous competition into China's market. In short term, local entrepreneurs are in a weak position compared with foreign rivals, which means a great challenge for China. Reform and economic pain are inescapable if China and Shanghai wishes to participate in the International Division of Labor. Protectionism and government monopoliza-tion will not work in promoting Shanghai from the investment-driven stage into the innovation-driven stage.

Conclusion

As a new member of the WTO and the community of global trade leaders, China has the chance to shape the global economy, not merely to be shaped by it (Frost 2001). Shanghai, the leading city in China, will be in the front line in participating in the International Division of Labor. WTO membership will bring great external reinforcement to Shanghai's market-oriented reform, and also create severe international competition. Transforming the role of government at such a turning point in Shanghai's development path is vital to enable the city to take advantage of the opportunities and tackle the challenges.

Given that the competitive advantage of Shanghai in its current development stage rests heavily on the availability of investment, the role of government is still substantial in its economic upgrading process. It can be important in such areas as channeling scarce capital into particular industries, promoting risk taking, stimulating and influencing the acquisition of foreign technology, etc. The enterprises, however, must begin to play an enlarged role as well. Government is the key actor in building up the entrepreneurial culture to nurture the growth of indigenous entrepreneurship. On the other hand, it should be cautious to distinguish between direct control and indirect guidance, and to avoid both over intervention and intervention deficiency.

References

Borja, J. and Castells, M. (1997) *Local and Global: The Management of Cities in the Information Age*. London: Earthscan Publications Ltd.

Brotchie, J. *et al.* (1995) *Cities in Competition: Production and Sustainable Cities for the 21st century*. Melbourne: Longman Australia Pty Ltd.

Buchholz, R. A. (1992) *Business Environment and Public Policy: Implications for Management and Strategy* (Fourth Edition). Englewood Cliffs: Prentice Hall.

Castells, M. (1989) *The Information City: Information Technology, Economic Restructuring, and Urban-regional Process*. Oxford: Basil Blackwell Ltd.

Castells, M. (1998) *End of Millennium*. Oxford: Blackwell.

Chai, J. M. (2000) "Measuring the formation of World Cities: the case of Shanghai," unpublished PhD dissertation, The University of Hong Kong, Hong Kong.

Chan, R. C. K. (2000) 'shanghai: developing strategies and planning implications," paper presented at International Conference (2000): *Re-inventing Global Cities*, The University of Hong Kong, Hong Kong.

Dicken, P. (1998) *Global Shift: Transformation the World Economy* (Third Edition). London: Paul Chapman Publishing Ltd.

Eng, I. (1997) "The rise of manufacturing towns: externally driven industrialization and urban development in the Pearl River Delta of China." *International Journal of Urban and Regional Research*, 21: 554–68.

Evans, P. (1995) *Embedded Autonomy: States and Industrial Transformation*. Princeton: Princeton University Press.

Frost, E. L. (2001) "China, the WTO and globalization: what happens next?" Downloaded from: http://www.chinaonline.com

Han, S. S. (2000) 'shanghai between state and market in urban transformation," *Urban Studies*, 37(11): 2091–112.

Hayter, R. (1997) *The Dynamics of Industrial Location: The Factory, the Firm and the Production System*. Chichester: Wiley.

Hong, W. (2001) "Assessment of business environment for hi-tech industrial development in Shanghai: implications for planning," paper submitted to the 2002 Annual Meeting of America Association of Geographer, America: Los Angeles.

Markusen, A. (1996) "Sticky places in slippery space: a typology of industrial districts," *Economic Geography*, 72(3): 293–313.

Msacitelli, R. (1999) *The Growth Warriors: Creating Sustainable Global Advantage for America's Technology Industries*. Northridge, CA.

Olds, K. (1997) "Globalizing Shanghai: the 'Global Intelligence Corps' and the building of Pudong," *Cities*, 14(2): 109–23.

Porter, M. E. (1990) *The Competitive Advantage of Nations*. New York: The Free Press.

Pounder, J. S. (1991) *Managing the Business Environment: Hong Kong and Beyond*. Hong Kong: Longman.

Rose, F. (1997) Shanghai: exception or rule? Consideration of urban development paths and processes in China since 1978, paper presented to the South Asian Urbanization Conference, 26–29 August, London.

Schneider, M. and Kim, D. (1996) "The effects of local conditions on economic growth, 1977–1990: the changing location of high technology activities," *Urban Affairs Review*, 32(2): 131–56.

Stare, M. (2001) "Advancing the development of business support services in Slovenia with foreign direct investment," *The Service Industries Journal*, 21(1): 19–34.

Storper, M. (1992) "The limits to globalization: technology districts and international trade," *Economic Geography*, 68: 60–93.

Storper, M. and Salais, R. (1997) *World of Production*. Cambridge, MA.: Harvard University Press.

Storper, M., Thomadakis, S. B. and Tsipouri, L. J. (eds) (1998) *Latecomers in the Global Economy*. London: Routledge.

Tang, Z. L. and Luan, F. (2000) "1990 nian dai shang hai de cheng shi kai fa yu yan biab" [Urban development and restructuring of Shanghai city in the 1990's], *Cheng Shi Gui Hua Hui Kan*, [*Urban Planning Forum*], 128: 32–7.

Wang, H. N. (1988) "Zhong guo bian hua zhong de zhong yang he di fang zheng fu de guan xi: zheng zhi de han yi" [The changing relationship between central and local state in China: its political meaning], *Fudan xue bao*, 1988(5): 1–8.

Worthington, I. and Britton, C. (1998) *The Business Environment* (Second edition). London: Pitman Publishing.

Wu, F. L. (2000a) "The global and local dimension of place-making: remaking Shanghai as a world city," *Urban Studies*, 37(8): 1359–77.

Wu, F. L. (2000b) "Place promotion in Shanghai, PRC," *Cities*, 17(5): 349–61.

Yatsko, P. (2000) *New Shanghai: The Rocky Rebirth of China's Legendary City*. Chichester: Wiley.

Yeung, W. C. (1998) "Capital, state and space: contesting the borderless world," *Royal Geographical Society*, NS 23: 291–309.

Yeung, W. C. (1999) "Grounding global flows: constructing an e-commerce hub in Singapore," paper presented to the conference on *Global networks, innovation and regional development*, UC Santa Cruz, November 11–13.

Yeung, W. C. (2000) "State intervention and neoliberalism in the globalizing world economy: lessons from Singapore's regionalization programme," *The Pacific Review*, 13(1): 133–62.

Zhao, M. and Zhang, Z. Y. (1998), "Metropolitan planning and governance in Asia and Pacific: the Shanghai case," unpublished paper, Tongji University, Shanghai, PRC.

11 Towards a model of the impacts of retail internationalisation

John Dawson

Introduction

The international activities of retailers increased in scale and complexity during the last quarter of the twentieth century. This phenomenon is seen in all the major markets. Whilst in 1980, only 6 of the 20 largest retailers based in Europe operated stores outside their domestic market, by 2000 all but 1 of the top 20 had internationalised their store network. By 2000, it is estimated that 12.8 per cent of British retail sales were accounted for by foreign-based firms (Clark *et al.* 2001). Throughout Central Europe foreign retailers have expanded dramatically since 1989. 'One of the consequences of the 50 years of communism is that the major retailers in these countries will be foreign owned' (Dawson 2001a: 27) through the early decades of the twenty-first century. European based retailers have been particularly active in opening stores in other countries both within Europe and in other cultural regions. Some of the most international firms, for example Carrefour, Body Shop, Zara and IKEA, are operating shops in twenty or more countries, including several in Asia. Others, for example Ahold, Signet and Courts have more than 50 per cent of sales accounted for by non-domestic activity. Whilst the activity of the major European retailers has been substantial, North American retailers also have been active, although not to the same extent. Nonetheless, Wal-Mart, Gap, Claire's, ToysRUs, and others have expanded into Europe and Asia whilst many others have opened stores in Canada and Mexico (Simmons and Kamikihara 1999).

Despite the substantial increases in activity over the last twenty years few, if any, retailers yet can claim to have a global scope to their operations. McDonalds and Benetton are probably the closest to having a truly global coverage of outlets and to be managing what could be termed a global firm. Many of the strongly active international retailers, including Wal-Mart, Ahold and Metro generally are absent from Africa, India and have a very small presence in China, in respect of store operations. Major European retailers with a strong international orientation often are absent from North America or have had less than satisfactory experiences there (Muniz-Martinez 1998). A relatively small number of retailers based in USA have moved beyond Canada or Mexico (Sternquist 1997a). The coming decades presage an increase in international activity with European and American retailers expanding particularly into Asia and joining Asian retailers who are moving internationally within their own broad culture realm. Truly global retailers may emerge over the next decade as the large firms from Europe and USA expand their presence rapidly in East Asia and South America and move slowly into India and Africa.

It is not only in shop operation that this internationalisation process has been evident. Retailers have increased the scope of international activity in three main areas (Dawson 1994). First, there is the sale of products in other countries, usually through shops but also including export activity.[1] Secondly, there is the sourcing from other countries of products for resale. Again there is a long history of such activity and the range of actions has increased in recent years. Thirdly, there is the internationalisation of managerial ideas and managers, including internationalisation of managerial activity amongst small independent traders. The internationalisation of management in the small firm is widespread, for example, the Chinese diaspora throughout Asia; East African and Pakistani traders in UK; Algerian shopkeepers in France; and the Koreans and Vietnamese in USA. This aspect of the internationalisation of retailing know-how is often ignored in discussions of retail internationalisation but has been a strong force in the sector with substantial impacts for many centuries. There are many countries where a substantial amount of small-scale retailing is operated by foreign retailers. The difference in these cases, from the more widely discussed internationalisation of the late twentieth century, is that with the larger firms the head-office and ultimate control remains in the home country. Nonetheless, the creation of operating subsidiaries, with substantial executive independence, begins to blur the distinction between what is and what is not an international retailer even for these larger firms.

Despite increased activity in all three areas, the internationalisation process in retailing, as it affects medium- and large-sized firms, remains in its early stages. It has probably extended furthest in sourcing and in the transfer of managerial ideas where the history of international activity has been longest. With a few notable exceptions, the operation of shops internationally by large firms, other than as a token presence in another country, is a relatively new phenomenon associated with the globalisation trends in economies. The pointers would suggest that this activity is likely to grow substantially over the next several decades. Increasing internationalisation of shop operation is, therefore, for the future, a long-term process affecting the retail sector.[2] It is this aspect of the internationalisation of retailing that is the focus of the remainder of this chapter.

Directions of previous research

Alongside the increase in internationalisation activity there has been an increase in academic study of the processes involved. Useful reviews have been provided by Burt (1991, 1995), Dawson (1994), Akehurst and Alexander (1995), Alexander (1997) and Alexander and Myers (2000). Much of the research has focused on

- *why* retailers internationalise their operations;
- the choice of entry country [*where*] and;
- the methods of entry [*how*].

These foci link directly to the immediate concerns of retailers as they consider and begin to undertake international activity. The studies have often been linked to considerations of strategic management in respect of the decision to move internationally. Much of the academic work has been empirical and often descriptive. These research studies have reported the results of surveys of which retailers have moved into new markets and of retailer responses to questionnaires about choice of new market.

Reflective of the relative volume of retailer activity most of the academic study of the topic has been based in Europe and reporting the activity of European retailers. In general, the topic has generated little interest, with some notable exceptions and until recently, among Asian and North American scholars. Notable exceptions in Japan are recent studies by Mukoyama (1997) and Kawabata (1999a,b) and in North America the seminal work of Hollander (1970) and Kacker (1985, 1988). International moves by American retailers, particularly since 1990, have encouraged some studies from the perspective of USA and Canada (Simpson and Thorpe 1995; Evans and Cox 1997; O'Grady and Lane 1997; Sternquist 1997a; Arnold and Fernie 1999, 2000; Vida 2000). There has also been a growing interest in China (Letosk *et al.* 1997; Wu 1997). The key studies since the mid-1980s, however, of Alexander (1990, 1995, 1997), Burt (1991, 1993, 1995), Davies (1994a,b, 2000), Dupuis and Prime (1996), Laulajainen (1987, 1991, 1992), Martenson (1981), McGoldrick and Ho (1992), Pellegrini (1991, 1994) and Wrigley (1989, 1997a,b,c, 2000) have tended to take a European perspective on retailer internationalisation even when considering moves to or in other continents.

The reasons for the surge in international activity of European retailers have been broadly established and these results can now be applied to forecasting developments in other culture realms. The reasons why particular markets are selected have also been identified and the potential attractiveness of markets for foreign retailer activity can now be established. The advantages and disadvantages of the different entry modes of retailers are also now better understood (Quinn 1998; Doherty 1999; Dawson 2001b; Quinn and Alexander 2002). There is still substantial empirical work to be undertaken outside the European region but the foundations for such empirical work have been laid. Conceptual and theoretical work remains to be developed on the empirically based answers to the questions of *why, where* and *how* but the general direction of research is clearly signed.

Two major gaps in the research are consideration of *when* retail internationalisation takes place and *what* the effects and impacts are on the domestic retail system of foreign retailer arrival in a country. There has been work on when moves take place in a temporal sense (Burt 1993; Quinn 1999) but not in a conditional one. Relevant conditional factors may refer to the home country or the host country. Research on the 'when' and 'what' topics involves moving forward from decisions related to entry (why, where, how) to exploration of development and growth following entry. This involves moving from the study of events to the study of processes. Work in these general areas is starting with studies of what competencies within the firm are internationalised. Burt and Carralero-Encinas (2000) have studied the international transferability of retail image and Goldman (2001) has identified transferable components of a format. Gielen and Dekimpe (2001) explore the link between mode of entry and subsequent performance of the retailer. The effects of Wal-Mart have been the focus of several studies. Burt and Sparks (2001) point to some of the ways that Wal-Mart may make changes to operations in ASDA, that they purchased in UK in 1997. Arnold *et al.* (1998) surveyed some of the impacts on consumers consequent on Wal-Mart's entry into Canada. Mondragón (1997) analysed the evolution of the Wal-Mart – CIFRA joint venture in Mexico. These studies are illustrative of this new phase of work, but are few compared with the work on entry. The development of a retailer in a foreign market involves adjustment to cultural and competitive conditions, a form of organisational learning associated with the management of intellectual capital, and issues of when and how fast development takes place. Few academic studies have yet addressed these issues of development paths of retailers in non-domestic markets.

The aims of this chapter are:

- to begin to explore some of the managerial and research issues associated with both the impact on domestic retailing of foreign retailer activity and the effects on the foreign retailer of operating in a new commercial environment;
- to provide a preliminary framework that can be used to consider the impacts of foreign retailer activity on both the domestic retail system and the foreign retailer.

The chapter is intended to stimulate discussion and debate. These issues currently lack a substantive research base both conceptual and empirical.

A framework for considering the impacts of retailer internationalisation

In considering the impacts of internationalisation it is proposed that it is necessary to distinguish:

- the types of impacts, including the institutions affected;
- the processes associated with impacts, for example, stages and timing of consequential changes; and,
- the degree of intensity of impacts.

Each of these will be considered in the following sections.

Types of impact

The types of impact can be classified into a number of broad categories that are related to the institutions and structures that are affected by foreign retailers.

These categories are:

- Impacts on vertical relationships including logistics and the behavioural relationships between retailers and suppliers. These are termed as changes in the *effectiveness of the demand chain*. The demand chain in this context extends beyond the chain of ownership of goods for resale and encompasses the provision of infrastructure and services, for example, the provision of property, marketing, and legal services and logistics.
- Impacts on the competitive structure and processes between retailers with the appearance and development of a new foreign retail company. These impacts comprise changes in retail *sectoral competitiveness*.
- Impacts on consumer behaviour and the processes of consumption that can be termed changes in *consumer literacy*.
- Impacts on the internationalising firm both in the host and home country that generate changes in the *performance of the firm*. These relate to many different financial and managerial processes that operate as the firm develops internationally.
- The expansion of foreign retailers often has impacts that generate implications for *public policy* at national, regional and local levels.
- There are broad scale impacts on *social and cultural values*, for example, those that have been popularly characterized as the 'McDonaldization' of society (Ritzer 1993; Belk 1996).

These six broad areas of impact are illustrated in Figure 11.1. Each of these six will now be considered and examples provided of the form of impacts that can occur within these types.

Within this general model there are specific situational effects so that, from an empirical viewpoint it is necessary to consider specific events of internationalisation in respect of a firm and a country. At this stage of our knowledge it is not realistic to generalize across countries or across retail sectors. Nonetheless, it is worthwhile considering the framework of Figure 11.1 in more detail through examples of the impacts of each type.

Changes in the effectiveness of demand chains

Moves by a retailer into another country mean the transfer of managerial knowledge relating to relationships with others in the demand (supply) demand. This can result in:

- changes in the role of intermediaries in the chain, as happened with Carrefour's development in Japan and with several major retailers in China (Au-Yeung 2002). New approaches to relationships with the various types of suppliers were introduced that have changed behaviours in the demand chain. Tesco's use in Thailand of slotting allowances and the passing of transport costs to suppliers, considered standard practice in many countries but new in Thailand, provides a further example of this type of impact;

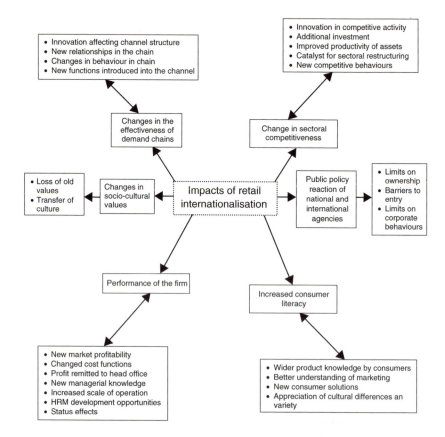

Figure 11.1 Types of impact of retail internationalisation in host country.

- innovation in logistics as happens with Zara and Hennes & Mauritz when they expand in foreign markets and introduce their short product cycle and new inventory control procedures into established channels (Vitzthum 2001);
- changes of trading terms (notably payment periods and discount structures) between retailers and suppliers as happened spectacularly with Promodès move into Greece;
- starting new relationships with suppliers in the host country providing these suppliers with new access to the market, as seen in Tesco's development of hypermarkets in Poland;
- introducing new processes into demand chains, for example, new quality control and monitoring processes introduced by Ahold in its demand chain in Czech Republic and Slovakia;
- supporting provision of services by other international firms, for example, West European retailers expanding their operations in Central Europe used the services of the international property agencies that also have sought to expand into these countries.

These changes introduced or strengthened by foreign retailers have a demonstration effect in that domestic retailers follow the lead and adopt the innovatory practices. For example, when Promodès entered Greece and negotiated new types of contract relations with suppliers that reduced prices, extended payment periods and changed discount structures in favour of the retailer, domestic Greek retailers quickly followed the lead of Promodès and sought to renegotiate their own contracts with suppliers. The result has been that across the whole sector, channel relationships have changed following the catalyst provided by Promodès (Bourlakis *et al.* 1996). Similar changes are reported in Taiwan, Korea and Thailand elsewhere in this volume. This demonstration effect is important in encouraging other changes in demand chain practices that diffuse through the body of domestic retailers.

Changes in sectoral competitiveness

The establishment of a foreign retailer in the market has impacts on horizontal competitive processes and so has effects on the competitiveness of retailers already in the market. Examples of these types of effect are:

- introduction and diffusion through the existing retail structure of new retail formats or retail formulae,[3] as exemplified by ToysRUs in Japan, Wal-Mart in Mexico, B&Q in Taiwan, HMV in Japan, Sephora in Spain and many other examples. The impacts are those of the introduction of a disruption to existing structure by the arrival of a retail format or retail formula with new cost structures, enabling new methods of competition through lower prices, higher service levels, new product ranges, etc. The cost structures, at a particular time, may be affected by the scale economies achieved by the foreign retailer, at that time, but this is then due to the situational impact of a specific firm rather than the impact of a new format or formula;
- introduction of improved information management methods that affect competitive success, for example, with the transfer of information systems from 7-Eleven Japan to the USA in their purchase of 7-Eleven USA (Sparks 1995, 2000);
- introduction of new marketing and merchandising methods using an existing format, for example, Aldi's expansion from Germany to other countries involved the introduction of new merchandising and pricing concepts within the existing small supermarket format. The internationalisation of Japanese department stores into the large cities in Asia and Europe also provide examples (Havens 1994; Davies and Fergusson 1995; Clarke and Rimmer 1997; Sternquist 1997b);
- injection of new and additional investment into the sector often with expectation of higher than average sectoral profitability and productivity returns on investment and consequential sectoral restructuring. Metro's substantial investment across several sectors in Poland with the development of hypermarkets, discount stores, DIY stores, electrical products stores and clothing stores had the effect of raising expectations of higher returns on investment across the whole retail sector. The impact therefore was to encourage a process of structural readjustment for the whole sector (Pütz 1997, 1998);

- reductions in profitability of small local retailers facing competition from more strongly capitalized foreign retailers can result in failure of the smaller firms. There is strong anecdotal evidence for large foreign retail firms acting as triggers for the closure of small retailers operating close to the margin of profitability. There is, however, little rigorous empirical evidence of direct causal links between foreign retailer growth and reduced profitability of small firms.

Existing retailers in the host markets have to make competitive responses to innovations from foreign retailers and the diffusion of these innovations. Horizontal competitive processes are therefore subjected to new forces brought by foreign retailers from outside the country. In order to remain competitive the existing domestic retailers have to respond to these new activities of foreign retailers.

Increased consumer literacy

The development of the activity of foreign retailers often brings new products to the retail market and may well introduce consumers to new methods of selling. In these ways, levels of consumer literacy of retailer activity are increased by foreign retailer activity and the subsequent copying of this activity by domestic retailers. Examples of situations when this has occurred are:

- the internationalisation of a style that is the distinguishing character of some internationalising retailers. Notable examples are Muji from Japan, IKEA from Sweden, Starbucks from USA and Laura Ashley from England, all of which have taken their design concepts into several foreign markets so bringing to consumers in the host country new design ideas in household goods, clothing and even coffee-drinking. The lifestyle brands of high fashion retailers provide other examples with consumers in host countries becoming aware of the distinctive styles and ranges of retailers such as Armani, Gucci and Escada (Laulajainen 1991, 1992). Consumer literacy of fashion trends is extended by these retailers creating stores in the host countries;
- extending consumer awareness and knowledge of products is exemplified by the activities of Sony. Sony has taken to many countries, in part through its Sony Centre store networks, sophisticated consumer technologies, widening and deepening the knowledge of consumers about such products. This is also an important aspect of the impact of Disney Stores and Warner Brothers Stores;
- widening consumer horizons of retail methods may also be an impact of retailers developing internationally. The spread of supermarkets into Turkey, Carrefour's development of hypermarkets in China, and Courts' development of furniture stores in Caribbean countries are examples but many others are to be seen.

Consumers become aware that some retailers are foreign retailers and so the consumers often have expectations that these retailers will present them with different products and different ideas. Consumer expectations of foreign retailers may be different from the expectations placed on foreign firms. Consumers in Japan expected Carrefour stores to be 'French' and were somewhat disappointed when this was not the case.

Consumers become susceptible to new cultural influences, perceived in both positive and negative terms, brought into a market by foreign retailers. This is a long established concept. Itinerant retailers, many centuries ago, travelled around European countries taking with them new and different products from those available from domestic retailers. This is conceptually no different from the internationalisation today of retailers such as Pier 1 and Body Shop that consciously introduce 'exotic' products to consumers in the host country.

Performance of the firm

The growth of store operations in a foreign country as well as affecting conditions in the host country also has substantial impacts on the performance of the firm involved. The impacts on the firm take many forms:

- impacts on profitability may be positive, as with the expansion into Spain and USA by Ahold, Wal-Mart into UK and Carrefour into Spain, or negative as with the experiences of Ahold in China and Wal-Mart, Carrefour, Sephora, and Marks and Spencer in Germany. Metro, over several years in the 1990s, showed a strong financial return from its investment in Poland that helped support a slowdown in profits from its domestic German operations. Signet has used the financial success of its foreign operation in USA to support the failures in its domestic operations in the UK. Tradehold, of South Africa, has used international expansion into UK, Australia and Poland, to sustain corporate profits that are under acute pressure in its domestic market in the late 1990s;
- managerial knowledge or intellectual capital may be obtained in the foreign country and brought back to benefit domestic operations. Wal-Mart is using ideas about retail brands obtained from ASDA in UK to benefit their operations in USA. Ahold have taken knowledge from their operations in USA back to be applied in the Netherlands and also in their operations in other countries. Cees van der Hoeven, Chief Executive of Royal Ahold has explained that in respect of the acquisition by Ahold of Giant in May 1998 and Pathmark in March 1999, 'We also see Giant-Landover giving Ahold a pool of talented retail professionals to populate other sister companies in the U.S. and abroad. That helps our globalization process' (van der Hoeven 1999: 78). The flow of 'know-how' within a firm, from the foreign operation to the domestic one is an important area of impact of international expansion of retailers;
- increases in scale of operation and resultant scale economies, particularly of purchasing, are obtained for the firm as it expands its international chain(s)

of stores. The basic rationale for retailers to move internationally is to increase the scale of their operations so clearly that there are impacts on the firm resulting from increased scale economies. Salto, as Deputy Operating officer of Promodès, claimed that the first reason for retail expansion in international markets was, 'so that the retail group can be of a comparable size to its main rivals and not suffer from lack of economies of scale' (Salto 1999: 6). These scale economies impact on the cost structure of the firm. Van der Hoeven wrote in respect of the acquisition by Ahold of Giant and Pathmark in USA, 'The economies of scale are yielding significant synergy effects in distribution and production, store operation and information technology. A major factor is the savings coming from synergies in buying and merchandising' (van der Hoeven 1999: 78). The expansion of Dixons from UK into Norway and Denmark has added to their scale of operation and has benefited their purchasing costs. The success of purchasing groups, for example, Intersport, depends on expansion into several countries to generate increasing purchase volumes for manufacturer branded items and for their own brand products. The same rationale lies behind the expansion of the store networks of limited range discount grocery firms, for example, Netto, Lidl, Aldi and Rema 2000. In these cases, because the international expansion increases the scale of the limited number of items being purchased, greater buying power is focussed onto the suppliers of these products;

- opportunities exist to use international expansion to support management development in the firm. IKEA, for example, uses its international store development network, to provide managers with a wide range of managerial experience in several countries;

- the status associated with the development of a successful international chain and the stigma of failure can be significant impacts for the retail firm. The pressure on Fast Retailing to extend its success in Japan by moving internationally has been great and the status of the firm will increase if the chain being built, from 2001 onwards, in UK is successful. Conversely failure will reduce status. The stigma of the failure of Boots in Japan had repercussions, more widely, on the status of the firm.

Impacts of internationalisation on the retail firm are considerable. As the firm expands its international operation so both the beneficial and detrimental aspects increase in magnitude. Cost structures in the firm may change. Major mistakes in internationalisation can have serious impacts for financial and capital performance of the firm. Examples are Yaohan's attempts to develop a chain of department stores outside Japan (Carlile 1998; Wong 1998) and the acquisition of store networks in Canada by Marks and Spencer and their attempts to build a European network of stores (Burt *et al.* 2002).

Public policy impacts

The activities of foreign retailers may bring responses from national governments concerned about potential social effects of the competitive impact on domestic retailers. International policy agencies, for example, the European Commission, may also take a view of the conduct of retailers, particularly where cross-border acquisition is involved. Typical of public policy impacts are:

- limits on the amount and type of foreign investment as is seen in India;
- licensing of foreign retailer activity as is practiced in China;
- introduction of controls over formats favoured by foreign retailers with consequential impact on domestic retailers operating these formats (Guy 2001);
- control over the extent to which foreign retailers may repatriate profits.

These controls are aimed at protecting domestic retailers from rapid development of foreign retailers (Davies 1993) who, as discussed above, can have major impacts on the structure, conduct and performance of the retail sector. The expansion of foreign retailers in a country can generate considerable political debate and the emergence of lobby groups espousing nationalist and protectionist views. The backlash to foreign retailers in Central European countries has tended to increase in the run-up to elections. Similar issues are emerging in East Asia with protests by small-scale retailers in Thailand in 2001, over the development of foreign-owned hypermarkets, is resulting in attempts in 2002, by the newly elected government, to control various activities of foreign firms.

Changes in socio-cultural values

The development of networks of foreign retailers can also have a profound impact on the socio-cultural values of a country. The moves of Sears Roebuck into Latin American countries, in the 1950s, were undertaken with the encouragement of the American government as an attempt to generate American-style economic development in the host countries (Galbraith and Holton 1955; Fritsch 1962). More recently the internationalisation of McDonalds, Starbucks, Benetton and IKEA, amongst many others, serve to diffuse a set of cultural values about American food, Italian fashion and Swedish household design into countries with very different indigenous food, fashion and furnishing values.

The framework provided in Figure 11.1 allows the types of impact to be disaggregated into those affecting existing retailers and structures, those affecting the firm involved and those affecting the society in which the foreign retailer is operating. By disaggregating the impacts in this way it is possible to develop a framework that can be applied although it ignores the interactions that create the totality of the impact. Nonetheless, with our current level of knowledge it can be argued that we need research at the disaggregated level before we can understand the synthesis of impact.

Processes of impact

The different types of impact involve different processes of interaction between the foreign retailers and the host country. There are several methods of expansion for retailers in foreign countries. The main methods of expansion are the same as those of entry, namely through acquisition, franchising, organic growth, joint ventures and, occasionally, store swaps. Each of the different expansion processes results in different forms of impact. For example, impacts on competitive structure are likely to be different if development is through acquisition rather than through organic growth; impacts on public policy may be different with joint ventures rather than acquisition; public policy issues may arise with franchise type activity but not with organic growth.

The processes that generate the impact will also be different with different economic conditions in one host country from another. For example, the impacts of Carrefour's activity in China will result from different processes to those in Brazil or Japan although similar types of impact may result from Carrefour's activity in all these countries. The infrastructure in the host country will also be a significant factor in influencing the processes of impact. The West European retailers that entered Central European countries, in the early 1990s, had to come to terms with very different levels of infrastructure provision than those they had encountered in international moves elsewhere. The nature of the infrastructure resulted in corporate processes, for example, those associated with compliance with legal requirements in land transfer, that affected the impacts of the firms on emerging public policies in the country. In a similar way, Western retailers entering China are faced with infrastructures and institutions with which the retailers are unfamiliar (Wu 1997). This results in a different set of processes of impact than occurs in international moves by the same retailers within Europe. Nonetheless, whilst situational factors are important there are some generic processes. The processes relating to the types of impact are summarized in Figure 11.2.

The processes affecting the impacts on the demand chain are ones of channel management. Important influences in channel management are the distribution of information amongst the channel members and the management of the technology needed to control the channel flows. The extent to which these processes are different for foreign retailers and for domestic ones is difficult to ascertain. It can be suggested, for example, that levels of information about the environment may be lower in foreign retailers than domestic ones and it will be lower for recent entrants compared to long established foreign firms. It may also be suggested that channel flows are more likely to be international in nature and that may affect some aspects of the management of the technology related to these flows. The channel management processes affect the relationships between retailer and suppliers and there is starting to be some empirical work, reported elsewhere (Chapters 2, 3 and 5) in this volume, of the nature of processes in relationships between foreign retailer and domestic suppliers. The channel management processes of foreign retailers will influence the impacts the retailer generates but we still know little about how this takes place.

The main processes affecting the sectoral competitiveness impacts are processes of marketing management. It is unclear how or whether marketing management processes are different for foreign retailers, as a group in a market, compared with domestic retailers. Specific foreign retailers may bring to a market

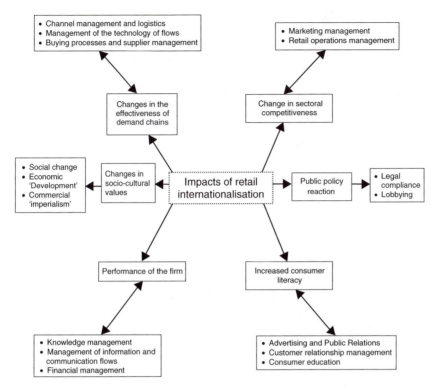

Figure 11.2 Key processes that relate to the types of impact of international retailers.

particular innovations in marketing management and so obtain first-mover advantage but this is unlikely to be sustainable given the openness of retail marketing and the ease with which copying can occur. Foreign retailers may target very specific consumer groups and in this way introduce new marketing practices into the market. The firm-specific element in marketing is considerable with some retailers introducing particular marketing processes, for example, pricing initiatives by Aldi, branding initiatives by Body Shop, store design initiatives by IKEA, customer relations by Tesco, promotional activities by Ahold, etc.

The processes of knowledge management and of knowledge transfer are important in understanding the impacts on the firm of the internationalisation activity. The impacts of internationalisation within the firm depend on the transfer of knowledge amongst the various managerial functions in the firm (Westney 2001). Knowledge may be categorised in a variety of ways. There is knowledge generated through experience – *experiential knowledge*. The knowledge an individual has, for example, of opening a new hypermarket for Carrefour in Poland. This knowledge comes from practical experience and is particularly useful as internationalisation progresses and, for example, Carrefour opens more hypermarkets in Poland or develops in other Central and East European countries.

Secondly, *routine knowledge* comes from learning about the way things work, for example, knowledge about how to operate a composite distribution depot for Tesco. This is important in internationalisation in the transfer from the home country to the host country. This knowledge enables transfer of retail know-how into a country. *Conceptual knowledge* is more explicit and results from the design and use of the symbols of the firm, for example, what can and cannot be done with brands. In an internationalisation context this category of knowledge is important in understanding the competitive impacts of developments. The use of conceptual knowledge in the internationalisation processes of Body Shop and Lush is different although both are using this type of knowledge in the same sector and often in the same countries. Finally, there is *systematic knowledge*. Systematic knowledge is codified into operating manuals that are widely used in any good retailer and define the operational activity of a foreign retailer in a host country. Research outside the retail sector (Nonaka *et al.* 2000a,b), has the potential to provide new insights on international retailing in respect of this knowledge creation and transfer in multinational firms. These processes of knowledge management are likely to be important in influencing the extent of improvement in performance as the firm develops internationally.

Impacts on consumer literacy are generated by processes of advertising, customer relationship management and consumer education. Some retailers, for example, Benetton, link their growth and expansion in a foreign market closely to explicit attempts to increase consumer literacy via advertising. Other firms transfer to their foreign operations the consumer education methods already in use in their home country. Sephora, for example, seeks to educate consumers in the nature and composition of perfumes with its help desk. IKEA seeks to illustrate and educate consumers in the principles of design. In such cases it is often difficult to disentangle the processes of consumer education from those of marketing.

The operations and processes undertaken by foreign retailers are, in many instances, likely to be similar to those of domestic retailers in the host country. That the processes are managed by foreign retailers is less important than that they are undertaken by a particular foreign firm. There are some exceptions to this generalisation that relate to the ability of foreign firms to introduce and diffuse innovations, and to transfer knowledge into the foreign market. Whilst there is anecdotal evidence that these processes of knowledge transfer occur there is little rigourous research on the issue. There is also virtually no research on how the information and communication networks change as the retail firm expands in a foreign market. The strategies and policies of the specific firm are important in defining the processes that generate the different types of impact.

In considering these processes the presence of considerable variety evident from empirical studies has resulted in a suggestion of a random element at work (Dawson 2001b). The apparent serendipity associated with many actions when once a foreign retailer is established in a country underpins this suggestion of a random factor. Randomness may be more apparent than real, however, and may simply be the amalgamation of several clearly defined processes that have been viewed together rather than deconstructed. For some of these processes there may be stages that are present and which become evident when there is study of a firm's actions over several years. For some processes it can be expected that there will be feedback effects and some process will be non-linear. When seen together this amalgam seems to have randomness but when disaggregated the individual processes may become discernable as having strategic consistency. These process issues will become clearer as we move forward with our understanding of international retailing from the basis of who, why and where to take a more dynamic view on when and what impacts occur.

Intensity of impact

The third aspect of impact is the degree or intensity of impact. A single store operated in a foreign country, for example, by Furla or Fratelli Rossetti, has a low intensity on most of the types of impact when compared to a network of stores, for example, Benetton or Zara. The number of stores, however, is not the sole determinant of impact as is evident from the impact of Nike Town, Harvey Nichols or Giorgio Armani; each has few international stores but their significance is considerable. The intensity of impact can be considered as a function of several variables:

- *extent of the retailer's adaptation to the culture and environment of the host country*: This is an influence on the intensity of impact but it is not a simple relationship. Foreign retailers that make minimal concessions to local culture, for example, IKEA, McDonalds and Laura Ashley, can have substantial impacts but similarly firms that adapt to local culture can also have significant impact, as exemplified by Ahold in USA, C&A in Europe and Carrefour in Spain. Nonetheless, intuitively there would seem to be a relationship between the degree of localisation and the intensity of impact, if all other variables could be held constant;
- *retailer's commitment to the new market*: In general higher levels of commitment, that may, but not necessarily, involve more extensive store networks, result in higher levels of intensity of impact. IKEA has strong commitment to the markets it enters but often develops relatively small networks. Marks and Spencer has exhibited relatively low levels of commitment to its international operations and has had low intensity of impact despite being large and having a strong domestic brand;
- *strength of retailer's brand*: The stronger the brand the more likely that impact will be more intense. This is evident, for example, with the strong brands of designer clothing and accessory retailers within the LVMH group. Again the generalisation has exceptions and the nature of the influence is complex with some strong domestic brands having a big impact but there are also examples of others having a weak impact, for example, Boots in its failed international activities in France and Japan and K-Mart's failure in Czechoslovakia;
- *method of expansion*: The different mechanisms of expansion (acquisition, franchising, organic growth, etc.) are likely to affect the intensity of impact because they affect the type of control the retailer exerts over the operations in the foreign market;

- *size of retail firm*: Larger firms with greater corporate resources are likely to have more intense impacts. Although tiny within the total market of China, Wal-Mart and Carrefour have significant impact on the Chinese market because of the widespread knowledge of the magnitude of the resource base of the firm;
- *level of competition*: In highly competitive markets with existing high levels of innovation and knowledge the intensity of impact is likely to be less. Impact has been higher in West European retailer development in Central Europe than in their moves into other West European countries and North America;
- *extent of public policy intervention*: Restrictive public policies limit the degree and intensity of impact. For example, Décathlon, the French operator of over 300 sports goods superstores worldwide, was refused permission to establish a large store at Høje Tåstrup near Copenhagen and so opened a smaller unit in Aalborg, thus lessening the intensity of impact. The firm decided, in 2002, to close the smaller store following the store's poor performance and withdraw from Scandanavia until land-use regulations became more relaxed.

The overall intensity of impact results from a combination of these various factors. Although it is possible to suggest the factors that affect the degree or intensity of impact, it remains a difficult concept to measure, given the various constituencies for the types of impact. Our understanding of both the processes and the intensity of impact is at an early stage.

Conclusion

A considerable amount of research has been undertaken in the last decade on retailer internationalisation. Relatively little research has considered the impacts on the host country and on the participant retailer of foreign retailer activity in the post-entry phases of development. As yet there is no established framework under which such studies would be undertaken. There are few empirical works monitoring international retailer activity in a systematic way and over a substantial period. There is minimal theory that addresses these issues with theories of retail competition generally still at a very early stage of development. This chapter has attempted to consider the issues associated with determining the impacts of foreign retailers on host countries. It has proposed an initial threefold structure that considers types of impact, the processes of impact and the intensity of impact. Each of these concepts has been expanded to derive a potential framework for gaining an understanding of impact.

The next steps in gaining a better understanding of the impacts of foreign retailers are likely to be:

- sharpening and further clarification of the framework, or substituting an alternative framework to that, presented in this chapter;

- identification of a series of propositions that could define a model of impact using this framework;
- exploration of the underlying theory behind the managerial and economic dynamics of international retail impacts;
- design and undertaking of empirical surveys to measure the presence, processes and intensity of the impacts of foreign retailers.

There are considerable benefits to be gained by a better understanding of foreign retailer impacts. These benefits lie in debates on corporate strategy and public policy. The likely increase in international activity of retailers over the next decade means that the internationalisation processes will become more central within corporate strategy and developments in New Commerce (Dawson 2001c). The requirements for retailers to grow will inevitably result in them extending their operations into other countries. The resultant impacts are important aspects of strategy with implications for all the stakeholders. As retailing moves away from being a domestic industry, the public policy regulation of retail activities takes on new dimensions. Foreign control of retailing can become a contentious political issue with conflict between local domestic entrepreneurs and large-scale foreign firms. Debates on the regulation of competition, rights of establishment, nature of financial reporting and employment conditions all need to accommodate the ownership structure of retailing, in effect the extent to which international retailing is developing in the economy. It is in this context that there is need for a clearer understanding of the impacts of international retail activity.

Notes

1 There are many examples of retailers, including Wal-Mart and Tesco, exporting their own brand product to retailers in countries where they have no store presence. This export activity is not new. Marks and Spencer, for example, by the late 1980s were exporting over £45 million (fob price) of product per year to retailers in countries where they did not operate shops.
2 It has been suggested (Dawson 1999) that there are three main forms of processes apparent in the transformation of retailing: sequential change processes, spatial change processes and structural change processes. Internationalisation represents on this basis a process of structural change.
3 The distinction between format and formula is important in this context and can be exemplified by the spread of the hypermarket (format) through Poland with the formulae of Casino, Carrefour, Real (Metro), Hit (Dohle), Jumbo (Jeronimo Martins) and Tesco (Dawson and Henley 1999). Each company-specific (branded) formula has its own operating characteristics within the general format.

References

Akehurst, G. and Alexander, N. (1995) 'The internationalisation process in retailing', *Service Industries Journal*, 15(4): 1–15.

Alexander, N. (1990) 'Retailers and international markets: motives for expansion', *International Marketing Review*, 7(4): 75–85.

Alexander, N. (1995) 'UK retail expansion in North America and Europe: a strategic dilemma', *Journal of Retailing and Consumer Services*, 2(2): 75–82.

Alexander, N. (1997) *International Retailing*. Oxford: Blackwell.

Alexander, N. and Myers, H. (2000) 'The retail internationalisation process', *International Marketing Review*, 17(4/5): 334–53.

Au-Yeung, A. Y. S. (2002) *Foreign Direct Investment of Food Retailers: The Case of People's Republic of China*, PhD thesis, The University of Edinburgh.

Arnold, S. J. and Fernie, J. (1999) 'Wal-Mart into the UK', *Journal of Enterprising Culture*, 7: 407–416.

Arnold, S. J. and Fernie, J. (2000) 'Wal-Mart in Europe: prospects for the UK', *International Marketing Review*, 17(4/5): 416–32.

Arnold, S. J., Handelman, J. and Tigert, D. J. (1998) 'The impact of a market spoiler on consumer preferences (or what happens when Wal-Mart comes to town)', *Journal of Retailing and Consumer Services*, 5: 1–13.

Belk, R. (1996) 'Hyperreality and globalization: culture in the age of Ronald McDonald', *Journal of International Consumer Marketing*, 8(3/4): 23–37.

Bourlakis, C., Bourlakis, M. and Dawson, J. (1996) 'The rise of retailer power in the Greek food retail sector 1988–1994', Paper to CREER seminar on *Channel Productivity: Efficiency in Retailing and Merchandising*, Mons, October 1996.

Burt, S. (1991) 'Trends in the internationalisation of grocery retailing: the European experience', *International Review of Retail, Distribution and Consumer Research*, 1(4): 487–515.

Burt, S. (1993) 'Temporal trends in the internationalisation of British retailing', *International Review of Retail, Distribution and Consumer Research*, 3(4): 391–410.

Burt, S. (1995) 'Retail internationalisation: evolution of theory and practice'. In: McGoldrick, P. J. and Davies, G. (eds) *International Retailing: Trends and Strategies*, London: Pitman, pp. 51–73.

Burt, S. and Carralero-Encinas, J. (2000) 'The role of store image in retail internationalisation', *International Marketing Review*, 17(4/5): 433–53.

Burt, S. and Sparks, L. (2001) 'The implications of Wal-Mart's takeover of ASDA', *Environment and Planning*, A33: 1463–89.

Burt, S., Mellahi, K., Jackson, T. P. and Sparks, L. (2002) 'Retail internationalization and retail failure: issues from the case of Marks and Spencer', *International Review of Retail, Distribution and Consumer Research*, 12(2): 191–219.

Carlile, L. E. (1998) 'The Yaohan group'. In: MacPherson, K. L. (ed.) *Asian Department Stores*, Richmond: Curzon, pp. 233–52.

Clark, R., Grant, C. and Leech, P. (2001) *International Retailers in the UK: The Future of UK Retailing*, London: Emap.

Clarke, I. and Rimmer, P. (1997) 'The anatomy of retail internationalisation: Daimaru's decision to invest in Melbourne, Australia', *Service Industries Journal*, 17: 361–82.

Davies, B. K. (1993) 'Trade barriers in East and South East Asia: the implications for retailers', *International Review of Retail, Distribution and Consumer Research*, 3(4): 345–66.

Davies, B. K. (1994a) 'The implications of foreign investment in the retail sector: the example of Singapore', *The Developing Economies*, 22(3): 299–330.

Davies, B. K. (1994b) 'Foreign investment in the retail sector of the Peoples Republic of China', *Columbia Journal of World Business*, 29(3): 56–69.

Davies, B. K. (2000) 'The international activities of Japanese retailers'. In: Czinkota, M. R. and Kotabe, M. (eds) *Japanese Distribution Strategy*, London: Business Press, pp. 227–41.

Davies, B. K. and Fergusson, F. (1995) 'The international activities of Japanese retailers', *Services Industries Journal*, 15(4): 97–117.

Dawson, J. A. (1994) 'The internationalization of retailing operations', *Journal of Marketing Management*, 10: 267–82.

Dawson, J. A. (1999) 'The evolution and future structure of retailing in Europe'. In: Jones, K. (ed.) *The Internationalisation of Retailing in Europe*, Toronto: Centre for Study of Commercial Activity, pp. 1–13.

Dawson, J. A. (2001a) 'Retail investment in central Europe and its implications', *Thexis*, 18(3): 23–8.

Dawson, J. A. (2001b) 'Strategy and opportunism in European retail internationalisation', *British Journal of Management*, 12(4): 253–66.

Dawson, J. A. (2001c) 'Is there a new commerce in Europe?', *International Review of Retail, Distribution and Consumer Research*, 11(3): 287–99.

Dawson, J. A. and Henley, J. S. (1999) 'Internationalisation of hypermarket retailing in Poland: West European investment and its implications', *Journal of East–West Business*, 5(4): 37–52.

Dupuis, M. and Prime, N. (1996) 'Business distance and global retailing: a model of the analysis of key success/failure factors', *International Journal of Retail and Distribution Management*, 24(11): 30–8.

Doherty, A. M. (1999) 'Explaining international retailers' market entry mode strategy: internalization theory, agency theory and the importance of information asymmetry', *International Review of Retail, Distribution and Consumer Research*, 9(4): 379–402.

Evans, W. and Cox, S. (1997) 'Retail border wars III: case studies of international retailers operating in Canada', *Research Report 1997–10, Centre for the Study of Commercial Activity, Ryerson Polytechnic University, Toronto*, 1997: 10.

Fritsch, W. (1962) *Progress and Profits: The Sears Roebuck Story in Peru*. Washington, DC: Action Committee for International Development.

Galbraith, J. K. and Holton, R. (1955) *Marketing Efficiency in Puerto Rico*. Cambridge, MA: Harvard University Press.

Gielen, K. and Dekimpe, M. G. (2001) 'Do international entry decisions of retail chains matter in the long run?', *International Journal of Research in Marketing*, 18(3): 235–59.

Goldman, A. (2001) 'The transfer of retail formats into developing economies: the example of China', *Journal of Retailing*, 77(2): 221–42.

Guy, C. (2001) 'Internationalisation of large-format retailers and leisure providers in western Europe: Planning and property impacts', *International Journal of Retail, Distribution and Consumer Research*, 29(10): 452–61.

Havens, T. R. H. (1994) *Architects of Affluence: The Tsutsumi Family and the Seibu–Saison Enterprises in the Twentieth Century'*. Cambridge, MA: Harvard University Press.

Hollander, S. (1970) *Multinational Retailing*. East Lansing: Michigan State University.

Kacker, M. P. (1985) *Transatlantic Trends in Retailing: Takeovers and the Flow of Know-how*. Wesport: Quorum Books.

Kacker, M. P. (1988) 'International flow of retailing know-how: bridging the technology gap in distribution', *Journal of Retailing*, 64(1): 41–67.

Kawabata, M. (1999a) 'Why have Japanese retailers crossed borders? Reconsideration of motive studies', *Journal of Business Studies Ryukoku University*, 39(2).

Kawabata, M. (1999b) 'An analysis of the overseas store expansion of Japanese retailers in Asian markets', *Journal of Japan Society of Marketing and Distribution*, 2(2).

Laulajainen, R. (1987) *Spatial Strategies in Retailing*. Dordrecht: D Reidel.

Laulajainen, R. (1991) 'Two retailers go global: the geographical dimension', *International Review of Retail, Distribution and Consumer Research*, 1(5): 607–26.

Laulajainen, R. (1992) 'Louis Vuitton Malletier: a truly global retailer', *Annals of the Japan Association of Economic Geography*, 38(2): 55–77.

Letosk, R., Murphy, D. and Kenny, R. (1997) 'Entry opportunities and environmental constraints for foreign retailers in China's secondary cities', *Multinational Business Review*, Fall: 28–40.

Martenson, R. (1981) *Innovations in Multinational Retailing: IKEA on the Swedish, Swiss, German and Austrian Furniture Markets*. Goteborg: University of Goteborg.

McGoldrick, P. J. and Ho, S. L. (1992) 'International positioning: Japanese department stores in Hong Kong', *European Journal of Marketing*, 26(8/9): 65–73.

Mondragón, C. (1997) *Strategic Alliances in Mexico: The Case of Wal-Mart-CIFRA*, PhD dissertation, University of Texas at Austin.

Mukoyama, M. (1997) 'Internationalizing Japanese distribution'. In: Tajima, Y. and Harada, H. (eds) *Introduction to Distribution Studies*, Tokyo: Nippon Keizai Shimbun, pp. 371–405.

Muniz-Martinez, N. (1998) 'The internationalisation of European retailers in America: the US experience', *International Journal of Retail and Distribution Management*, 26(1): 29–37.

Nonaka, I., Toyama, R. and Konno, N. (2000a) 'SECI, Ba and leadership: a unified model of dynamic knowledge creation', *Long Range Planning*, 32: 5–34.

Nonaka, I., Toyama, R. and Nagata , A. (2000b) 'A firm as a knowledge creating entity: a new perspective on the theory of the firm', *Industrial and Corporate Change*, 9(1): 1–20.

O'Grady, S. and Lane, H. O. (1997) 'Culture: an unnoticed barrier to Canadian retail performance in the USA', *Journal of Retailing and Consumer Services*, 4: 159–70.

Pellegrini, L. (1991) 'The internationalisation of retailing and 1992 Europe', *Journal of Marketing Channels*, 1(2): 3–27.

Pellegrini, L. (1994) 'Alternatives for growth and internationalization in retailing', *International Review of Retail, Distribution and Consumer Research*, 4(2): 121–48.

Pütz, R. (1997) 'New business formation, privatisation and internationalisation. Aspects of the transformation of Polish retail trade', *Die Erde*, 128: 235–49.

Pütz, R. (1998) *Einzelhandel im transformatioonsprozess*. Passau: L.I.S.

Quinn, B. (1998) 'Towards a framework for the study of franchising as an operating mode for international retail companies', *International Review of Retail, Distribution and Consumer Research*, 8(4): 445–67.

Quinn, B. (1999) 'The temporal context of UK retailers' motives for international expansion', *Service Industries Journal*, 19(2): 101–16.

Quinn, B. and Alexander, A. (2002) 'International retail franchising: a conceptual framework', *International Journal of Retail and Distribution Management*, 30(5): 264–76.

Ritzer, G. (1993) *The McDonaldization of Society*. Thousand Oaks, CA: Pine Forge Press.

Salto, L. (1999) 'Towards global retailing: the Promodès case'. In: Dupuis, M. and Dawson, J. (eds) *European Cases in Retailing*, Oxford: Blackwell, pp. 5–14.

Simmons, J. and Kamikihara, S. (1999) 'The internationalisation of commercial activities in Canada', *Research Report, Centre for the Study of Commercial Activity, Ryerson Polytechnic University, Toronto*, 1999: 7.

Simpson, E. M. and Thorpe, D. I. (1995) 'A conceptual model of strategic considerations for international retail expansion', *Service Industries Journal*, 15(4): 16–24.

Sparks, L. (1995) 'Reciprocal retail internationalisation: the Southland Corporation, Ito Yokado and 7-Eleven convenience stores', *Service Industries Journal*, 15(4): 57–96.

Sparks, L. (2000) 'Seven-Eleven Japan and the Southland Corporation: a marriage of convenience?', *International Marketing Review*, 17(4/5): 401–15.

Sternquist, B. (1997a) 'International expansion of US retailers', *International Journal of Retail and Distribution Management*, 25(8): 262–8.

Sternquist, B. (1997b) 'Internationalization of Japanese department stores', *International Journal of Commerce and Management*, 7(1): 57–73.

Vida, I. (2000) 'An empirical inquiry into international expansion of US retailers', *International Marketing Review*, 17(4/5): 454–75.

van der Hoeven, C. (1999) 'Royal Ahold: a global strategy based on local independence', *International Trends in Retailing*, 16(1): 73–80.

Vitzthum, C. (2001) 'Zara's speed sells fashion', *Wall Street Journal Europe*, May 11–12: 21–2.

Westney, D. E. (2001) 'Multinational enterprises and cross-border knowledge creation'. In: Nonaka, I. and Nishiguchi, T. (eds) *Knowledge Emergence: Social, Technical and Evolutionary Dimensions of Knowledge Creation*, Oxford: Oxford University Press, pp. 147–75.

Wong, W. H. (1998) 'From Japanese supermarket to Hong Kong department store'. In: MacPherson, K. L. (ed.) *Asian Department Stores*, Richmond: Curzon, pp. 253–88.

Wrigley, N. (1989) 'The lure of the USA: further reflections on the internationalisation of British grocery retailing capital', *Environment and Planning*, A21: 283–8.

Wrigley, N. (1997a) 'British food retail capital in the USA – part 1: Sainsbury and the Shaw's experience', *International Journal of Retail and Distribution Management*, 25(1): 7–21.

Wrigley, N. (1997b) 'British food retail capital in the USA – part 2: Giant prospects', *International Journal of Retail and Distribution Management*, 25(2): 48–58.

Wrigley, N. (1997c) 'Foreign retail capital on the battlefields of Connecticut: competition regulation at the local scale and its implications', *Environment and Planning*, A29: 1142–52.

Wrigley, N. (2000) 'Strategic market behaviour in the internationalization of food retailing: interpreting the third wave of Sainsbury's US diversification', *European Journal of Marketing*, 34(8): 891–918.

Wu, J. P. (1997) *The Development of China's Retail Industry since the Economic Reform of 1978*, PhD thesis, Cornell University.

12 Conclusion

The direction of future research on the internationalisation of retailing

Masao Mukoyama

That industrialisation, or more accurately modernisation, in the retail distribution sector has lagged behind that of the manufacturing sector is well known. Certainly this lag was the position in past years. Retail companies in the Western economies that have gone through industrialisation in both the manufacturing and retailing sectors have developed advanced retail technologies. These firms are expectedly taking the lead in the internationalisation of retailing. Some major Japanese retailers at the end of the 1980s and beginning of the 1990s were in a similar position but are now no longer amongst the leading companies. As a result, current trends in retail internationalisation show that European and North American retailers are the main players, moving strongly across national boundaries in the European and North American consumer realms.

Research on international retailing has analysed the state of internationalisation and is characterised by Western researchers working with Western paradigms of business, focusing on Western retail firms, from the viewpoint of the why, where and how of internationalisation. This issue is raised in Chapter 11 by John Dawson. However, the reality of the retail internationalisation on which these research studies were built, changed in the 1990s, and, particularly so, in the later half of that decade. There was a shift towards moving into the Asian market which had yet to experience 'industrialisation' in the retail distribution sector. The Asian market became the battlefield for Western retail companies. However, although there has been a big shift in the target markets and in the activity of retailers, the research on retail internationalisation has not fully taken this into account. The theme of this book, which is the question 'What is happening in the Asian market in respect of the development of retail internationalisation?', is a pressing question for both the retail business world and researchers on retail internationalisation.

In answering this question, first it is essential to know, 'What are the histories and characteristics of the retail industries of Asian countries, and how are they changing?' These histories and characteristics include not only ones of economic structure but also of distribution policy and distribution systems. Unfortunately, so far, we have to say that Western countries and Asian countries do not understand each other in these areas. With this in mind the First Asian Distribution Workshop was convened by the University of Marketing and Distribution Science in Kobe in November 2001. The papers of that workshop constitute this book.

The chapters of Jirapar Tosomboon, Han Jinglun, Shuguang Wang and Victor Savage provide insights into the retailing in Thailand, China and Singapore and so begin to bridge this gap in understanding. These studies make a substantial contribution to the gathering of fundamental information for research into the internationalisation of retailing. More are needed.

However now, we also must take the next step in our research. There are many different views as to what this 'next step' should be, but the chapters in this book provide us with several indications as to what research topics are of value for us at this next stage.

Analysis of the unique phenomena that are occurring in each country

Jirapar Tosomboon, for example, outlines the situation in Thailand where local capital is inviting international retailers into the market. Not only are the retail companies entering the market under their own volition but on the Thai side there are specific moves aimed at industrialising the retail sector using the abilities of foreign firms. Seong Mu Suh and Choi Sang Chul introduce the emergence of new forms of retailing in Korea where the local retailers are competing with Western companies such as Carrefour and Wal-Mart on an equal, if not higher, level. Furthermore, Hitoshi Tsuchiya investigates the various conflicts that arose between the local manufacturers and retailers when Carrefour moved into Taiwan. There is a greater need for us to know what phenomena are going to occur and be important in the future in each country. And once we know what is going on, we must come up with the answers to the questions of why international retailers in certain countries operate in specific ways and cause change, maybe conflict, through the channel.

Analysis of the behaviour of international retailers

Among Western retailers there are those that have succeeded in moving into overseas markets and there are those who have failed. Why did some international retailers succeed? And what are the reasons for the failure of others? Although there are retailers who have aggressively internationalised and succeeded, it is not always the case that they have succeeded in every country. Why is it that the same retailers sometime succeed in some countries but in other situations fail? Is the reason due to the differences in the environment in the home country versus the environment in the host country?

On this point, Roy Larke shows that the mode of entry into the foreign market by the retailer can affect the outcome, and Amelia Yuen Shan Au-Yeung puts forward a model for analysing the behaviour of retailers in the host country whereby retail internationalisation is treated as a process of technology transfer. This research shows that international retailers possess some form of strategic strength which other retailers do not have (such as an ability to choose their entry mode or an ability to transfer their retail technology to the host country) and that by using these advantages they can be successful, and that in cases where their strengths are not enough to overcome the differences in environments they can also fail. In research terms we need to clarify the strategic strengths held by international retailers and analyse what conditions are essential for their success.

Analysis of the impact of international retailers on the distribution systems of host countries

John Dawson proposes a framework for comprehensively analysing the impact that international retailers have on the local markets in which they move into. Roger Chan and Wen Hong discuss how foreign investment can be used to modernise economies and raise the economic value of urban areas, through the example of Hong Kong. This research does not simply focus on international retail business but also shows the importance of thinking about how international retailers are affecting the countries into which they move. In the past in Japan, within the process whereby revolutionary retail formats grew from things learnt from the West, conflicts have arisen between traditional small and medium retailers and the innovative new formats. This in turn affected distribution policy and caused a social problem related to the survival of small and medium retail operators, with the result that the structure of the distribution system changed greatly. In this way, when revolutionary retail technologies are introduced there is a resulting change in the domestic distribution system. This set of impacts, however, is different depending on the country in question and indeed the level of the impacts effects is probably different too. There is, therefore, a need to analyse the impact on countries which undergo penetration by international retailers, from multiple perspectives.

Analysis of the relationship between the strategies and market consciousness of international retailers

In the research on the motivations for entering overseas markets, many factors have been pointed out. These include the existence of overseas niche markets and unopened markets with a high growth potential, both of which are pull factors, and the maturation of domestic markets and the existence of pressure for competition both of which act as a push factor. These research studies, however, are rooted in environmental theory. That is to say, such research is based on the idea that 'If the environmental conditions are right then retailers will move overseas'. But, the question of whether or not the market conditions in the target country are really attractive depends on the retailers themselves and how they perceive these conditions. For example, it is possible that one retailer might recognise a market as a market to move into, whereas another retailer might not consider it so. Not only that, two companies might recognise the same market as being a market they should move into, but the way they enter and the way they act after entry may not necessarily be the same. What decides the result is not just the environmental factors but also subjective factors within the retailers themselves. What decides the relationship between the retailer and the market they move into is the strategic competitiveness of the company, or the quality and quantity of the management resources of the company, or the nature of the decision-making systems of the company. When a retail company internationalises how do they see the market and why do they see it that way? How is this difference in recognising markets related to differences in behaviour? Research on motivations for entering overseas markets must move forward to a comprehensive analysis that is linked to internationalisation.

Analysis of Asian retailers moving into overseas markets

Internationalisation is not the sole right of Western countries. We must not forget that it is possible for any retailer to internationalise their activity. At the present time, although it is not the centre of attention and although there are still few examples, there exist already local Asian retail companies that are moving into overseas markets. Taiwanese retailers are moving into China and several Hong Kong and Singapore speciality stores are opening stores in Asian markets. The internationalisation processes of these Asian companies are likely to be different from those of Western companies. Whereas Western retailers have built up their own know-how and technologies for internationalisation, Asian local retailers have learnt this from being subjected to foreign competition, and then have moved overseas using this gained knowledge. This process of technological transfer is something that is very worth researching as little research exists in this area.

Up until now, Western researchers in retail distribution have hardly looked at Asia as a research topic. Analysis of the Asian retail market, however, is becoming an important research area for Western researchers, as international retailers target Asia. On the other hand, in the various Asian countries research on retail and distribution is still at a preliminary stage and there is a shortage of researchers. Nonetheless, Asian researchers are the ones who know the Asian market best. This has very important implications. That is, the driving force for advancing research on internationalisation in retailing is the melding of knowledge between the three main players: Asian researchers, Western researchers and international retailers. This book is an attempt to start this process and to stimulate more activity. The opportunities for the three groups to come together are considerable as they create new knowledge in this exciting area.

Index